MOBILIZATION,
PARTICIPATION,
AND DEMOCRACY
IN AMERICA

MOBILIZATION, PARTICIPATION, AND DEMOCRACY IN AMERICA

STEVEN J. ROSENSTONE

University of Michigan

JOHN MARK HANSEN

University of Chicago

MACMILLAN PUBLISHING COMPANY

New York

MAXWELL MACMILLAN CANADA

Toronto

MAXWELL MACMILLAN INTERNATIONAL

New York   Oxford   Singapore   Sydney

For Dana, Maria Antonia, Sara, and Anna

Editors: *Bruce Nichols and Robert Miller*
Production Supervisor: *Sharon Lee*
Production Manager: *Roger Vergnes*
Text Designer: *Patrice Fodero*
Cover Designer: *Cathleen Norz*

This book was set in 10/12 Janson by Publication Services, Inc., and was printed and bound by R. R. Donnelley & Sons. The cover was printed by Philips Winson, Inc.

Macmillan Publishing Company
866 Third Avenue, New York, New York 10022

Macmillan Publishing Company is a part of the Maxwell Communication Group of Companies.

Maxwell Macmillan Canada, Inc.
1200 Eglinton Avenue East
Suite 200
Don Mills, Ontario, M3C 3N1

LIBRARY OF CONGRESS CATALOGING-IN-PUBLICATION DATA

Rosenstone, Steven, J.
    Mobilization, participation, and democracy in America / Steven J. Rosenstone, John Mark Hansen.
       p. cm. — (New topics in politics)
    Includes bibliographical references and index.
    ISBN 0-02-403660-9
    1. Political participation—United States. 2. Elections—United States. 3. United States—Politics and government—1945–
I. Hansen, John Mark. II. Title III. Series.
JK1764.R67 1993
323'.042'0973—dc20   92-34552
                                            CIP

Printing: 1 2 3 4 5 6 7   Year: 3 4 5 6 7 8 9

ACKNOWLEDGMENTS

This book has been a long time in the making. Back in 1982, when Steven Rosenstone was an assistant professor and Mark Hansen was a graduate student at Yale, we met over lunch to see whether we had common interests that might lead to a joint project. We went to work on this project that summer, and in 1984 we presented a first draft at the Weingart–Caltech Conference on the Institutional Context of Elections. Then we left it. Rosenstone got busy getting tenure and starting a family; Hansen got busy on a dissertation and a new job. Promises to return to the project became our yearly ritual.

That we finally did return to the project ten years later owes much to the interest of our editor at Macmillan, Bruce Nichols. Bruce read our 1984 paper, liked it, and encouraged us to pick it up again.

We are glad we did. Our 1984 paper posed the central questions and laid the foundations of the theoretical perspective that informs this work. In writing the book, however, we transformed some vague ideas about mobilization into a systematic way of understanding political participation.

The conception, the theorizing, the data collection, the analysis, and the writing were entirely joint ventures. Through this process, we have learned much from each other, managing to emerge from the decade not only as trusted colleagues but also as good friends. We differed on much, but we disagreed on only one point: on whose name should appear first on the cover. Hansen argued it should be Rosenstone; Rosenstone argued it should be Hansen. We resolved the issue with a coin toss.

Many people have contributed to this project over the years, and we are grateful for their help. Lois Timms-Ferrara, Marilyn Potter, and Ann-Marie Mercure of the Roper Center at the University of Connecticut, Donald DeLuca and Jane Draper of the Roper Center at Yale, Jo Ann Dionne of the Yale Social Science Data Archives, and Tom Smith of the National Opinion Research Center all helped us secure the data gathered by the Roper Organization. Brad Fay of the Roper Organization approved early release of some data, which greatly facilitated our analysis.

Our work also draws upon the National Election Studies conducted by the University of Michigan's Center for Political Studies under grants from the National Science Foundation. Ricardo Rodriguiz aided our acquisition of the NES data from the Interuniversity Consortium for Political and Social Research archives. Santa Traugott and Pat Luevano helped us interpret some coding of the NES data. Neither the original collectors of these data, the ICPSR, nor the Roper Center are responsible for our analysis and interpretations.

Many colleagues and friends provided detailed advice along the way. Christopher Achen, David Mayhew, Donald Kinder, Ron Jepperson, Paul Abramson, and Shanto Iyengar read our 1984 paper and made suggestions that proved invaluable as we revived this project. Laura Scalia and Robert Sherman commented on early drafts of Appendix F. Gerald Rosenberg, Guy Stuart, Daniel Carpenter, Jane Junn, Patricia Conley, Burdett Loomis, Hanes Walton, Erik Austin, Michael Dawson, and Christopher Achen offered wise counsel and helpful suggestions as we saw our way to the final manuscript.

Lynn Harris, Paul Freedman, Yoshitaka Nishizawa, Peter Harbage, and Kyungjoon Kim helped by tracking down the examples and references that appear throughout. Alyson Reed of the League of Women Voters Education Fund graciously provided materials on voter registration laws, and Gary Jacobson generously shared his data on congressional elections. Mary Jo Stofflet helped prepare the bibliography.

We are grateful for the support that the Falk Fund and the Mag Foundation provided us through Yale University. Hansen received funding from the Division of the Social Sciences of the University of Chicago; Rosenstone received support from the Carnegie Corporation of New York and from the Center for Political Studies of the Institute for Social Research at the University of Michigan.

Dana, Maria Antonia, Sara, and Anna came into our lives long after this project had begun but long before it was finished. They will be the first to tell you that this work has dragged on long enough. Their infinite patience, tolerance, encouragement, and support made this collaboration possible. It is to the joy that they have brought to our lives that we dedicate this book.

CONTENTS

CHAPTER 5
PARTICIPATION IN
ELECTORAL POLITICS   128

TABLES AND FIGURES

Tables

xv

Figures

INTRODUCTION: THE PUZZLE OF PARTICIPATION IN AMERICAN POLITICS

Distinct among the world's political systems, democracies offer citizens opportunities to participate in their own governance. In democracies, the people elect their own leaders. They assemble to speak and act in concert. They petition their governors for redress of their grievances.

In every democracy, some citizens heed while others neglect their opportunities to take part in politics. Sometimes people vote, sometimes they lobby, sometimes they petition, and sometimes they do nothing. What does it mean in a democracy when citizens exercise their right to take part in elections and government? What does it mean when they do not?

The answers to these questions are of real political importance — especially in the United States, where the record of citizen participation over the last half of the twentieth century presents a set of vexing puzzles.

Participation in American national elections has declined steadily since the 1960s. Turnout in presidential elections fell nearly 13 percentage points between 1960 and 1988. Only half the American electorate cast a ballot in the 1988 presidential contest and barely one-third turned out to vote in the 1990 midterm elections. In 1988, citizens were also substantially less likely than they were three decades before to contribute time or money to a political party or candidate, to attend political meetings or rallies, or to try to convince others how to vote.

Yet at precisely the same time that participation in elections was sliding, Americans were becoming increasingly likely to take part in other kinds of political activities. Whereas only 5 percent of the adult population wrote a letter to a representative or senator in 1961, 16 percent did so in 1983. Over the same period political organizations of all kinds—interest groups, community organizations, and political action committees—swelled in numbers at both the local and national levels.

What does it mean that fewer Americans exercise their right to vote or to take part in electoral campaigns? Does it indicate an electorate that is basically satisfied with the way things are going, or does it betoken a massive withdrawal of popular support and legitimacy, a "diffuse, systemwide crisis" of alienation and distrust?[1] What does it mean that more Americans are taking advantage of their right to organize and lobby government? Does it mark a populace that is more eager to effect change for the better, or does it signify a cynical and manipulative abuse of the political process by selfish special interests?[2]

It is not at all clear that we know the answer to any of these questions. First, we have remarkably little empirical evidence bearing upon them. Few analysts have examined the ebb and flow of political participation systematically; fewer still have examined the changes outside of elections. Moreover, most of what we know about participation comes from studies of cross sections, from comparisons of individuals at a single moment, usually in a single election.

Second (partly a consequence of the first), our current theoretical understanding of political participation is incapable of answering

[1] Walter Dean Burnham, "Shifting Patterns of Congressional Voting Participation in the United States," paper presented at the annual meeting of the American Political Science Association, 1981, p. 47; Curtis B. Gans, "The Empty Ballot Box: Reflections on Nonvoters in America," *Public Opinion* (September/October 1978), pp. 54–57; Warren E. Miller, "Disinterest, Disaffection, and Participation in Presidential Elections," *Political Behavior* 2 (November 1980), pp. 7–32; Stephen E. Bennett, *Apathy in America, 1960–1984: Causes and Consequences of Citizen Political Indifference* (Dobbs Ferry, N.Y.: Transnational Publishers, 1986); E. J. Dionne, *Why Americans Hate Politics* (New York: Simon and Schuster, 1991).

[2] Benjamin Ginsberg and Martin Shefter, *Politics by Other Means: The Declining Importance of Elections* (New York: Basic Books, 1990); Walter J. Stone, *Republic at Risk: Self-Interest in American Politics* (Pacific Grove, Calif.: Brooks/Cole Publishing Co., 1990); Lawrence N. Hansen, "Our Turn: Politicians Talk about Themselves, Politics, the Public, the Press, and Reform" (Washington, D.C.: Centel Corporation, 1992).

the questions. The reigning theories of participation in American politics, amazing as it may seem, do not have much to say about politics. Instead, they trace activism to the characteristics of individual American citizens, to their educations, their incomes, and their efficacy. They assume that attitudes determine behavior. When asked to account for the changes in citizen involvement over the last half century, these explanations largely fail.

We know, for instance, that education usually promotes participation. The most educated are much more likely to turn out to vote than the least educated, and Americans have never been better educated. In 1950, the average American adult had barely a ninth-grade education; in 1990, the average adult had completed almost a year of college. Still, Americans' willingness to vote has waned. Why is that? Why has turnout declined, despite increasing levels of education that would otherwise give rise to higher and higher levels of participation?

We know, likewise, that the public's confidence in its ability to act effectively in politics usually promotes participation. The most efficacious citizens are much more likely to try to influence political decisions than the least efficacious. Nearly 75 percent of the American population had a positive sense of their own effectiveness in politics in 1960; barely 40 percent did in 1988. Americans have not felt less politically efficacious since scholars began to ask these questions in national surveys, but their eagerness to contact their representatives in Washington has increased. Why is that? Why has citizen contact risen despite the public's withering belief that its actions are effective? We really do not know.

These questions, as Richard Brody put it more than a decade ago, constitute "the puzzle of political participation in America."[3] Our task in this book is to resolve this puzzle. Why do some citizens participate in politics while others do not? Why is public involvement in American politics plentiful at some times and scarce at others? Who participates, when do they participate, and why do they participate, as they do and when they do?

[3] Richard A. Brody, "The Puzzle of Political Participation in America," pp. 287–324 in Anthony King, ed., *The New American Political System* (Washington, D.C.: American Enterprise Institute, 1978).

In this book, we elaborate a way of thinking about the puzzle that helps us to understand political participation and why it varies, across people, time, contexts, and types of actions. To that end, we develop new theory and we offer new evidence.

By way of evidence, we analyze a wide range of citizen involvement in American politics, both in elections and in government. Using data from studies of national elections since 1952, we examine voter turnout, efforts to persuade others how to vote, work performed for political parties, and contributions to campaigns. Using data from studies of governmental politics since 1973, we investigate citizen contacts with representatives and senators, attendance at meetings of local governments, and signing of petitions.

Along the way, we encounter a raft of interesting questions: Why did participation in many kinds of electoral politics peak in the 1960s and plunge in the 1980s? Why did attendance at the meetings of local governments decline in the 1970s? Why did letter writing to Congress surge in the early 1980s? Why did participation in many kinds of governmental politics typically rise in the summer and dip in the winter? These questions, and others, we raise and address in turn.

Voting, persuading, campaigning, giving, contacting, attending, and signing, of course, do not by any means exhaust the possibilities for citizen involvement in American politics. We hold an expansive definition of citizen activism: Political participation is action directed explicitly toward influencing the distribution of social goods and social values. Admittedly, the definition is much broader than our analysis, encompassing public pressures on private as well as public actors, indirect as well as direct pressures, "outsider" as well as "insider" activities.[4] The limits on our empirical analysis, though, are purely pragmatic: We are constrained by the kinds of information that social scientists and pollsters have gathered over

[4]Our definition is also much broader than the conventional focus on "the selection of government personnel and the actions they take." See Sidney Verba and Norman H. Nie, *Participation in America: Political Democracy and Social Equality* (New York: Harper & Row, 1972), p. 2; Lester W. Milbrath and M. L. Goel, *Political Participation*, 2nd ed. (Chicago: Rand McNally, 1977), p. 2; Joseph LaPalombara, "Political Participation as an Analytical Concept in Comparative Politics," pp. 167–94 in Sidney Verba and Lucian W. Pye, eds., *The Citizen and Politics: A Comparative Perspective*

the last four decades and thus are able to focus our research only on voting, persuading, campaigning, giving, contacting, attending, and signing—and on nothing else. Even so, our investigation includes a mix of electoral and governmental, national and local, and mass and elite, political activities that are both important analytically and consequential politically. We reflect, in Chapter 8, on how well our analysis of these political activities generalizes to other kinds of political actions in other times and other places.

Along with new evidence, we offer new theory. Our argument has two main elements, one personal and one political. Taking individuals in theoretical isolation, we first evaluate the personal costs and benefits of political participation and link their burdens and attractions to personal resources, interests, preferences, identifications, and beliefs. Placing individuals in society, we then identify the aspects of social and political life that make people accessible and amenable to the appeals of political leaders. We trace patterns of political participation— who participates and when they participate—to the strategic choices of politicians, political parties, interest groups, and activists. People participate in politics not so much because of who they are but because of the political choices and incentives they are offered.

Throughout this book we build upon, depart from, and elaborate upon earlier theories of political participation and collective action. We argue most emphatically, however, for the centrality of strategic mobilization. Political analysts, we contend, have until now told only half of the story of participation in America, the half that stresses the resources, interests, identifications, and beliefs of individual citizens. We complete the story. Political leaders, in their struggles for political advantage, mobilize ordinary citizens into American politics. The strategic choices

---

(Stamford, Conn.: Greylock, 1978), pp. 170–71; Samuel P. Huntington and Joan M. Nelson, *No Easy Choice: Political Parties in Developing Countries* (Cambridge: Harvard University Press, 1976), p. 4; M. Margaret Conway, *Political Participation in the United States*, 2nd ed. (Washington, D.C.: Congressional Quarterly Press, 1991), pp. 3–4. Our definition is not, however, all-encompassing. It requires action that is directed toward the achievement of social outcomes. Thus, it rules our psychological involvement, social involvement, and prosecution of private conflicts as forms of political participation.

they make, the strategic decisions they reach, shape the contours—
the whos, whens, and whys—of political participation in America.

Plan of the Book

We begin in the next chapter by presenting our theoretical argument. To state it broadly, citizens participate in elections and government both because they go to politics and because politics comes to them.

The first half of Chapter 2 focuses on the personal attributes of individuals that inspire them and enable them to become involved in politics. When people choose to take part, they bear costs and gain benefits. Accordingly, to take part, people must have both the resources to meet the costs and the interests, identifications, and beliefs to appreciate the benefits. Because neither resources nor interests are distributed evenly across the population, some people find the costs less burdensome and the benefits more attractive than others do. The wealthy, the educated, the experienced, and the efficacious can more easily afford the demands on their money, time, skill, and self-confidence. Likewise, people who see more at stake in politics, whether because policies affect them more, identities beckon them more, options appeal to them more, or duty calls them more, are more attracted by the many benefits that politics offers. Taken together, resources and interests help to explain why some people participate in politics and others do not.

The second half of Chapter 2 concentrates on the elements of the political system that pull people into politics. Left to their own devices, we argue, the public's involvement in the political process would be defeated by two difficult problems: the paradoxes of participation and rational ignorance. The social nature of political life, however, makes it possible for individuals in concert with political leaders to overcome those disincentives to take part. Working through individuals' networks of friends, family, co-workers, and associates, politicians, political parties, interest groups, and activists supply the information that conquers rational ignorance and occasion the creation of the particularized social benefits that surmount the paradox of participation. Locked into struggles for political advantage, political leaders mobilize public involvement strategically. They target and time their efforts for maximum effect. They target their efforts on people they know, people who are well positioned in social networks, people who are influential in politics, and people who are likely to participate. They organize their efforts around salient issues, time them to avoid other distractions, calibrate them to impending decisions, and escalate them when outcomes hang in the balance. Thus, in deciding who to mobilize, political leaders help to determine which people participate. Correspondingly, in deciding when to mobilize, they help to determine when people participate. Their strategic choices determine the shape of political participation in America.

In the next five chapters, we evaluate our argument in light of the evidence—and there is lots of it. From chapter to chapter, the topics change, but the story does not. Whether the subject is participation in elections or in government, participation in local politics or in national politics, participation of the many or of the few, the key to understanding who takes part and who does not, when they take part and when they do not, is mobilization.

Chapter 3 begins the empirical analysis by describing the data and identifying the particular puzzles that we will confront. We show that political involvement is not the exclusive reserve of a small band of inveterate activists, but the open province of episodic participants who advance and withdraw as the situation requires. Here we display the longitudinal patterns of citizen involvement in American politics, identifying some important similarities and some equally important differences, posing the questions that are the subject of the chapters that follow.

Chapter 4 examines citizen participation in governmental politics. Using both cross-sectional and time-series data, we assess the contributions of resources, interests, and strategic mobilization to public involvement in signing petitions, writing letters to Congress, and attending local meetings on town or school affairs. Resources, interests, and social involvements, we show, distinguish people who participate in governmental politics from people who do not. The strategic opportunities that political leaders face, on the other hand, distinguish when people participate in governmental politics from when they do not. Mobilization by political leaders around issues and opportunities is the key to understanding public involvement in American government.

When we turn to electoral involvement, the story is very much the same, as it should be. In Chapters 5, 6, and 7, we use data from national surveys conducted since 1952 to analyze popular involvement in campaigns and elections, examining voter turnout, work performed for political parties, contributions to campaigns, and attempts at persuading others.

Chapter 5 shows that cynicism toward the political process makes little difference to citizen participation in electoral politics. Instead, resources, attitudes toward parties and candidates, and social embeddedness again distinguish who participates and who does not, when they participate and when they do not.

Chapter 6 explores the many facets of strategic electoral mobilization. Political leaders, we find, contact people discerningly, focusing their efforts on those who stand a good chance of participating if encouraged and on those who stand in a position to mobilize others. The efforts of political parties, candidates, campaign organizations, and the movement for black civil rights substantially increase the likelihood that people will in fact participate. They promote participation not because they change people's ideas about the election or the political system, but because they offset some of the costs of participation and exploit social relationships to create social rewards for participation.

Chapter 7 concludes our consideration of electoral participation by solving the puzzle of citizen involvement in American elections, accounting for the decline of electoral participation since the 1960s. We show that part of the solution arises from the ways in which the American people have changed, the ways in which their resources, their social ties, and their evaluations of their choices have changed. We also show, however, that an equally large part of the solution arises from the ways in which the political world has changed, the ways in which political parties, electoral campaigns, and social movements have changed. Our theory of political participation not only explains who participates in politics but also when they participate. In governmental politics and in electoral politics, the story is the same.

Finally, in the conclusion, Chapter 8, we ponder what the findings mean in the context of the theory. We document the relationship between the extent of popular involvement in American politics and the degree of social equality in the American system. Declining political participation, we find, has been accompanied by growing inequality. Mobilization has typically worsened the situation, although it has sometimes made things better. By bringing some people in and leaving others out, mobilization orders the incentives that political leaders hear and heed. We close, then, where we began: with reflections on the meaning of political participation in democratic society.

THE POLITICAL LOGIC OF POLITICAL PARTICIPATION

While spontaneous popular action warms the heart of any good demo-crat, a moment's reflection shows that the people initiate little of what we normally call participation. . . . Acts of participation are stimulated by elites — if not by the government, then by parties, interest groups, agitators, and organizers.

Jack Nagel[1]

Why do people get involved in politics? Why do some people par-ticipate in politics while others do not? Why are citizens deeply committed to participation in politics at some times and wholly passive at other times?

We offer two answers, one personal, one political. Working from one side, the personal, we trace participation to the individual char-acteristics of citizens. People participate in politics when they get valuable benefits that are worth the costs of taking part. Working from the other side, the political, we trace participation to the strate-gic choices of political leaders. People participate in politics when political leaders coax them into taking part in the game. Both sides are necessary: Strategic mobilization without individual motivation is impossible, and individual motivation without strategic mobiliza-tion is illogical.

The complex interaction of the personal and the political stems from the nature of democratic politics. We view democratic pol-itics as a struggle for political power among competing political

---

[1]Jack Nagel, *Participation* (Englewood Cliffs, N.J.: Prentice-Hall, 1987), pp. 3–4.

10

leaders.[2] In such a system, citizen activism has *two* beneficiaries: It is a source of policy benefits for citizens and a source of political advantage for leaders. Accordingly, to understand political participation, we must appreciate how it is used, both by individual citizens and by their leaders.

In this chapter, we lay out the political logic of citizen activism in politics. First, working from the individual perspective, we lay out the benefits and costs of political participation and show how individual resources, interests, preferences, identifications, and beliefs determine the relative attractions of the benefits and the relative burdens of the costs. Next, we consider individuals in political society. We show how the social nature of political life affects the individual rewards of involvement. We show how the social nature of political life makes people accessible and amenable to the appeals of political leaders. And we show how the strategic choices of political leaders determine who participates and when.

Political participation, we conclude, cannot be explained entirely by the orientations and endowments of individual citizens. The competitive pressures of the democratic system encourage political leaders to mobilize their fellow citizens, and if we are to understand participation, we must also comprehend their choices.

Individual Influences on Political Participation

People participate in politics for a variety of personal reasons. Some people participate because it does not cost them much; some participate because they receive lots of benefits. As stated, this personal explanation of political activism is both obvious and tautological: It explains everything because it rules out nothing.

Even so, as political theorist Brian Barry noted, "it is still a quite potent tautology, because it can be combined with empirical assertions to produce significant implications."[3] Our task in this

[2]Joseph A. Schumpeter, *Capitalism, Socialism, and Democracy* (New York: Harper & Row, 1950); Anthony Downs, *An Economic Theory of Democracy* (New York: Harper & Row, 1957); Robert A. Dahl, *A Preface to Democratic Theory* (Chicago: University of Chicago Press, 1956).
[3]Brian Barry, *Sociologists, Economists and Democracy* (London: Collier–Macmillan, 1970), p. 33; for a similar approach, see John Mark Hansen, "The Political Economy of Group Membership," *American Political Science Review* 79 (March 1985), pp. 79–96.

section is to supply empirical linkages, to develop the implications of different resources for the relative costs of participation, and to develop the implications of different interests and attitudes for the relative benefits of participation.

Costs and Resources

Participation in politics puts demands on people's scarce resources. Working on a political campaign requires time; writing a letter requires verbal acuity; making a donation to a candidate requires money; signing a petition requires a sense of personal competence. Participation in politics, that is, has a price, a price that is some combination of money, time, skill, knowledge, and self-confidence.

Some people are better able to pay the price than others. In economic life people with greater resources can consume more of (almost) everything, from fancy meals to fast cars to flashy clothes. In social life people with greater resources can do more of (almost) everything, from entertaining friends to joining organizations to volunteering at schools, churches, and charities.[4] So, too, in political life. People with abundant money, time, skill, knowledge, and self-confidence devote more resources to politics, not because politics gives them more in return (although it might) but because they can more easily afford it. Many of the most familiar empirical regularities in American politics follow from this simple observation.

First, the wealthy vote, write, campaign, and petition more than the poor.[5] This should come as no surprise. Citizens with lots of income can simply afford to do more—of everything—than citizens with little money. The wealthy have discretionary income that they can contribute directly to political parties, candidates, political action committees, and other causes. Moreover, money is fungible—it

[4]Paul F. Lazarsfeld, Bernard Berelson, and Hazel Gaudet, *The People's Choice* (New York: Columbia University Press, 1948); Sidney Verba and Norman H. Nie, *Participation in America: Political Democracy and Social Equality* (New York: Harper & Row, 1972), chap. 11; Howard V. Hayghe, "Volunteers in the U.S.: Who Donates the Time?" *Monthly Labor Review* (February 1991), pp. 17–23.
[5]Among many, Verba and Nie, *Participation in America*, chap.8; Raymond E. Wolfinger and Steven J. Rosenstone, *Who Votes?* (New Haven: Yale University Press, 1980), pp. 20–26.

can be freely converted into other political resources that make it easier for people to take part in politics. A car is not a necessary condition for political action, for example, but having one makes it much easier to get to a school board meeting, a political rally, or a candidate's campaign headquarters. Money can be used to hire someone to do the daily chores—to clean the house, buy the groceries, cook dinner, baby-sit the kids—and free up time for politics. Thus, if people want to participate in politics, money makes it easier for them to do so.

The costs of political activity can also be measured in opportunities forgone. Taking part in politics requires that people forfeit or postpone other activities, and these opportunity costs of participation are higher for some people than for others.[6] Because the resources of the wealthy are more ample, they do not face the same hard tradeoffs that the poor face every day of their lives. As important and interesting as politics may be, its significance pales in comparison with paying the rent, maintaining the car, keeping the children in school, and putting food on the table. In short, for people whose resources are limited, politics is a luxury they often cannot afford, particularly when political outcomes may have only a modest impact on their own economic situations.[7]

Second, the more educated are more likely to take part in politics than the less educated.[8] Again, no surprise. In the United States,

---

[6]In general, politics does not compete very well with the other things that demand people's attention. See John P. Robinson and Philip E. Converse, "Social Change Reflected in the Use of Time," pp. 17–86 in Angus Campbell and Philip E. Converse, eds., *The Human Meaning of Social Change* (New York: Russell Sage Foundation, 1972); John P. Robinson, Philip E. Converse, and Alexander Szalai, "Everyday Life in Twelve Countries," pp. 113–44 in Alexander Szalai, ed., *The Use of Time: Daily Activities of Urban and Suburban Populations in Twelve Countries* (The Hague, Netherlands: Mouton, 1972).

[7]Wolfinger and Rosenstone, *Who Votes?*, p. 20: Steven J. Rosenstone, "Economic Adversity and Voter Turnout," *American Journal of Political Science* 26 (February 1982), pp. 25–46; Benjamin Radcliff, "The Welfare State, Turnout, and the Economy: A Comparative Analysis," paper presented at the annual meeting of the Midwest Political Science Association, 1991.

[8]Angus Campbell, Philip E. Converse, Warren E. Miller, and Donald E. Stokes, *The American Voter* (New York: Wiley, 1960), chap. 17; Verba and Nie, *Participation in America*, chap. 8; Wolfinger and Rosenstone, *Who Votes?*, pp. 18–26.

the educational experience fosters democratic values and nurtures a sense of citizen competence, both of which encourage participation. [9] More important, however, education provides skills that facilitate participation in politics. As Wolfinger and Rosenstone argue, "education imparts information about politics and cognate fields and about a variety of skills, some of which facilitate political learning.... Schooling increases one's capacity for understanding and working with complex, abstract and intangible subjects, that is, subjects like politics." [10] Skills in research, writing, and speaking, developed through education, help citizens to negotiate the maze of demands that participation places on them. To cast a ballot, citizens must figure out how to register to vote; they must make sense of the candidates and issues; they must locate polling places. To write a letter to a senator, citizens must compose a persuasive message once they have identified the senator and looked up her address. For the grade-school educated, these are daunting tasks; for the college educated, they are easy. The better educated have been better trained to participate in politics.

Finally, those with many years of formal schooling are substantially more likely to read newspapers, follow the news, and be politically informed, all of which makes them more aware of the opportunities to participate and more likely to possess information with which to do so.

This is not to say that politically useful knowledge and skills derive only from the classroom. Lessons picked up from the "school of hard knocks" can compensate for formal education, imparting equivalent knowledge, experience, and skills. [11] With experience comes familiarity with the political process, familiarity with and increased attachment to the political parties and their candidates, and familiarity with the ins and outs of political action: what people need

---

[9] One of the unusual features of American schools is their historic emphasis on citizenship education, an emphasis born in response to the massive waves of immigration in the nineteenth century. Wolfinger and Rosenstone elaborate more fully the connection between education and citizenship values in *Who Votes?*, chap. 2. Here, this effect is considered to work through the attitudes it fosters: a sense of duty and a sense of efficacy.

[10] Wolfinger and Rosenstone, *Who Votes?*, p. 18.

[11] Wolfinger and Rosenstone, *Who Votes?*, chaps. 2–3.

to do to take part and where people need to go to do it.[12] Hence, older citizens vote, write, campaign, and petition more than young citizens who have had less experience in politics.

Finally, people with a sense of political efficacy are more likely to take a more active part in politics than those without this belief. By efficacy we mean both a sense of personal competence in one's ability to understand politics and to participate in politics (what political scientists call internal efficacy), as well as a sense that one's political activities can influence what the government actually does (external efficacy).[13] Some people come to believe in their personal competence because they have been told again and again, by parents, teachers, and friends, that their efforts make a difference. Other people come to believe in their personal competence because they have acted and in fact found their actions consequential. As defined, it is already evident that efficacy is an important political resource.[14] Working in a campaign or signing a petition involves some sense that the cause is not hopeless (even if the particular effort is). Participation is a waste of time if one does not believe that one's

---

[12] Philip E. Converse, *The Dynamics of Party Support: Cohort-Analysing Party Identification* (Beverly Hills: Sage, 1976); John M. Strate, Charles J. Parrish, Charles D. Elder, and Coit Ford III, "Life Span Civic Development and Voting Participation," *American Political Science Review* 83 (June 1989), pp. 444–64; John M. Strate, Charles J. Parrish, Charles D. Elder, and Thomas Jankowski, "Life Span Civic Development and Campaign Participation," paper presented at the annual meeting of the American Political Science Association, 1990.

[13] For a discussion of the distinction between internal and external efficacy see Robert E. Lane, *Political Life: Why and How People Get Involved in Politics* (New York: Free Press, 1959); George I. Balch, "Multiple Indicators in Survey Research: The Concept of 'Sense of Political Efficacy,' " *Political Methodology* 1 (1974), pp. 1–43; Stephen C. Craig, "Efficacy, Trust, and Political Behavior: An Attempt to Resolve a Lingering Conceptual Dilemma," *American Politics Quarterly* 7 (April 1979), pp. 225–39; and Stephen C. Craig and Michael A. Maggiotto, "Measuring Political Efficacy," *Political Methodology* 8 (1982), pp. 85–109.

[14] Among others, Campbell et al., *The American Voter*, chap. 5. It is so evident, in fact, that one fears circularity: People participate because they feel efficacious, but they feel efficacious because they participate. Analysts have long seen citizen participation as productive of efficacy; see Carole Pateman, *Participation and Democratic Theory* (Cambridge: Cambridge University Press, 1970) and Steven E. Finkel, "Reciprocal Effects of Participation and Political Efficacy: A Panel Analysis," *American Journal of Political Science* 29 (November 1985), pp. 891–913. More troubling is the argument
(continued)

efforts make a material difference to political outcomes. Those who have confidence that their participation will make a difference are more likely to act than those who lack that basic confidence.[15]

In summary, the costs of political activism affect different people in different ways, depending on their resources. For people with abundant money, time, knowledge, skills, and efficacy, involvement costs very little. Consequently, they participate more.

Rewards, Interests, and Beliefs

People participate in politics because they get something out of it. The rewards take many forms.[16] Participants sometimes enjoy *material benefits*, tangible rewards that are easily converted into money, like a government job or a tax break. Those active in politics can also receive *solidary benefits*, intangible rewards that stem from social interaction, like status, deference, and friendship. And participation can also yield *purposive benefits*, intrinsic rewards that derive from the act of participation itself, such as a sense of satisfaction from having contributed to a worthy cause.

(continued)
that the relationship between involvement and efficacy might be an artifact of human psychology. Some work in psychology has cast doubt on the idea that people can identify their internal attitudinal states (e.g., Richard E. Nisbett and Timothy D. Wilson, "Telling More than We Can Know: Verbal Reports of Mental Processes," *Psychological Review* 84 (May 1977), pp. 231–59). When asked to identify their internal attitudinal states, they instead infer their attitudes from their own behavior (see Daryl J. Bem, "Self-Perception: An Alternative Interpretation of Cognitive Dissonance Phenomena," *Psychological Review* 74 (May 1967), pp. 183–200; and Richard Nisbett and Lee Ross, *Human Inference: Strategies and Shortcomings of Social Judgment* (Englewood Cliffs, N.J.: Prentice-Hall, 1980). The concern, then, is that survey respondents infer beliefs from their behaviors: "I must feel like my actions make a difference because otherwise all of the time I spend participating in politics would be wasted."

[15]Among more recent arguments, Terry M. Moe, *The Organization of Interests* (Chicago: University of Chicago Press, 1980); Paul R. Abramson and John H. Aldrich, "The Decline of Electoral Participation in America," *American Political Science Review* 76 (September 1982), pp. 502–21.

[16]James Q. Wilson, *Political Organizations* (New York: Basic Books, 1973), chap. 3; Peter B. Clark and James Q. Wilson, "Incentive Systems: A Theory of Organizations," *Administrative Science Quarterly* 6 (September 1961), pp. 129–66; Robert H. Salisbury, "An Exchange Theory of Interest Groups," *Midwest Journal of Political Science* 13 (February 1969), pp. 1–32.

This typology, suggested by James Q. Wilson, gives an idea of the great variety of possible benefits from participation, but for our purposes, the distinction between collective and selective rewards is more important.[17] *Collective rewards*, on the one hand, benefit every resident of a particular place or every member of a particular group, whether she took part in politics or not. Most, but not all, are material. A clean air bill, for example, benefits every resident of Los Angeles, New York, or Denver. A residential parking ordinance benefits every resident of the neighborhoods surrounding a hospital. A mortgage interest deduction for homeowners benefits every homeowner, homebuilder, and realtor. An end to the ban on interstate sales of firearms benefits every gun owner and gun dealer. People receive collective rewards regardless of whether they participate. *Selective rewards*, on the other hand, benefit only those people who take part in politics. Some selective rewards are material: Government jobs in Brooklyn, for instance, may go exclusively to campaign workers. Others are solidary: Recognition as a leader falls only to neighborhood activists. Many are purposive: A sense of having done one's duty accrues only to those who have done their duty. Unlike collective rewards, people receive selective rewards because they participate; by the same token, people forgo selective rewards because they do not.[18]

Each form of citizen participation in politics offers a unique mix of collective and selective benefits. Citizens find each combination of benefits more or less worthwhile depending on their interests, preferences, identifications, and beliefs. A man who works for the park district of the city of Chicago might view campaign work as a requirement of his job. A woman who lives on a farm in west Texas might see attendance at county commission meetings as a rare opportunity for visiting with friends and neighbors. A man who has been socialized with a deep sense of obligation to participate

---

[17]This distinction has a long history in economics, where the equivalent terms are "public" and "private" goods, but it was most influentially applied to the problem of political action by Mancur Olson, Jr., *The Logic of Collective Action* (Cambridge: Harvard University Press, 1965).

[18]The definitional distinction between collective and selective rewards—namely, whether people have to take part in order to get them—will become very important to our argument later on.

in the community might see voting as a way to live up to his duty. Depending on their needs, certain kinds of participation make more sense for certain people than other kinds of participation.[19]

These observations help to structure our ideas about the role that interests, preferences, identifications, and beliefs play in promoting participation in politics.

First, people who have a direct stake in political outcomes are obviously more likely to participate in politics than people who do not have such an immediate stake.[20] Parents who have children in public schools, for instance, are much more likely to attend school board meetings than other people, simply because the school board makes decisions that affect the welfare of their children directly, broadly, and consequentially. Although everybody in the community has an interest in the financial decisions that school boards make, only parents typically care very much about such matters as curricular requirements, athletics and activities, bus routes, crossing guards, and dress codes. People with direct interests anticipate greater material rewards, both collective and selective, from their actions.

Second, people who strongly prefer one political outcome to another are more likely to enter politics than people who have weaker preferences.[21] Voters consistently complain that American elections offer no choices, only echoes. Their complaint, however, is not always on the mark. Some people see differences where others see none. For many Americans in 1948, Harry Truman and Thomas Dewey were Tweedledum and Tweedledee: Both supported the New Deal welfare state and both were anticommunist cold warriors. But for members of industrial labor unions the differences between them were clear: Truman was the defender of the National Labor Relations Act against the anti-union Republicans in Congress. Likewise, the system sometimes offers a real choice. Although voters might be

---

[19] Wilson, *Political Organizations*, chap. 3.

[20] Wolfinger and Rosenstone, *Who Votes?*, chap. 5; Raymond E. Bauer, Ithiel de Sola Pool, and Lewis Anthony Dexter, *American Business and Public Policy: The Politics of Trade*, 2nd ed. (Chicago: Aldine-Atherton, 1972), chaps. 9–13.

[21] Campbell et al., *The American Voter*, chap. 5; John F. Zipp, "Perceived Representativeness and Voting: An Assessment of the Impact of 'Choices' vs. 'Echoes,' " *American Political Science Review* 79 (March 1985), pp. 50–61.

forgiven for confusing Gerald Ford and Jimmy Carter in 1976, few could fail to discern the differences between Lyndon Johnson and Barry Goldwater in 1964 or Ronald Reagan and Walter Mondale in 1984.

The variations in preferences are important. Those who strongly prefer one candidate or one party or one policy to another anticipate greater policy benefits from the outcome than those whose preferences are weaker. Accordingly, they are more likely to get involved in politics.

Third, people who identify closely with political contenders are more likely to participate in politics than people whose psychological identifications are weaker.[22] This may sound, on its face, like a restatement of the preceding point, but it is not. Before, we argued that strong preferences heighten the value of extrinsic rewards of participation, of material and solidary benefits that arise as a consequence of political action. Here, we argue that strong psychological attachments heighten the value of intrinsic rewards from participation, of the internal satisfactions that derive from taking part. Just as sports fans take pleasure in cheering on their favorite teams, so partisans take pleasure in acting on behalf of their favorite politicians, parties, or groups. The more committed the fans, the more lusty their cheers; the more committed the partisans, the more likely their participation.

Because of their psychological attachments, then, issue activists are more likely to write letters to their representatives in Congress. Because of their psychological attachments, likewise, strong Democrats and strong Republicans are more likely to be active in elections than independents or weak partisans. Political participation appeals more to the strongly than the weakly committed because the strongly committed derive greater personal satisfaction from it.

Finally, some people hold beliefs and preferences that motivate their participation internally. The most common is a sense of citizen duty. Because of their socialization by family, teachers, or friends, some people believe it is their responsibility to participate in politics—and in particular to vote—regardless of whether their participation has any effect on the outcome. Obviously, people who

---

[22]Campbell et al., *The American Voter*, chap. 6; Verba and Nie, *Participation in America*, chap. 12; Abramson and Aldrich, "The Decline of Electoral Participation."

hold these beliefs are more likely to participate: Taking part makes them feel that they have discharged their obligations.[23] The purposive rewards of participation are selective.

Thus, the benefits of political participation appeal to different people in different ways, depending on their interests, preferences, identifications, and beliefs. People who perceive more at stake in politics—because policies affect them more, identities beckon them more, options appeal to them more, or duty calls them more—participate more in politics.

People get involved in politics, then, in predictable ways: Because of their resources, some people can better afford politics than others; because of their interests, preferences, identifications, and beliefs, some people get more benefit from politics than others. Clearly, the two work together. No matter how valuable the benefits of participation, people cannot take part unless they have sufficient resources to do so. No matter how ample the resources, people will not take part unless they get more out of politics than other pursuits. Taken together, these considerations help to explain why some people take part in politics and others do not.

Political Influences on Participation: Strategic Mobilization

When applied to the question of *which* people participate in politics, the individual explanations of political activism that we have just discussed seem to satisfy. But when applied to the question of *when* people participate in politics, their inadequacies begin to show.

Suppose, for instance, that people participate in politics because of the solidary or the purposive benefits they receive—the approba-

---

[23] Campbell et al., *The American Voter*, chap. 5; William H. Riker and Peter C. Ordeshook, "A Theory of the Calculus of Voting," *American Political Science Review* 62 (March 1968), pp. 25–42. Again, the connection between belief in a duty to participate and participation itself is distressingly close. Undoubtedly, many people vote because they believe it is the right thing to do. Still, many people might identify their duty as a reason for their participation because they cannot identify any other reason for it. As with a sense of personal efficacy, people may infer a sense of duty from their participation: "I have voted in every election in the last ten years; thus, I must believe that it is important to vote." See the references in note 14.

tions of their friends or the satisfactions from a duty performed. It stands to reason, then, that participation should not fluctuate very much from month to month or from year to year because fundamental social identifications and political beliefs change only slowly, if at all. The same people should turn out for politics time and time again.

Yet this prediction is wrong, as we will show in Chapter 3. Both the level of political participation and the people who participate change significantly from month to month, year to year, and election to election. That being the case, we need to turn to the *political* circumstances that change over time and induce people to take part at one moment and not another: the personal qualities and policy stands of the candidates for office; the issues that appear and disappear on the political agenda; the actions of the politicians, parties, and interest groups that compete for political advantage. These considerations, in turn, lead to an explanation of political participation that emphasizes the collective benefits that people receive from political outcomes, such as military spending, abortion rights, tax breaks, and other public policies. But this line of thinking immediately runs up against two deadly logical conundrums.

Two Paradoxes: Participation and Rational Ignorance

The first difficulty is the famous "paradox of voting," or, more broadly, the "paradox of participation in politics."[24] If people are rational, the paradox holds, and if they receive only collective benefits, they will not turn out to vote, and for very good reason: The result of the election will be the same whether they participate or not. In any election, hundreds or thousands or millions of voters will cast ballots; the chance that a single ballot will determine the result is exceedingly small. In 1960, for example, the closest presidential election in the twentieth century, John F. Kennedy's victory over Richard M. Nixon hinged on 115,000 votes, only 0.2 percent of the total, but still a very large number. At the same time, casting a vote is costly. At a minimum, voters must spend time, energy,

---

[24]Downs, *An Economic Theory of Democracy*, chap. 14; Olson, *The Logic of Collective Action*, chap. 1; Barry, *Sociologists, Economists and Democracy*, chap. 2.

and money rousting themselves to polling places and marking their ballots. Thus, even if the outcome of the election really matters to people, trying to affect it does not make any sense. Rational people choose the most efficient means to achieve their goals; they do not knowingly waste their scarce resources. Voting, it follows, is irrational: It consumes resources but achieves no results that would not be achieved otherwise.

The same paradox holds with equal force for other forms of political activity. Objectively, the probability that any one person's one lonely act will determine a political outcome is vanishingly small. One more letter mailed to Congress, one more person attending a meeting, one more dollar sent to a campaign, one more person persuaded to vote will not make a bit of difference to the result, but it will cost the participant. If people receive only collective benefits from political outcomes, therefore, they will not participate in politics. Political action, if it occurs, is irrational.[25]

The second difficulty is "rational ignorance."[26] If political involvement is irrational, so, for much the same reason, is political learning. First, information about politics and government must be gathered, and its cost is far above zero. Washington is a distant place, government is a complicated business, and the press can be relied on to cover only a fraction of what the government is up to. Likewise, candidates for office are unfamiliar people, their records are voluminous, and the media are quite selective in their coverage of the campaigns. Second, the value of information, once obtained, is very small, precisely because of the paradox of participation in politics. Even if voters had lots of information about the issues debated in Washington and the issues contested in campaigns, what good would it do them? It makes no sense for them to act on it anyway: The outcome will be the same regardless. Thus, citizens have few incentives to inform themselves about politics. They stay "rationally ignorant."

Thus, the question of when people involve themselves in politics cannot be addressed solely within the context of individual motives and behaviors. One approach fails to provide an answer,

---

[25] On this more general point, Olson, *The Logic of Collective Action*, chap. 1. See also Barry, *Sociologists, Economists and Democracy*, chap. 2.

[26] Downs, *An Economic Theory of Democracy*, chaps. 12–13.

and the other gets tangled in its own logic. Instead, the explanation of participation, to make any sense, must move beyond the worlds of individuals to include family, friends, neighbors, and co-workers, plus politicians, parties, activists, and interest groups.

The Social Nature of Political Life

With few exceptions, people are deeply embedded in a web of social relationships with family, friends, neighbors, and co-workers. Within these circles, people convey expectations to others about the kinds of behaviors, some political, that are appropriate and desirable. Sometimes they relate their expectations overtly: They ask acquaintances directly to do something. More often they relate their expectations subtly: They simply raise their concerns. What's more, people in these networks reward those who comply with expectations, and they sanction those who do not. They praise, esteem, and owe favors to those who do act, and reprove, shun, and take note of those who do not. Social networks, in short, create solidary rewards and bestow them, selectively, on those who act in the common interest.[27]

For most people, the obligations and rewards of friendship, camaraderie, neighborliness, and family ties are very powerful. People want to be accepted, valued, and liked. As a consequence, social networks play a key role in overcoming the paradoxes of participation and rational ignorance.[28]

[27] Wilson, *Political Organizations*, chap. 3; Robert Huckfeldt, "Political Participation and the Neighborhood Context," *American Journal of Political Science* 23 (June 1979), pp. 579–92; Robert Huckfeldt and John Sprague, "Political Parties and Electoral Mobilization: Political Structure, Social Structure, and the Party Canvass," *American Political Science Review* 86 (March 1992), pp. 70–86; Carole Jean Uhlaner, "'Relational Goods' and Participation: Incorporating Sociability into a Theory of Rational Action," *Public Choice* 62 (September 1989), pp. 253–85; Stephen Knack, "Civic Norms, Social Sanctions, and Voter Turnout," *Rationality and Society* 4 (April 1992), pp. 133–56.

[28] Gerald M. Pomper and Loretta Sernekos, "The 'Bake Sale' Theory of Voting Participation," paper presented at the annual meeting of the American Political Science Association, 1989; Huckfeldt, "Political Participation and the Neighborhood Social Context"; Huckfeldt and Sprague, "Political Parties and Electoral Mobilization"; Christopher B. Kenney, "Political Participation and Effects from the Social Environment," *American Journal of Political Science* 36 (February 1992), pp. 259–67.

Social networks address rational ignorance. They provide information.[29] Participants in family, work, and friendship groups communicate, and in doing so they learn about politics from others in the group. They likewise reward contributions of information. Family, work, and friendship groups favor those who offer their knowledge to the collegium. Thus, because of social networks, each person bears the cost of collecting only a fraction of the political information she receives.

Too, social networks address the paradox of participation. People take part in family, work, and friendship groups on a regular and sustained basis. Consequently, members of social networks can identify readily those who comply with social expectations and those who do not, that is, those who vote and write and attend and otherwise participate in politics and those who do not. In turn, because members of social networks can distinguish participants from pikers, they can also selectively reward the one and sanction the other. Finally, because they can reward and sanction discerningly, they can also create and enforce expectations that many will act in concert.[30] Although one letter to Congress is not likely to have any impact, one thousand letters is, and although one vote for governor is not likely to make a difference, one hundred thousand votes is. Social networks, the everyday groupings of friends, family, and associates, make effective, coordinated, political action possible.

They do not, however, make effective, coordinated, political action probable. Most citizens are not in positions to know what is occurring in politics, nor do they know anybody who is. Neither they nor their families, friends, and co-workers really know whether their interests are enough at stake at the moment to warrant political action—of whatever kind—being undertaken to advance or defend them.

[29] Gabriel A. Almond and Sidney Verba, *The Civic Culture* (Boston: Little, Brown, 1965); Bonnie H. Erickson and T. A. Nosanchuk, "How an Apolitical Association Politicizes," *Canadian Review of Sociology and Anthropology* 27 (May 1990), pp. 206–19; Robert Huckfeldt and John Sprague, "Networks in Context: The Social Flow of Political Information," *American Political Science Review* 81 (December 1987), pp. 1198–1216.
[30] Russell Hardin, *Collective Action* (Baltimore: Resources for the Future, 1982), chaps. 10–11; Robert Axelrod, *The Evolution of Cooperation* (New York: Basic Books, 1984).

Others in the system have such knowledge close at hand. Because they are in the thick of political battles, political leaders, be they candidates, party officials, interest groups, or activists, know exactly what is on the political agenda and exactly how it affects people. And because they are in the thick of political battles, they have a tangible incentive to convey such information to the people who can help them to win.

For politicians, political parties, interest groups, and activists, citizen involvement is an important political resource. In a democracy, the people's wants are supposed to matter. In elections, for example, candidates for office and their organized supporters need citizens' votes, money, and time. In national government, likewise, elected officials, interest groups, and activists want votes in Congress, favors from the White House, and rulings from the bureaucracy, and they can use citizens' letters, petitions, and protests to help get them. In local government, finally, neighborhoods want stop signs from city councils and parents want computer labs from school boards, and they can use citizens' contacts, presence, and pressures to try to get them. Citizen participation is a resource that political leaders use in their struggles for political advantage.[31] We call their efforts to deploy it "mobilization."

Political Mobilization

Mobilization is the process by which candidates, parties, activists, and groups induce other people to participate. We say that one of

---

[31] Gerald H. Kramer, "The Effects of Precinct Level Canvassing on Voter Behavior," *Public Opinion Quarterly* 34 (Winter 1970), pp. 560–72; James N. Rosenau, *Citizenship between Elections: An Inquiry into the Mobilizable American* (New York: Free Press, 1974); Carole J. Uhlaner, "Rational Turnout: The Neglected Role of Groups," *American Journal of Political Science* 33 (May 1987), pp. 390–422. Unsurprisingly, mobilization arguments show up most often in comparative works on political participation, e.g., Sidney Verba, Norman H. Nie, and Jae-on Kim, *Participation and Political Equality* (New York: Cambridge University Press, 1978), chap. 6; G. Bingham Powell, Jr., "American Voter Turnout in Comparative Perspective," *American Political Science Review* 80 (March 1986), pp. 17–43; Robert W. Jackman, "Political Institutions and Voter Turnout in the Industrial Democracies," *American Political Science Review* 81 (June 1987), pp. 405–23.

these actors has *mobilized* somebody when it has done something to increase the likelihood of her participation.[32] We distinguish two types of mobilization. Leaders mobilize people *directly* when they contact citizens personally and encourage them to take action. Door-to-door canvasses by campaign organizations, direct mail solicitations by political agitators, televised appeals for aid by presidents, and grass-roots letter drives by interest groups are examples of direct mobilization. Leaders mobilize people *indirectly* when they contact citizens through mutual associates, whether family, friends, neighbors, or colleagues. When candidates solicit employers for campaign money and bosses in turn encourage their employees to give, when local activists push their friends to attend meetings and friends ask family to accompany them, when parties contact workers in a plant and the workers ask their co-workers to vote, that is indirect mobilization.[33]

Direct Mobilization
Through direct mobilization, political leaders provide opportunities for political action that citizens would not have otherwise. They build the organizations that give people the chance to contribute their time and money to political causes. They sponsor the meetings and rallies that give people the opportunity to attend. They circulate petitions that give people the chance to sign. They request contributions to causes that people may never have heard of until the moment of contact. The mobilization efforts of political leaders create the very opportunities for citizens to participate.

[32] Charles Tilly, *From Mobilization to Revolution* (Reading, Mass.: Addison-Wesley, 1978), p. 69.
[33] Huckfeldt and Sprague, "Political Parties and Electoral Mobilization"; Rosenau, *Citizenship between Elections*, chap. 3. This conjecture about indirect mobilization is analogous to the notion of the "two-step flow" of communication in which information flows first to opinion leaders who in turn pass on the information to the less active members of the population. See Lazarsfeld, Berelson, and Gaudet, *The People's Choice*; Elihu Katz, "The Two-Step Flow of Communication: An Up-to-Date Report on an Hypothesis," *Public Opinion Quarterly* 21 (Spring 1957), pp. 61–78; John P. Robinson, "Interpersonal Influence in Election Campaigns: Two Step-Flow Hypotheses," *Public Opinion Quarterly* 40 (Fall 1976), pp. 304–19. With respect to mobilization, we think that people who are the most attentive to and active in politics are most likely to be directly mobilized, but once they are mobilized, they are likely to influence others in their family, in their neighborhood, and in the place of work.

Through direct mobilization, likewise, political leaders subsidize political information. Because information is costly and because politics is far from the most pressing concern in most people's lives, few citizens know much about politics unless somebody tells them. People remain rationally ignorant. Through the mobilization efforts of political leaders, however, they are informed about the issues on the congressional agenda, alerted to the meetings of the school board, and reminded about the upcoming city council elections. In short, they are given information about the issues at stake and the opportunities to affect them. The mobilization efforts of political leaders help citizens to overcome their rational ignorance.

Through direct mobilization, finally, political leaders subsidize the costs of citizen activism. They distribute voter registration forms and absentee ballots. They drive people to the polls on election day. They provide child care to free parents to attend meetings and demonstrations. They supply people with the texts for letters to representatives and senators. By underwriting the costs of political participation, the mobilization efforts of political leaders help to overcome the paradox of participation.

Indirect Mobilization

The impact of political mobilization, though, extends far beyond the effect it has on the limited number of people who are contacted directly. Membership in social networks makes people available to politicians, organizations, and activists. Membership in social networks makes people responsive to mobilization. Social networks, that is, convert direct mobilization into indirect mobilization. Political leaders mobilize citizens for political action through social networks.[34]

For politicians, parties, interest groups, and activists, access to social networks reduces the costs of making contact. Leaders need not communicate with every person directly. Instead, leaders contact their associates, associates contact their colleagues, and colleagues contact their friends, families, and co-workers.[35] Through social

[34]Elihu Katz and Paul F. Lazarsfeld, *Personal Influence: The Part Played by People in the Flow of Mass Communications* (Glencoe, Ill.: The Free Press, 1955).

[35]Doug McAdam, *Political Process and the Development of Black Insurgency, 1930–1970* (Chicago: University of Chicago Press, 1982), p. 44; Luther P. Gerlach and Virginia H. Hine, *People, Power, Change: Movements of Social Transformation* (Indianapolis: Bobbs-Merrill, 1970), p. 79; and Anthony Oberschall, *Social Conflict and Social Movements* (Englewood Cliffs, N.J.: Prentice-Hall, 1973), p. 125.

networks, leaders get the word out, and citizens get the word. Social networks multiply the effect of mobilization: Direct mobilization reverberates through indirect mobilization.[36]

Even more important, for politicians, parties, interest groups, and activists, access to social networks makes it possible to mobilize people to participate. Absent the involvement of social networks, leaders usually have only collective rewards to offer to potential participants: They hold out the prospect that favored candidates will win or that the government will formulate beneficial policies.[37] Because rewards are collective, however, citizens receive them whether they act or not. Mobilization runs aground on the paradox of participation.[38]

With the involvement of social networks, however, mobilization occasions the creation of selective rewards. When friends, neighbors, and co-workers present the opportunities to partici-

[36] Bauer, Pool, and Dexter, *American Business and Public Policy*, chaps. 11–13. Social networks ensure that information spreads rapidly even to people the initiator does not know at all. One amazing bit of evidence comes from the experimental investigations of the "small world problem" in the 1960s. The experimenters asked their subjects in Nebraska to get a letter to a person in Massachusetts without finding the address and sending it directly. Instead, they were to send it to a "first-name acquaintance" who might know somebody who knew the intended recipient. Each intervening recipient of the letter received the same instructions. Over a quarter of the letters reached their destination. The average number of people — all mutual acquaintances — through whose hands the letters passed on their way from Nebraska to Massachusetts was 5.5. (Presented with the same task, people in Massachusetts got about a third of the letters through to the target, using an average of 4.4 intermediaries.) See Jeffrey Travers and Stanley Milgram, "An Experimental Study of the Small World Problem," *Sociometry* 32 (December 1969), pp. 425–43; Stanley Milgram, "Interdisciplinary Thinking and the Small World Problem," pp. 103–20 in Muzafer Sherif and Carolyn W. Sherif, eds., *Interdisciplinary Relationships in the Social Sciences* (Chicago: Aldine Publishing Co., 1969); Charles Korte and Stanley Milgram, "Acquaintanceship Networks between Racial Groups: Application of the Small World Method," *Journal of Personality and Social Psychology* 15 (June 1970), pp. 101–08.

[37] William A. Gamson, *The Strategy of Social Protest* (Homewood, Ill.: Dorsey Press, 1975); David A. Snow, "Social Networks and Social Movements," *American Sociological Review* 45 (October 1980), pp. 787–801. In some cases, which are rare and becoming rarer, political leaders are able to provide material incentives (such as jobs, contracts, and access to leaders) to those who take part. See Wilson, *Political Organizations*, pp. 97–101; and Raymond E. Wolfinger, *The Politics of Progress* (Englewood Cliffs, N.J.: Prentice-Hall, 1974), chap. 4.

[38] Olson, *The Logic of Collective Action*, chap. 1.

pate, they also convey social expectations about desirable courses of action. Citizens who comply and participate reap the rewards of social life. They enjoy the attentions and esteem of their friends and associates; they enjoy the instrinsic satisfactions of having helped their colleagues' cause. Citizens who fail to comply and refuse to participate receive no rewards; in fact, they may suffer social sanctions.[39]

Indirect mobilization promotes participation, then, by allowing political leaders to exploit citizens' ongoing obligations to friends, neighbors, and social groups. Citizens feel an obligation to help people they like, people they identify with, people who are like them, and people who have helped them in the past—an obligation, that is, to help their friends, family, and daily associates.[40] Likewise, citizens are more likely to contribute when they know that the people who expect them to help can tell whether or not they have done so.[41] Political organizers have long thought personal, face-to-face contacts to be much more effective than impersonal mobilization through the mail or the media, and this is why.[42]

Contact through social networks adds the power of social expectations to the message of mobilization.

Thus, by working through social networks, political leaders need not provide selective incentives themselves, need not coax, cajole, and persuade people to take part. Social networks do it for them. Family, friends, neighbors, and co-workers echo leaders' calls to action, and participants respond to please their neighbors and co-workers and to

[39] Uhlaner, "Rational Turnout"; Uhlaner, "'Relational Goods.'"

[40] E. E. Sampson and C. A. Insko, "Cognitive Consistency and Conformity in the Autokinetic Situation," *Journal of Abnormal and Social Psychology* 68 (February 1964), pp. 184–92; C. D. Batson and J. S. Coke, "Empathy: A Source of Altruistic Motivation for Helping?" pp. 167–87 in J. P. Rushton and R. M. Sorrentins, eds., *Altruism and Helping Behavior* (Hillsdale, N. J.: Lawrence Erlbaum, 1981); C. D. Batson and J. S. Coke, "Empathic Motivations for Helping Behavior," pp. 417–33 in J. T. Cacioppo and R. E. Petty, eds., *Social Psychophysiology: A Sourcebook* (New York: Guilford Press, 1983); H. W. Simmons, N. N. Berkowitz, and R. J. Moyer, "Similarity, Credibility and Attitude Change: A Review and a Theory," *Psychological Bulletin* 73 (January 1970), pp. 1–16; D. Byrne, *The Attraction Paradigm* (New York: Academic Press, 1971).

[41] B. Latane and J. M. Darley, *The Unresponsive Bystander: Why Doesn't He Help?* (New York: Appleton-Crofts, 1970); Hardin, *Collective Action*, chap. 11.

[42] Saul D. Alinsky, *Reveille for Radicals* (Chicago: University of Chicago Press, 1946), pp. 94–99, 108–10; Si Kahn, *Organizing* (New York: McGraw-Hill, 1982), p. 109;

(continued)

honor their obligations to friends. Working through social networks, politicians, parties, interest groups, and activists piggyback political action onto the everyday hum of social relationships.

The Strategy of Political Mobilization

Of course, mobilization is not a universal or a constant occurrence. Political leaders do not try to mobilize everybody, and they do not try to mobilize all of the time. Mobilization, after all, is not their real goal; they have little interest in citizen activism per se. Rather, they seek to use public involvement to achieve other ends: to win elections, to pass bills, to modify rulings, to influence policies. Mobilization is one strategy they may use, but it is neither the only one nor, always, the best one. Alternatively, politicians, parties, interest groups, and activists might (among other things) incite other politicians, ally with other interest groups, compile facts and figures, muster experts, or even (we hope rarely) pay bribes. Because each strategy is costly, and because resources are scarce, political leaders simply cannot use every tool in their toolkit on every job.

Consequently, citizen participation is a resource that political leaders use selectively in their fights for political advantage. For maximum effect, they *target* their efforts on particular people, and they *time* them for particular occasions.

Targeting Mobilization
Once political leaders decide to pursue a mobilization strategy, they want to get the most effective number of people involved with the least amount of effort. This simple—indeed obvious—criterion suggests four kinds of citizens whom leaders are most eager to contact.

(*continued*)
Lazarsfeld, Berelson, and Gaudet, *The People's Choice;* Katz, "The Two-Step Flow"; Paul Carton, *Mobilizing the Black Community: The Effects of Personal Contact Campaigning on Black Voters* (Washington, D.C.: Joint Center for Political Studies, 1984). It is also possible that the framing of the messages conveyed by political leaders promotes participation by changing people's attitudes toward politics. Leaders often try to play on people's sense of civic responsibility. They try to bolster feelings of political efficacy and to increase the intensity of political beliefs. They try to portray a situation of life-or-death issues hanging in the balance. As appealing as these ideas might be, we find little evidence in Chapter 6 that mobilization reshapes people's political values and perceptions about political conflict.

First, politicians, parties, and other activists are most likely to mobilize the people they already know. For one thing, they are close at hand, easy to contact, and responsive to requests—because they are friends or associates.[43] For another thing, they are familiar. Political leaders, naturally, want their allies to participate, not their enemies. Democrats want Democrats to vote, not Republicans, and abortion rights advocates want pro-choice voters to write letters, not pro-life voters. When leaders mobilize people they know, they have a good idea of how they are going to act.[44]

Second, politicians, groups, and other activists are more likely to mobilize people who are centrally positioned in social networks. They are easier to identify, simply because they are more visible and because they know more people. More important, because they are in the middle of things they are in a good position to mobilize others. They turn direct mobilization into indirect mobilization.

Third, politicians, parties, groups, and agitators are more likely to mobilize the people whose actions are most effective at producing political outcomes. Like it or not, some citizens are more influential in politics than others, and legislators, executives, or bureaucrats like, fear, respect, or depend on them more. Because political leaders are interested in outcomes, they concentrate their mobilization efforts on the powerful.

Finally, politicians and activists are more likely to mobilize people who are likely to respond by participating.[45] As we already argued earlier in this chapter, some people, because of their resources, interests, preferences, or beliefs, are more likely to participate in politics than other people. Because political leaders cannot afford to mobilize everyone, they concentrate their efforts on people they have the greatest chance of mobilizing.

A number of simple predictions follow from these observations. First, people who are employed, especially in large workplaces, are more likely to be mobilized than people who are not; they are

---

[43] See Fenno's idea of a "personal constituency." Richard F. Fenno, Jr., *Home Style: House Members and Their Districts* (Boston: Little, Brown and Co., 1978).

[44] Rosenau, *Citizenship between Elections*; Kramer, "The Effects of Precinct Level Canvassing"; Huckfeldt and Sprague, "Political Parties and Electoral Mobilization."

[45] Huckfeldt and Sprague, "Political Parties and Electoral Mobilization."

more likely, consequently, to participate. Their jobs make them visible. Political leaders know where to find them—at work—and know what they care about—their jobs. Their jobs make them powerful. Workplaces represent concentrations of numbers, wealth, and power, the currencies to which politicians respond. Finally, their jobs incline them toward participation. They have powerful incentives to act in defense of their livelihoods, and they have powerful incentives to live up to the expectations of their employers and co-workers.

Second, people who belong to associations are more likely to be mobilized and more likely to participate than people who do not belong.[46] Group members are more visible. Labor unions, service clubs, and churches meet daily, weekly, or monthly, and their purposes often reveal their politics. Group members are more influential. In politics, organizations have the power of numbers, attentiveness, and singular purpose. Finally, through their organizations, group members get greater encouragement to participate. They voluntarily associate with people who share their identities and their interests; accordingly, they find it difficult to resist the entreaties of other members. Indeed, their very involvement in organizations signals their susceptibility to social expectations.

Third, leaders of organizations, businesses, and local governments are more likely to be mobilized: They are better known to political leaders,[47] more likely to be effective, and more likely to participate, for the reasons we have already discussed. In addition, their positions atop organizations and institutions give them the ability to reach other people. Business owners have access to employees, union stewards to rank-and-file, club presidents to members, and church deacons to the faithful. They occupy the center of social networks. They turn direct mobilization into indirect mobilization.

Finally, the wealthy, the educated, and the partisan are more likely to be targeted for mobilization than the poor, the uneducated, and the uncommitted, which is part of the reason for their greater potential for political action. The advantaged are better

---

[46]Among many, Verba and Nie, *Participation in America*, chap. 11; Erickson and Nosanchuk, "How an Apolitical Association Politicizes."

[47]Sidney Verba and Gary Orren, *Equality in America: The View from the Top* (Cambridge: Harvard University Press, 1985), p. 67.

known to political leaders because they travel in the same social circles. Politicians and activists are usually wealthier, better educated, and more partisan than ordinary citizens, and so are their friends and associates. Likewise, their actions are more likely to produce favorable political outcomes. Because of their social positions, they often know legislators, executives, and bureaucrats personally. Moreover, because of their status and wealth, they stand as benefactors of many politicians and government officials: campaign contributors, information sources, former and future employers. Consequently, political elites know them, like them, respect them, and depend on them. They, in short, have power. Finally, they are more likely to respond to political leaders' requests. They have more resources. They have the money, the leisure, and the skills to meet the demands that participation places on them.[48] Likewise, they receive more rewards. Because of their social status they have a greater stake in political decisions, and because of their socialization they have a bigger psychological investment in political affairs. Perhaps most important, they are part of social networks that esteem, expect, and reward activism in politics; hence, they receive greater selective and solidary rewards from their activism. The greater propensity of the advantaged toward participation, that is, stems not only from their individual characteristics but also from their placement in the political system.[49]

Thus, the strategic calculations of political leaders determine a lot about who participates. Intent on creating the greatest effect with the least effort, politicians, parties, interest groups, and activists mobilize people who are known to them, who are well placed in social networks, whose actions are effective, and who are likely to act. Their efforts to move the organized, the employed, the elite, and the advantaged into politics exacerbate rather than reduce the class biases in political participation in America.

[48]This is most obviously important in the case of campaign fundraising: The wealthy get hit up for money and the poor do not. Recalling the famed remark of the bank robber Willie Sutton, political fundraisers target the wealthy because that is where the money is.

[49]See Michael W. Giles and Marilyn K. Dantico, "Political Participation and Neighborhood Social Context Revisited," *American Journal of Political Science* 26 (February 1982), p. 149.

Timing Mobilization

Political leaders likewise identify favorable times to move citizens into politics. Sometimes mobilization of public participation is a worthwhile enterprise—it is likely to accomplish its purpose—and sometimes it is not.

Clearly, for mobilization of citizen activism to be an effective strategy, two conditions must obtain. First, people must be ready to follow their leaders into politics. If people are not interested in the issues or are distracted by other concerns, mobilization is wasted effort. Second, citizen participation must have a consequential effect on political outcomes. If important decisions are not on the docket, if political outcomes are foregone conclusions, or if public officials are unmoved by citizens' pleas, mobilization is wasted effort. Unless citizens are likely to act and action is likely to yield outcomes, leaders' resources are better spent on strategies other than mobilization.

These observations provide some perspective on when people are likely to be mobilized, and when in turn people are likely to participate in politics.

First, people participate in politics more when salient issues top the agenda. Leaders can only lead, after all, when the public is willing to follow. Big pocketbook issues, such as pensions and jobs, and big moral issues, such as prohibition and abortion, draw greater public attention than more arcane issues, such as deregulation of natural gas pipelines and accounting rules for capital depreciation. Salient issues affect more people more directly. Knowing that, political leaders adopt mobilization strategies when the issues excite people and adopt other strategies when they bore people. Because of their strategic calculations, citizens receive more pressure to participate when the issues are salient than when they are not.

Second, people participate more in politics when other concerns do not demand their attentions. As important as politics is, for most people other things come first: making a living, spending time with the family, and so forth.[50] Leaders understand this, and they hesitate to mobilize citizen activism when more pressing needs dominate.

---

[50] Robinson and Converse, "Social Change Reflected in the Use of Time"; Robinson, Converse, and Szalai, "Everyday Life in Twelve Countries"; Rosenstone, "Economic Adversity and Voter Turnout."

On campus, for instance, college politicos rarely schedule political events during midterms and finals. In real politics, likewise, activists curb their efforts during holidays, when people want only to spend time with family, and during hard spells, when people want only to get back to work or to pay their bills. Because political leaders accommodate the more pressing concerns of the public, people feel less encouragement and pressure to participate when more important events distract them.

Third, people participate more in politics when important decisions are pending. Politics moves to its own distinctive rhythms. Elections, for example, are cyclic: Presidential elections occur every four years, House elections every two years, Senate elections every six years, and state and local elections idiosyncratically, some in presidential years, some in midterm years, and some in off years. Legislation, on the other hand, is seasonal: The U.S. Congress and the larger state legislatures formulate proposals in committees in the spring and summer, debate policies on the floor in the summer and fall, and recess in the winter. Cyclic or seasonal, calendars regulate the activities of political leaders. For maximum effect, these leaders mobilize citizens at the moment when conflicts near resolution. Because leaders are more likely to contact them when decisions are imminent, citizens respond to the rhythms of the calendar as well.

Fourth, people participate more in politics when outcomes hang in the balance. Some elections are so close that a few votes can make a difference, whereas others are so lopsided that hundreds of thousands could not affect them.[51] Similarly, some legislative battles are so evenly matched that a burst of public involvement could clinch them, whereas others are so settled that nothing could perturb them. Given scarce resources, political leaders focus their efforts on the tight contests and forget about the cakewalks. Because leaders are more likely to contact them when decisions come down to the wire, citizens respond to political competition.

[51]There is a large literature on closeness and turnout. See Downs, *An Economic Theory of Democracy;* William H. Riker and Peter D. Ordeshook, *An Introduction to Positive Political Theory* (Englewood Cliffs, N.J.: Prentice-Hall, 1973), pp. 62–63; John Ferejohn and Morris Fiorina, "Closeness Counts Only in Horseshoes and Dancing," *American Political Science Review* 69 (September 1975), pp. 920–25.

Finally, people are more likely to be mobilized to participate in politics when issues come before legislatures than when they come before bureaucracies and courts. The institutions of American government expose legislators to popular pressures, but they insulate bureaucrats and judges. Representatives, senators, county commissioners, and members of city councils submit regularly to the discipline of the voters, but bureaucrats and judges do not. Accordingly, public participation potentially has more impact when elected officials make decisions than when civil servants and judges do. Accordingly, politicians and activists pursue mobilization strategies when issues are before legislatures, but they favor other strategies when decisions are before agencies and courts. Because leaders are more likely to contact them when the outcomes they seek are laws, people participate more in legislative politics than in bureaucratic and judicial battles.

Thus, the strategic choices of political leaders determine a lot about when people are mobilized, and hence about when they participate. Eager to time their efforts so that they will have the greatest effect, candidates, parties, interest groups, and activists mobilize people when their efforts are most likely to be effective: when issues are salient, when distractions are few, when resolutions are imminent, when decisions are closely contested, and when decision makers depend on the evaluations of the public.

Conclusion

Political participation arises from the interaction of citizens and political mobilizers. Few people participate spontaneously in politics. Participation, instead, results when groups, political parties, and activists persuade citizens to take part. Personal characteristics—resources, perceived rewards, interests, and benefits from taking part in politics—define every person's predisposition toward political activity. The strategic choices of political leaders—their determinations of who and when to mobilize—determine the shape of political participation in America.

In mobilizing citizens for political action, political leaders intend only their own advantage. Seeking only to win elections, pass bills, amend rulings, or influence policies, they target their appeals selectively and time them strategically. Nevertheless, in doing so, they extend public involvement in political decision making. They bring people into politics at crucial times in the process. Their strategic choices impart a distinctive *political* logic to political participation. Through mobilization of both kinds—direct contact, and indirect contact through social networks—political leaders supply information about politics that many citizens otherwise would not have. Politics is remote from the experience of most people. Absent mobilization, rational ignorance would defeat much citizen involvement in politics. Through mobilization of both kinds, moreover, political leaders create selective, solidary inducements to participate that many citizens otherwise would not have. Politics is not a priority for most people; absent mobilization, the paradox of participation would defeat much citizen involvement in politics.

People participate in politics for a host of reasons, but mobilization makes citizen participation both more common and more consequential. As Rosenau summarized,

> Most citizens... are not autonomous actors who calculate what ought to be done in public affairs, devise a strategy for achieving it, establish their own resources, and then pursue the course of action most likely to achieve their goals. Their instrumental behavior is often suggested, if not solicited, by others, either directly in face-to-face interactions or indirectly through the mass media; either explicitly through calls for support by mobilizers or implicitly through the statements of leaders, journalists and acquaintances that situations might be altered (or preserved) if support were available. Thus, to conceive of the practices of citizenship as being largely sustained by independent action toward the political arena initiated by individuals is to minimize the relational context in which people participate in public affairs.[52]

[52] Rosenau, *Citizenship between Elections*, p. 96.

PARTICIPATION IN AMERICAN POLITICS, 1952–1990

The puzzle of participation in American politics finds its solution in mobilization. The choices of politicians, parties, and interest groups among strategies, accomplices, and opportunities delineate the pool of political participants and direct its expansion and contraction. These claims are contentious, and in the rest of this book we undertake to document them. This chapter introduces the empirical analysis. Its aims, for now, are purely descriptive. We first describe our data, then report the characteristics of political activists, and finally depict the patterns of citizen involvement in American politics over the last forty years. In doing so, however, we also identify specific puzzles, the precise features of participation in American politics on which we bring our argument to bear in the chapters that follow.

Analysis and Evidence

In Chapter 2, we traced citizen involvement in American politics to three main sets of factors: personal resources, interests and identifications, and the mobilization efforts of strategic political elites. That argument makes three special demands on our empirical analysis.

First, Chapter 2 offered a theory of political participation, not just a theory of voter turnout. To test it and elaborate it, we must examine citizen participation in *both* electoral politics *and* governmental politics.

38

Second, the argument holds that differences in resources, interests, social involvements, and contacts with political leaders account for variations across individuals in the propensity to participate. Thus, to assess this claim, we must examine variations in citizen activism across individuals, in cross section.

Finally, the theory holds that differences in strategic situations—differences in the competitiveness of elections, for example, or in the contents of congressional agendas—account for variations in the timing of citizen participation in politics. To test these ideas, we cannot make do only with cross-sectional data, which include individuals from a single slice in time: Cross-sectional analyses hold constant almost every element of the strategic context. We cannot learn a thing about the effect of hotly contested presidential campaigns, for example, by looking at only a single election. We obviously need to compare people who were exposed to the hot contests with those who suffered through the dull ones.[1] Thus, to understand *when* people participate we must examine variations in citizen activism over time.

To meet these requirements, our analysis draws on two distinct data sources; the first provides information about citizen participation in electoral politics, and the second furnishes data about public involvement in governmental politics.

For our analysis of electoral participation, we use the data gathered in the nineteen national surveys that comprise the National Election Studies (NES), conducted by the Center for Political Studies at the University of Michigan. In election years since 1952, NES has interviewed a random sample of Americans of voting age in person. In every study but one, NES asked a core set of questions about respondents' political outlooks, personal characteristics, and participation in that year's campaign. We combined the eighteen surveys from 1952 to 1988 into a single pooled data set with 33,852 respondents. These data form the basis for our analysis of participation in electoral politics: voter turnout, work for political parties and candidates, monetary contributions to campaigns, and attempts

---

[1] Gerald H. Kramer, "The Ecological Fallacy Revisited: Aggregate- versus Individual-Level Findings on Economics and Elections and Sociotropic Voting," *American Political Science Review* 77 (March 1983), pp. 92–111.

to influence the votes of others. By pooling four decades of cross-sectional data, we are able simultaneously to assess variations across individuals and over time.[2]

Our analysis of governmental participation relies chiefly on data from 173 national surveys that the Roper Organization conducted between September 1973 and December 1990. Every five to six weeks, Roper interviewed, in person, a national cross section of around 2,000 people of voting age.[3] On each of the surveys, Roper asked exactly the same questions about political participation. Aggregated responses to these questions give us a seventeen-year time series on citizen involvement in writing letters to members of Congress, signing petitions, and attending local meetings on town or school affairs. The explanatory variables, some weekly, some monthly, and some yearly, but all aggregated, come from a variety of sources.[4] The Roper surveys, conducted ten times yearly for almost two decades, allow us to examine the effects of both short- and long-term changes in political context.

Because we cannot disaggregate the Roper time series,[5] we supplement it with an analysis of very similar questions about citizen involvement in governmental politics that appeared on the 1976 National Election Study (NES). The 2,248 respondents to the 1976

[2]Our descriptions of variations in electoral participation over time also draw from the 1990 National Election Study, although our causal analysis is confined to data from the studies between 1952 and 1988, which have been pooled in the "American National Election Studies Cumulative Data File, 1952–1988," and distributed by the Inter-University Consortium for Political and Social Research. In each election study, NES employed a multistage area probability design to sample randomly from citizens of voting age living in households. Appendix B details the wording of the questions and the coding.

[3]The sampling method, a multistage, stratified probability sample with quotas for sex, age, and employed women, remained essentially constant over the seventeen-year period. In each survey, the interviews were conducted in person over a period of one to two weeks. Up to three callbacks were made in an effort to reach people who were not immediately available for interview. In December 1986, Roper implemented a more involved sampling procedure, but it appears to have no effect on our analysis.

[4]Appendix A identifies the sources of the variables and their coding.

[5]Although the political participation battery remained on the Roper Surveys throughout the seventeen-year period, the contents of the rest of the survey changed constantly. Thus, there is no useful information to be gotten from the individual responses to the Roper Surveys, aside from demographic descriptions of respondents, which we obtained and present for sixteen of the surveys.

NES were a random sample of Americans of voting age, 1,005 of whom participated in the final wave of the 1972–1974–1976 NES panel study and 1,243 of whom were new to the study. These data allow us to analyze what kinds of people wrote letters to Congress, signed petitions, and attended the meetings of local governments.[6]

Political Activity and Political Activists

We begin by describing the nature of political participation in America: how much, by what kinds of people, in which kinds of activities, and with what degree of concentration and continuity.

By far the most common form of citizen participation in American politics is voting. Since 1952, on average, 57 percent of the voting age population has cast a ballot in presidential election years and 42 percent has turned out in midterm election years (see Table 3-1).[7] Beyond voting, electoral politics draws many fewer participants, especially as the costs of political involvement become more substantial. In presidential election years, 32 percent of the electorate has tried to influence how other people vote, but only 10

---

[6]Appendix A also presents the exact wording of the 1976 NES questions and their coding.

[7]The turnout percentages displayed in Table 3-1 and later in Figure 3-1 are aggregate estimates based on votes cast in national elections. In presidential election years, turnout is the number of ballots cast for president divided by the U.S. Census Bureau's estimate of the voting-age population. In midterm election years, the calculation is more difficult. Although nearly everybody who votes in presidential election years casts a presidential ballot, many more people in midterm years vote for governor or U.S. senator than for U.S. representative. These estimates take the drop-off into account. In each state, we compared the total votes cast in the House races, the Senate race, and the gubernatorial race (if they were held). Within each state, we chose the highest of these three vote totals, summed across all the states and divided by the estimate of voting-age population, to get midterm turnout. (Of course, there may still be some people who turn out but do not cast a ballot for the office receiving the most votes, meaning that midterm turnout may still be underestimated.) Accordingly, these estimates are different from those based solely on the number of votes cast for the House of Representatives. Forty percent of the electorate went to the polls in 1982, for example, but only 37.7 percent voted for a House candidate. In general, the gap between the "actual" midterm turnout and the vote cast for the House has grown since 1962.

Table 3-1   Participation in Electoral Politics, 1952–1990

| | Percentage Taking Part | |
| | Presidential Elections | Midterm Elections |
Activity		
Voted	57	42
Tried to influence how others voted	32	20
Contributed money to a party or candidate	10	9
Attended a political meeting or rally	8	8
Worked for a party or candidate	4	5

Source: 1952–1990 National Election Studies, except for voter turnout. See Appendix B.

percent has contributed money to parties or candidates, and just 4 percent has worked for campaigns.

The extent of citizen participation in governmental politics also ranges from common to rare. On average, between 1973 and 1990, 35 percent of the voting-age population said they had signed a petition, 18 percent said they had attended a public meeting on a town or a school affair, and 15 percent said they had written a representative or a senator within the previous year (see Table 3-2). Nine percent of all Americans had attended a political rally or speech; less than 5 percent had written a letter to a newspaper, had made a speech, or had written a newspaper or magazine article.[8]

[8]For purposes of analysis in Chapter 4, we have selected only the three most common of the activities in governmental politics: signing a petition, attending a meeting, and writing a representative or senator. There are both substantive and methodological reasons for the choice. First, taken together, these three activities represent participation both in national and in local government, in high-cost activities and in low-cost activities. Second, each has a range of observed values that well exceeds sampling error. For these three items, the sampling error varies from 1.6 to 2.2 percentage points. The percentage of Americans writing Congress ranges from 9 to 19; the percentage attending meetings ranges from 14 to 24; and the percentage signing petitions ranges from 28 to 44.

Table 3-2 Participation in Governmental Politics, 1973–1990

Now here is a list of things some people do about government or politics. Have you happened to have done any of these things in the past year?

Activity	Percentage Taking Part
Signed a petition	35
Attended a public meeting on town or school affairs	18
Written your congressman or senator	15
Attended a political rally or speech	9
Written a letter to the paper	5
Made a speech	5
Written an article for a magazine or newspaper	2

Source: Roper Reports. See Appendix A.

In both electoral politics and governmental politics, participants come disproportionately from the most advantaged sectors of society: from among wealthy, well-educated, white Americans.

Whites are more likely than African-Americans to take part, as shown in Table 3-3. There are racial disparities across every form of political activity in both the electoral and governmental arenas. In electoral politics, whites are 15 percent more likely than blacks to vote, 5 percent more likely than blacks to try to influence how others vote, and 6 percent more likely than blacks to contribute money. In governmental politics, whites are twice more likely than blacks to sign petitions and three times more likely to write to representatives and senators.

In addition, wealthy Americans are more likely than poor Americans to take part in political activities. Rates of turnout among the most affluent citizens are nearly 35 percentage points higher than the rates of turnout among the most needy (see Figure 3-1). The prosperous are two and a half times more likely than the poor to attempt to influence how others vote and over ten times more

Table 3-3   Participation in American Politics, by Race

Participation in Electoral Politics

Activity	Percentage Taking Part	
	Black	White
Voted	53	68
Tried to influence how others voted	22	27
Contributed money to a party or candidate	4	10
Attended a political meeting or rally	7	8
Worked for a party or candidate	4	5

Participation in Governmental Politics

Activity	Percentage Taking Part	
	Black	White
Signed a petition	18	38
Attended a public meeting on a town or school affair	12	18
Wrote a letter to a congressman or senator	5	16

Sources: Electoral: 1952–1988 National Election Studies. See Appendix B. Governmental: Roper Surveys, 1976, Nos. 76–1, 76–2, 76–6, 76–7; 1980, Nos. 80–1, 80–2, 80–6, 80–7; 1984, Nos. 84–1, 84–2, 84–6, 84–7; 1988, Nos. 88–1, 88–2, 88–6, 88–7.

likely to contribute money to campaigns. In governmental politics, the best off are around twice more likely than the worst-off to sign a petition, to attend a public meeting, and to write a letter to Congress.

Finally, better educated Americans are more prone than the lesser educated to participate in politics. The turnout of college graduates exceeds that of the grade school educated by almost 30 percentage points (see Figure 3-2). The most schooled are over two times more likely to try to influence others and over four times more likely to work for a campaign. They are four times more likely to sign petitions and attend public meetings. [9] We will comment on the causes and consequences of these racial and class disparities throughout this book, but especially in the concluding Chapter 8.

Aside from voting, most participants in American politics take part in only one or two political activities: Some people contribute money to campaigns, others work for parties or candidates, still others write letters to representatives and senators or attend the meetings of local governments. For example, only 32 percent of those who either voted or tried to influence how others voted engaged in both activities (see Table 3-4). Only 15 percent of those who either voted or signed a petition did both, and only 30 percent of those who either signed a petition or attended a local meeting engaged in both. [10]

Clearly, some participants engage in several different political activities, but not to the point that they cluster in identifiable "modes" of political participation. [11] Activism in electoral politics mixes as much with activism in governmental politics as with involvement in other kinds of electoral activities. Participants tend to overlap in activities that require the same kinds of resources—for instance, making a speech, writing a letter to the newspaper, and writing an article for a magazine, all of which require verbal acuity—and in activities that are by-products of other activities—for example, party workers have more opportunities to attend rallies. [12]

---

[9] There are also gender disparities in participation—men usually participate more than women—but these differences are small and declining. In some cases, however, women are more active than men, for instance in attendance at local meetings on town or school affairs.

[10] Another way to gauge these figures is to compare them to the percentage who would have participated in both activities, if everybody who had participated in the least common of the two also participated in the other. That percentage is equal to the ratio of the percentage that participated in the less common activity to the percentage that participated in the more common activity.

[11] Sidney Verba and Norman H. Nie, *Participation in America: Political Democracy and Social Equality* (New York: Harper & Row, 1972), pp. 32–80.

[12] The substantial overlap between those who attended political meetings or rallies, on the one hand, and who worked for a political party or candidate or contributed money, on the other hand, suggested that there was little marginal return from analyzing all three items. Accordingly, we dropped the attending political meetings or rallies question from the analysis that follows.

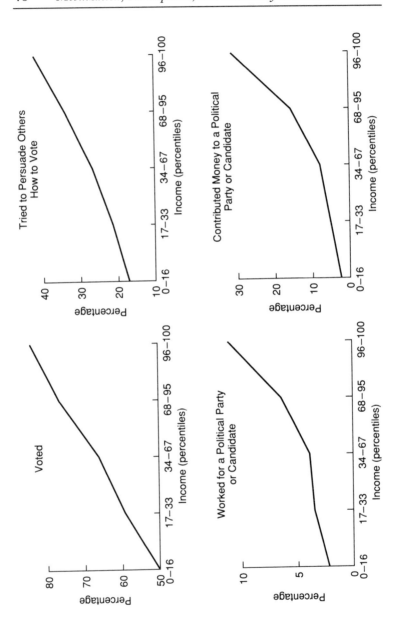

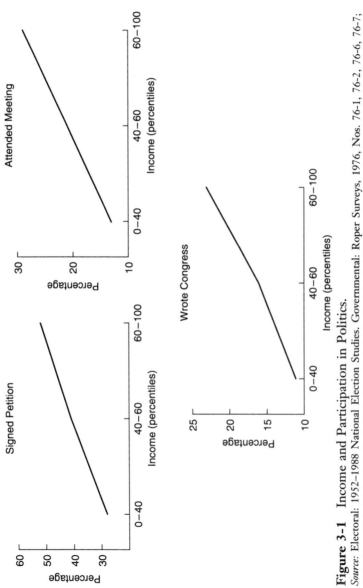

Figure 3-1 Income and Participation in Politics.

Source: Electoral: 1952–1988 National Election Studies. Governmental: Roper Surveys, 1976, Nos. 76-1, 76-2, 76-6, 76-7; 1980, Nos. 80-1, 80-2, 80-6, 80-7; 1984, Nos. 84-1, 84-2, 84-6, 84-7; 1988, Nos. 88-1, 88-2, 88-6, 88-7.

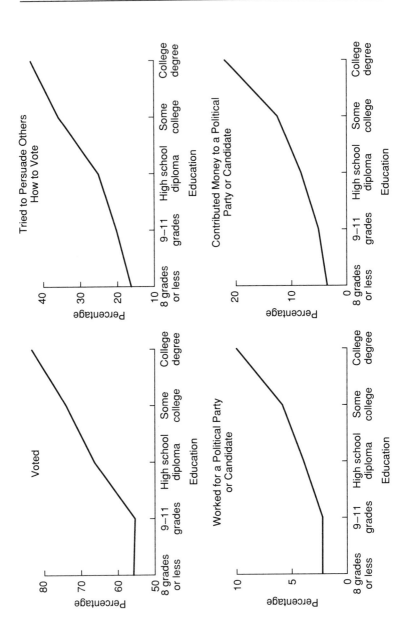

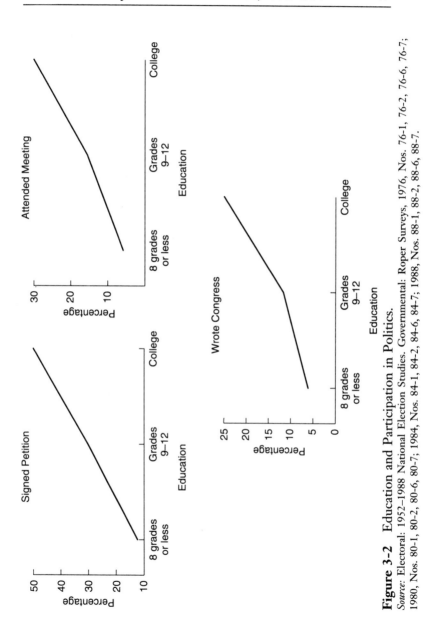

Figure 3-2   Education and Participation in Politics.

Source: Electoral: 1952–1988 National Election Studies. Governmental: Roper Surveys, 1976, Nos. 76-1, 76-2, 76-6, 76-7; 1980, Nos. 80-1, 80-2, 80-6, 80-7; 1984, Nos. 84-1, 84-2, 84-6, 84-7; 1988, Nos. 88-1, 88-2, 88-6, 88-7.

Table 3-4 Overlap of Participation in American Politics

	Voted	Influence	Money	Rally	Work
	Participation in Electoral Politics				
	Of Those Who Did Either, Percentage Who Did Both				
Voted	—				
Tried to influence	32	—			
Contributed money	13	18	—		
Attended rally	10	16	23	—	
Worked for party	6	13	18	25	—

	Voted	Influence	Money	Rally	Work
	Participation in Electoral and Governmental Politics				
	Of Those Who Did Either, Percentage Who Did Both				
Signed petition	15	18	12	8	8
Attended meeting	21	21	15	12	9
Wrote Congress	36	33	15	10	9

	Petition	Meeting	Congress	Rally	Letter	Speech
	Participation in Governmental Politics					
	Of Those Who Did Either, Percentage Who Did Both					
Signed petition	—					
Attended meeting	30	—				
Wrote Congress	24	22	—			
Attended rally	16	20	17	—		
Wrote letter	10	13	15	13	—	
Made speech	9	13	10	13	12	—
Wrote article	5	6	6	8	13	17

Sources: Electoral: 1952–1988 National Election Studies. See Appendix B. Electoral and Governmental: 1976 National Election Study. See Appendix A. Governmental: Roper Surveys, 1976, Nos. 76-1, 76-2, 76-6, 76-7; 1980, Nos. 80-1, 80-2, 80-6, 80-7; 1984, Nos. 84-1, 84-2, 84-6, 84-7; 1988, Nos. 88-1, 88-2, 88-6, 88-7.

As the limited amount of overlap implies, the vast majority of people who do take part participate in only one endeavor in any given election or any given year. Leaving aside voting, 70 percent of electoral participants engaged in a single campaign activity and nothing more (see Table 3-5). In total, only 7 percent of the American electorate took part in two of the four campaign activities, only

Table 3-5   Concentration of Participation in American Politics

Participation in Electoral Politics		
Number of Activities	Percentage of Population	Percentage of Activists
0	66	—
1	24	70
2	7	19
3	3	7
4	1	4

Activities include trying to influence how others vote, contributing money to a party or candidate, attending a political meeting or rally, working for a party or a candidate. Activities do not include voting.

Participation in Governmental Politics		
Number of Activities	Percentage of Population	Percentage of Activists
0	64	—
1–2	35	69
3–11	11	31

Activities include attending a meeting, writing to Congress, serving as a club officer, serving on an organization's committee, attending a rally, writing a letter to the newspaper, making a speech, working for a party, being a member of a group, writing an article, and running for office. Activities do not include signing a petition.

Sources: Electoral: 1952–1988 National Election Studies. See Appendix B. Governmental: Roper Surveys, 1973–1990. See Appendix A.

3 percent took part in three, and barely 1 percent tried to influence others' votes, worked on a campaign, contributed money, *and* attended political rallies.[13] Complete activists are very rare.

Participation in governmental politics is more concentrated, at least on its face.[14] Even so, leaving aside signing a petition, more than two-thirds of the people who took part in any governmental activities participated in only one or two (see Table 3-5). This analysis included participation in organization activity, which almost certainly accounts for the relatively large proportion of the population that was involved in three or more kinds of participation—11 percent. As we have argued before and as we will demonstrate later, associations expose people to opportunities for participation in a wide variety of political endeavors.[15]

---

[13] Another way to gauge the degree of overlap is to compare the percentages of people who participate in multiple activities to the percentage that we would expect if the activities were independent of each other. To oversimplify greatly, assume that the probability that people participate in each activity is one in ten (a probability in the middle of the range for the activities reported here). Then the binomial distribution (with $p = .1$, $n = 4$) gives the expected percentages of participants taking part in multiple activities. The comparison:

Number of Activities	Expected Percentage	Actual Percentage
0	66	66
1	29	24
2	5	7
3	0	3
4	0	1

Clearly, using this crude analysis, the percentages of people who take part in multiple activities is higher than it would be if the activities were independent, but not by a lot.

[14] In this analysis we were constrained by the form in which the Roper data were made available to us. In addition to the governmental activities that we present, Roper also asked questions about participation in electoral politics and involvement in associations. Thus, there will certainly appear to be more concentration in the Roper data simply because Roper respondents chose from twelve activities while National Election Study respondents chose from only four.

[15] Once again, we can compare the percentages who take part in multiple activities to the percentages we would expect if the activities were independent. Here, we assume that people have a 7.5 in 100 chance of taking part (once again in the middle

(continued)

The relatively limited concentration of political activity is matched by relatively limited continuity. On two occasions, in 1956, 1958, and 1960 and in 1972, 1974, and 1976, the NES interviewed the same respondents over a series of three elections. As the evidence from those two panel studies indicates, the people who participate in American politics changes from year to year. Very few of the people who take part in one election do so in the next.

As Table 3-6 shows, most of the people who vote in presidential elections turn out election after election. Eighty-four percent of the citizens who cast ballots in either the 1956 election or the 1960 election participated in both, and 81 percent of the people who voted in either the 1972 or the 1976 election turned out in both. Inclusion of midterm elections, in which voter turnout is always much lower, reduces the continuity further, but even so, 80 percent of the voters cast ballots in all three elections in the 1950s, and 61 percent of the voters participated in all three elections in the 1970s. Voter turnout is, in a sense, habitual.

The stability of citizen participation in the most ceremonial act of American politics is the exception rather than the rule, however. As Table 3-6 also shows, the number of people who move in and out of the pool of participants is strikingly large. In both the 1956 and 1960 and the 1972 and 1976 pairs of presidential

---

(continued)
of the range of probabilities for the activities considered here). Using the binomial distribution (with $p = .075$ and $n = 11$), the expected and actual percentages are:

Number of Activities	Expected Percentage	Actual Percentage
0	42	64
1–2	53	25
3–11	5	11

From this considerably oversimplified analysis, people are more likely both to take part in many activities and to take part in no activities than we would expect if participatory acts were independent.

Table 3-6   Continuity of Participation in Electoral Politics,
1956–1960 and 1972–1976

1956–1958–1960 Panel

Activity	Percentage Who Participated in 1956 or 1960 Who Participated in Both Years	Percentage Who Participated in 1956, 1958, or 1960 Who Participated in All Three Years
Voted	84	80
Tried to influence how others voted	36	24
Contributed money to a party or candidate	29	*
Attended a political meeting or rally	19	*
Worked for a party or candidate	20	*

1972–1974–1976 Panel

Activity	Percentage Who Participated in 1972 or 1976 Who Participated in Both Years	Percentage Who Participated in 1972, 1974, or 1976 Who Participated in All Three Years
Voted	81	61
Tried to influence how others voted	42	17
Contributed money to a party or candidate	34	16
Attended a political meeting or rally	20	8
Worked for a party or candidate	16	7

*Not ascertained in 1958 wave of study.
Source: National Election Studies, 1956–1958–1960 Panel Study and 1972–1974–1976
Panel Study.

elections, only a little more than a third of those who tried to influence how others voted in either year did so in both years; only around a third of those who contributed money in either year did so in both years; and only about a fifth of those who worked on a campaign in either year did so in both years.[16] Put differently, only one *participant* in three participates regularly; over two-thirds of the *participants* take part sporadically.[17] The core group of people that participates election after election, time after time, is remarkably small.[18]

[16]It is still the case, however, that participating in one election makes people more likely to participate in another. If participation in each activity were independent over time, we would expect many fewer participants to take part in both elections than we actually observe (say, in 1956–1960):

Activity	Expected	Actual
Voting	40	84
Influencing	19	36
Contributing	5	29
Attending	4	19
Working	2	20

Clearly, participation over time is far from independent. Especially striking are the larger differences between actual and expected participation for contributing money and working for a party. As we argued in Chapter 2, political leaders direct their mobilization efforts especially toward people they have mobilized before: In raising money, campaigns call up people who have contributed before, and in mustering volunteers, parties contact people who have worked in campaigns before.

[17]The overall lack of continuity in participation in electoral politics is all the more impressive because the NES panel data probably *overestimate* it. The National Election Study is an unusually effective form of civic education: Somehow, answering an hour of questions about politics gets people interested enough to become more involved in it. For this reason (and a variety of others), the professed voter turnout among NES respondents is 9 to 11 percentage points higher, on average, than the voter turnout calculated from aggregate statistics. The repeated interviewing of the panel study no doubt increases the probability of participation through successive waves of the study, thereby inflating estimates of continuity.

[18]See also M. Margaret Conway and Judith Garber, "Stability and Change in Political Participation: A Panel Analysis," paper presented at the annual meeting of the Southern Political Science Association, 1983. Because questions about participation in governmental politics do not appear throughout the 1972–1974–1976 panel, we are unable to obtain comparably precise estimates of continuity in governmental

(continued)

One reason for this lack of continuity in who participates in politics, as we will show in more detail throughout this book, is the lack of continuity in who is mobilized to take part. Only 22 percent of the people who were contacted by a political party in either 1956 or 1960 were contacted in both years; 78 percent were contacted in one year, but not the other. The same pattern holds two decades later: Only 31 percent of the people contacted by a political party in either 1972 or 1976 were contacted in both years; 69 percent were contacted in one year, but not the other.

This initial overview of activism in American politics yields an important lesson, one that informs our analysis in the chapters that follow. The various types of political participation that we examine in this book do not boil down to one or two modes of activity that draw the same set of participants year in and year out. Rather, they are distinctive kinds of political activities that attract participants selectively. People participate in some activities but not in others; they participate at some times but not at others. As we show, there are good reasons for this. Participation makes distinctive demands on resources and yields distinctive rewards. And, most important, participation contributes in distinctive ways to the strategies of politicians, political parties, and interest groups.

Trends in Citizen Participation in Elections and Government

These same resources, rewards, and strategic opportunities, we argued in Chapter 2, cause participation in American elections and

---

(continued)
participation, but less adequate evidence places it in the same general range. In both 1972 and 1976, NES asked panel respondents whether they had "ever" written to a public official or to the editor of a newspaper. Of those who answered "yes" either in 1972 or in 1976, 48 percent indicated in both years that they had ever written public officials, and 29 percent indicated in both years that they had ever written editors of newspapers. These figures raise some questions about the reliability of the items, but they probably also represent an upper bound to the continuity. For other panel evidence, dealing with participation in boycotts and protests, see Max Kaase, "Mass Participation," pp. 23–64 in M. Kent Jennings and Jan W. van Deth, eds., *Continuities in Political Action* (New York: Walter de Gruyter, 1990).

government to vary over time. The 19 National Election Studies and 173 Roper Surveys enable us to trace the flow of citizen activism longitudinally, as we do here, first for participation in electoral politics and then for participation in governmental politics.

Participation in Electoral Politics, 1952–1990

The most important, most familiar, most analyzed, and most conjectured trend in recent American political history is the thirty-year decline of voter turnout in national elections. As shown in Figure 3-3, the percentage of the voting-age population that participated in presidential contests rose into the 1950s and reached a postwar peak, at 62.8 percent, in 1960. After 1960, voter turnout plummeted: rapidly in 1972, when citizens between the ages of eighteen and twenty first gained the right to vote, and steadily—though with a slight revival in 1984—through 1988, when a bare majority of the eligible electorate, 50.1 percent, took part in the election of George Bush to the presidency.

Voter participation in midterm years reached a postwar high of 48.2 percent in 1966; then it turned down. Midterm turnout crashed in 1974, the year eighteen- to twenty-year-olds entered the midterm

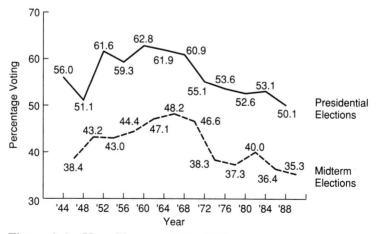

Figure 3-3 Voter Turnout, 1944–1990.
Source: See Appendix B.

electorate, and after 1974 it continued slowly to fall, declining in every midterm year except one, 1982. In 1990, barely a third of the eligible voters participated in elections for senators, governors, and representatives.

The declining propensity of Americans to exercise their franchise did not afflict every sector of American society, however. As shown in Figure 3-4, whites participated in elections at rates consistently above those of African-Americans.[19] In the 1960s, however, the

---

[19] In this figure and in the remaining figures, the estimates of participation in national elections rely on the reports of respondents to the 1952 through 1988 National Election Studies. The estimates of voter turnout from sample surveys are always higher than the estimates from aggregate counts of ballots cast. Each estimate has its own pluses and minuses.

Aggregate figures drawn from reports of ballots cast *underestimate* turnout because the voting-age population, the denominator in the calculation, includes millions of people who are not eligible to vote (aliens, felons, and those confined to penal and mental institutions). The numerator, the number of votes cast, also fails to count people who voted but who spoiled a ballot or who voted for write-in candidates whose votes were not tallied. In presidential years, the numerator omits people who voted but not for president; in midterm years, it misses people who voted but not for the office that received the highest total in the state.

Survey estimates, on the other hand, *overestimate* turnout. The National Election Studies exclude people living in rooming houses and in institutions (dormitories, military bases, nursing homes, and so forth) from the sample, thereby omitting groups of people who are eligible to vote but unlikely to do so. Groups of people who tend not to vote are also less likely to be included in the samples because they are less likely than people who tend to vote to agree to be interviewed. (See John Brehm, "Opinion Surveys and Political Representation," Ph.D. dissertation, University of Michigan, 1990.) Finally, some respondents do not report accurately, most often claiming to have voted when in fact they did not. Estimates of overreporting of turnout, made by comparing survey responses to official voting records, are in the neighborhood of 11 percent (although some of the apparent overreporting may be owing either to faulty recordkeeping by public clerks or to faulty retrieval of voter records by NES).

For a sampling of the literature on the validity of various measures of voter turnout, see John P. Katosh and Michael W. Traugott, "The Consequences of Validated and Self-Reported Voting Measures," *Public Opinion Quarterly* 45 (Winter 1981), pp. 519–35; Brian D. Silver, Barbara A. Anderson, and Paul R. Abramson, "Who Reports Voting," *American Political Science Review* 80 (June 1986), pp. 613–24; U.S. Bureau of the Census, "Studies in the Measurement of Voter Turnout," *Current Population Reports Special Studies*, Series P-23, No. 168, November 1990; Stanley Presser, Michael Traugott, and Santa Traugott, "Vote 'Over' Reporting in Surveys:

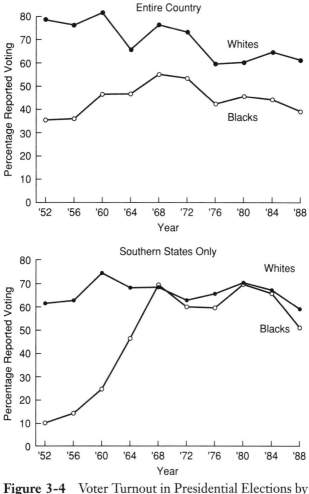

Figure 3-4   Voter Turnout in Presidential Elections by
Race, 1952–1988.
Source: 1952–1988 National Election Studies.

The Records or the Respondents," paper presented at the International Conference
on Measurement Errors, 1990; Paul R. Abramson and William Claggett, "Racial Differences in Self-Reported and Validated Turnout in the 1988 Presidential Election,"
Journal of Politics 53 (February 1991), pp. 186–97.

gap between whites and blacks narrowed rapidly. Although turnout among white Americans held steady, turnout among black Americans nearly doubled nationally and more than quintupled in the South. In 1968, in fact, the participation of Southern blacks equaled the participation of Southern whites, erasing a 50-percentage-point turnout differential in the old Confederate states. After 1968, the racial disparity in voter turnout again worsened: Voter participation declined among both racial groups, but much more quickly among blacks than among whites. Still, white Americans turn out less now than they did forty years ago. Black Americans—especially in the South—turn out more.[20]

The number of people who work for a political party or candidate has also declined over the last three decades (Figure 3-5).

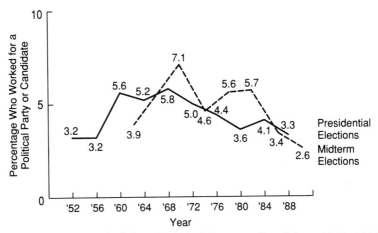

Figure 3-5   Worked for a Political Party or Candidate, 1952–1990.
Source: 1952–1990 National Election Studies.

[20]These numbers possibly underestimate the true racial gap in voter participation. There is some evidence that blacks are significantly more likely than whites to over-report turnout in national elections. Silver, Anderson, and Abramson, "Who Reports Voting"; and Abramson and Claggett, "Racial Differences." Other analyses have challenged this finding, suggesting instead that the recordkeeping by public offices that serve blacks may be less reliable than reporting by offices that serve whites. Presser, Traugott, and Traugott, "Vote 'Over' Reporting."

Volunteer work in campaigns in presidential election years, low during Eisenhower's term, climbed to over 5 percent throughout the 1960s, then declined steadily to bottom out at 3.3 percent in 1988. Party activism in midterm election years reached its peak—at an extraordinary 7.1 percent—in 1970, then also declined over the next two decades, with a spurt of revival in 1978 and 1982. By the close of the 1980s, the percentage of the population that worked for a political party was just about half what it was two decades earlier.

Citizen participation in other electoral activities, however, followed slightly different patterns. Between 1952 and 1956, for example, the percentage of the voting-age population that contributed money to election campaigns more than doubled, to nearly 10 percent (see Figure 3-6). Throughout the 1960s and into the 1970s, campaign giving in presidential years remained relatively high, then it declined through the 1980s to just over 8 percent of the voting-age population. Even as contributions fell in presidential election years, however, they actually rose in midterm election years, most strikingly in the late 1970s and early 1980s, although they fell off dramatically in 1990.

Likewise, public involvement in efforts to influence how other people voted mostly increased between 1952 and 1980 before drop-

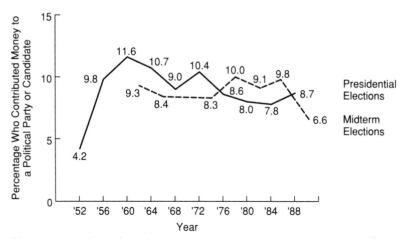

Figure 3-6 Contributed Money to a Political Party or Candidate, 1952–1990.

Source: 1952–1990 National Election Studies.

ping off again more recently. As Figure 3-7 shows, the percentage of the electorate that tried to persuade others rose during the presidential elections in the 1960s and 1970s to a high of 36.7 percent in 1976. Persuasion remained high in 1980, but then it fell rapidly to 28.9 percent in 1988, returning to the level at which it began in the 1950s.

Participation in American electoral politics, then, has seen neither uniform increases nor uniform declines. Between 1952 and 1990, voter participation fell among whites but rose among blacks. Between 1952 and 1990, voter turnout and work for political parties diminished, but financial contributions to campaigns remained steady, and attempts to influence others increased. Still, having emphasized the differences, it also helps to highlight the similarities. First, voter turnout, work for parties, contributions to campaigns, and attempts to influence rose, without exception, in the 1950s and fell in the 1980s. Second, participation in electoral politics was relatively high throughout the 1960s. Contributions to candidates and voter turnout reached their peaks in presidential elections. Finally, participation in many activities revived, for a time, in the early 1980s. Involvement in political parties and contributions to midterm campaigns quickened in the first part of the 1980s, and voter turnout

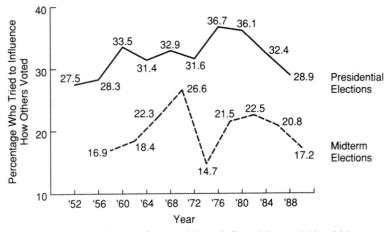

Figure 3-7   Tried to Influence How Others Vote, 1952–1990.
Source: 1952–1990 National Election Studies.

increased in 1982 and 1984 after more than a decade of unbroken decline.

These are the puzzles we take up later in this book: Why the increases and why the declines, why the similarities and why the differences? For now, in light of Chapter 2, some hypotheses come readily to mind. First, participation varies with the resources of the electorate: its education, its age, its efficacy. Participation varies with the engagement of the interests of the electorate: its attachment to political parties, its affinity for the candidates. Finally, participation varies with the opportunities presented by the political system: the mobilizing activities of political parties and social movements, the competitiveness of elections, the extent of the franchise. In Chapters 5, 6, and 7, we show that the evidence supports these expectations.

Participation in Governmental Politics, 1973–1990

If the longitudinal patterns of participation in electoral politics put the focus on long-term changes in citizen activism, the longitudinal patterns of participation in governmental politics put the spotlight on short-term fluctuations. After all, people cannot participate in elections when there are no elections, but they can participate in government at almost any time.

As shown in Figures 3-8, 3-9, and 3-10, the short-term variations in opportunities to participate are very important. The figures display the (almost) monthly levels of citizen involvement in three activities designed to influence national and local public policies: writing a letter to a representative or senator, attending a local meeting on a town or school affair, and signing a petition. Each of the time series has two striking features.

First, public participation in all three activities has declined over the last seventeen years. The decline in local politics was steep, in congressional politics moderate, and in petition signing slight. The percentage of people who attended local meetings dropped by almost 4 percentage points between 1973 and 1990 (see Figure 3-9). The percentage who wrote members of Congress fell by about one and a half percentage points (see Figure 3-8). The percentage who signed a petition declined by only half a percentage point (see Figure 3-10).

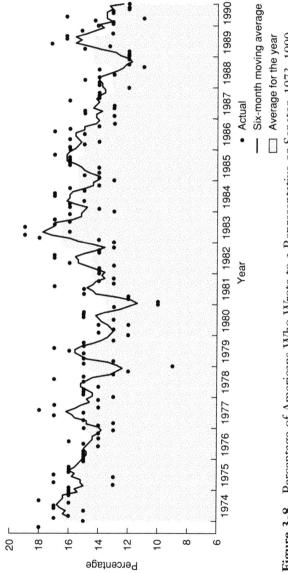

Figure 3-8 Percentage of Americans Who Wrote to a Representative or Senator, 1973–1990.
Source: See Appendix A.

64

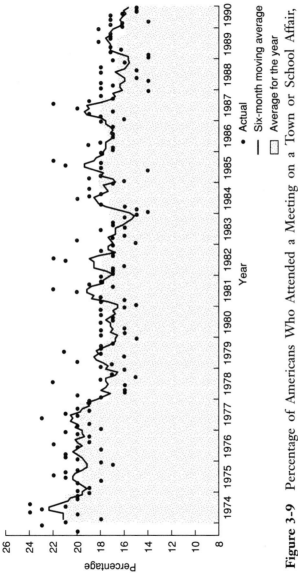

Figure 3-9 Percentage of Americans Who Attended a Meeting on a Town or School Affair, 1973–1990.

Source: See Appendix A.

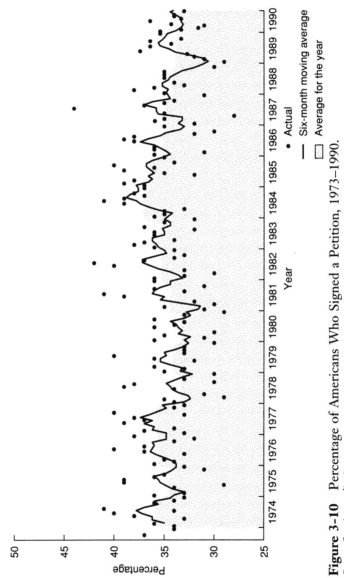

Figure 3-10 Percentage of Americans Who Signed a Petition, 1973–1990.
Source: See Appendix A.

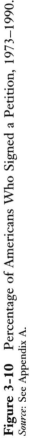

The pattern of the decline of citizen involvement in governmental politics varied across the three activities. Attendance at local meetings declined steadily: It dropped quickly in the mid-1970s and fell slowly thereafter. Correspondence with Congress and petition signing, on the other hand, declined in the 1970s, revived in the early 1980s, and declined again in the late 1980s.

Second, and perhaps even more intriguing, public participation in governmental politics showed a definite annual cyclicity, which statisticians call "seasonality." The percentages of the population who wrote letters to Congress, attended local meetings, and signed petitions were consistently higher in the summer than in the winter.[21] On average, 2.9 percent more Americans wrote representatives in July than in December, 2.9 percent more attended meetings in July than in January, and 5.2 percent more signed petitions in July than in December. (See Figure 3-11.) For all three, the seasonal

---

[21] The seasonality in each of the time series strongly suggests that survey respondents did not think back a full year, as they were asked, in answering the Roper questions. If they had, the series would show slow-moving trends rather than annual cyclicity.

As a number of studies suggest, the inability to recall specific instances—or, more accurately, to recall exactly when specific instances occurred—is common. Forty-four percent of the people who signed a petition in Idaho did not recall having done so sixteen months later; 31 percent did not even remember having seen the petition. Even experiences that are presumably more salient, like hospitalizations, crime victimizations, and major home improvement expenditures, fade rapidly from memory. Asked nine to twelve months later, people who were involved in automobile accidents neglected to report 37 percent of the incidents that had caused injuries and 22 percent of the incidents that had only damaged property. Likewise, 42 percent of the people who said they were unemployed in November 1982 also said in July 1983—eight months later—that they had *not* been unemployed within the last year. See Norman M. Bradburn, Lance J. Rips, and Steven K. Shevell, "Answering Autobiographical Questions: The Impact of Memory and Inference in Surveys," *Science* 236 (April 10, 1987), pp. 157–61; Charles F. Cannell, Kent H. Marquis, and Andre Laurent, "A Summary of Studies of Interviewing Methodology," n.d.; Nancy A. Mathiowetz, "The Problem of Omission and Telescoping Error: New Evidence from a Study of Unemployment," *Proceedings of the Section on Survey Research Methods*, American Statistical Association (1985), pp. 482–84; John Neter and Joseph Waksberg, "A Study of Response Errors in Expenditure Data from Household Interviews," *Journal of the American Statistical Association* 59 (March 1964), pp. 18–55; Betye K. Eidson Penick, *Surveying Crime* (Washington, D.C.: National Academy of Sciences, 1976); John C. Pierce and Nicholas P. Lovrich, "Survey Measurement of Political Participation:

(continued)

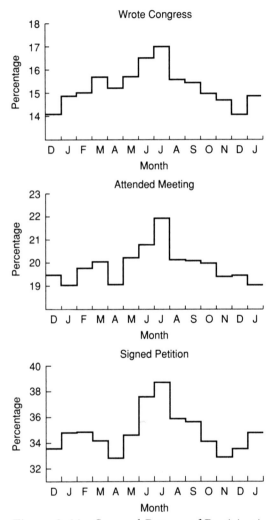

Figure 3-11   Seasonal Pattern of Participation in Governmental Politics, 1973–1990.

Source: See Appendix A.

variations within years were almost as large as the trend variations across years.

As before, the precise seasonal pattern of citizen involvement in governmental politics differed across the three activities. Starting from a low point in December, correspondence with Congress rose steadily in the spring to a high point in July, fell sharply in August, and declined slowly thereafter to the end of the year. In contrast, meeting attendance and petition signing grew only slowly in the spring, exploded in June and July, and then decreased steadily throughout the fall and into the winter.

The longitudinal patterns of citizen participation in governmental politics raise interesting puzzles that we will address in the rest of this book, particularly in Chapter 4. How is it that participation in local government fell so steadily while participation in national government declined and then rose and then declined? How is it

---

(continued)
Selective Effects of Recall in Petition Signing," *Social Science Quarterly* 63 (March 1982), pp. 164–71; Steven J. Rosenstone, John Mark Hansen, and Donald R. Kinder, "Measuring Change in Personal Economic Well-Being,"*Public Opinion Quarterly* 50 (Summer 1986), pp. 176–92.

Throughout our analysis, accordingly, we assume that the time frame for responses is much shorter than a year and that people recall recent instances more readily than distant ones. Two additional bits of evidence reassure us that these assumptions are reasonable. First, in an experiment we conducted in 1983, we put the Roper questions to a national sample, asking half of them to think back one year and half of them to think back only six months. The two time frames elicited roughly the same percentage of participants. Second, and more strikingly, other estimates of citizen activism in governmental politics show the same seasonal patterns. Since 1973, the Post Office of the House of Representatives has presented monthly tallies of the number of letters it has received. Those figures also show a striking annual cyclicity: The volume of mail peaks in the spring and summer and bottoms out in the winter. In fact, the monthly averages for the Post Office estimates (normalized for population) and the monthly averages for the Roper estimates correlate at r = .67. John Mark Hansen and Steven J. Rosenstone, "Participation outside Elections," report submitted to the Board of Overseers, National Election Study, October 1983; *Hearings before a Subcommittee of the Committee on Appropriations*, House of Representatives, "Legislative Branch Appropriations for 1991," 101st Congress, 2d session, 1990, part 2, p. 96; *idem*, "Legislative Branch Appropriations for 1987," 99th Congress, 2d session, 1986, part 2, p. 98; *idem*, "Legislative Branch Appropriations for 1981," 96th Congress, 2d session, part 2, p. 108.

that participation in governmental politics varies with the seasons, rising in the summer and declining in the winter?

Casual reflections on the patterns of participation in governmental politics already begin to suggest some of the right and wrong answers. Clearly, the long- and short-term fluctuations in governmental participation cannot have much to do with changes in the attitudinal and demographic characteristics of the American public: The public's level of activism changes much more quickly than its personal characteristics do. Instead, the patterns of participation in governmental politics must have something to do with the agendas of the governments and the activities of the politicians and interest groups that seek to influence them. In Chapter 4, we will elaborate and test this conjecture—and find it to be substantially true.

Conclusion

Four lessons should be taken from this chapter. First, citizen participation in American politics is extensive but hardly universal. In any given presidential election about half of the eligible population turns out to vote, and in any given year about a sixth of the population writes a letter to Congress. Second, citizen participation in American politics is episodic. It is not the exclusive province of a limited number of hard-core activists who take part in everything all the time. Third, citizen participation in American politics is dominated by the most advantaged, but the degree of bias differs across political activities and over time. Finally, citizen participation in American politics changes from election to election, year to year, month to month. Involvement in elections and government waxes and wanes.

In the next four chapters, we move to explain these many aspects of public involvement in American politics, first for participation in government and then for participation in elections. We demonstrate the impact of resources, interests, identifications, and attitudes. Most important, we show that the strategic calculations of politicians, parties, interest groups, and social movements are crucially important in accounting for the pulse of citizen activism in American elections and government.

C H A P T E R   4

PARTICIPATION IN GOVERNMENTAL POLITICS

Every day, local, state, and national governments make decisions that affect the lives of millions of Americans. They decide how to raise money and how to spend it, who will pay taxes and who will receive benefits. They decide whether parking will be permitted on both sides of the street, whether highway contractors will be required to hire women, whether gun enthusiasts will be allowed to own semiautomatic weapons.

With so much at stake, politicians, political parties, interest groups, and ordinary citizens all attempt to influence these government decisions. They try to persuade legislators, bureaucrats, and judges to see things their way and mobilize others to do the same.

In this chapter, we begin to sort out how and why citizens participate in politics, examining three activities designed to influence the decisions of national and local governments: writing a U.S. representative or senator, attending a local meeting on town or school affairs, and signing a petition. Two separate analyses, one longitudinal and one cross-sectional, help us to determine what leads people to take part. Using data from the Roper Surveys, the longitudinal analysis models the month-to-month changes in political involvement from late 1973 to the end of 1990. Table 4-1 shows a summary of the results. The entries represent the partial effect of each variable on the aggregate level of participation holding the other causes constant.[1] Using the data drawn from the National Election

---

[1] Each entry is the ordinary least squares regression coefficient reported in Appendix C multiplied by the range of the independent variable. Thus, it shows the effect on participation when the independent variable increases from its lowest to its highest value.

Table 4-1 Summary: Causes of Participation in Governmental Politics, 1973–1990

Variable	Wrote Congress	Attended Meeting	Signed Petition
Social Involvement			
Officer of organization	.8	.9	1.8
On committee of local group		1.5	
Mobilization by Political Leaders			
Worked for party	.9		3.0
Freshman Representatives and Senators	−1.8		−2.2
Congressional policy activism	1.2		
Presidential calls for letters	1.1		
Mobilization around Issues			
Children in school per 1,000 voting-age population		2.6	
Change in property tax collected		.6	.7
Watergate period	1.4		
Unemployment rate	1.5		
Presidential budget request relative to current (largest versus no change)	1.1		
Mobilization around Opportunities			
Holiday in preceding month		−.2	
Days Congress in session	.7		
Bills on floor	1.3		
Percentage with local budgets due		1.7	2.7
Percentage within two months of ballot access closing date			1.6

Note: Entries are the partial effects (in percentages) of independent variables on participation (ordinary least squares coefficients multiplied by ranges of variables).
Source: Appendix C.

Study (NES), the cross-sectional analysis accounts for the person-to-person differences in political participation in 1976. Table 4-2 summarizes those results. These entries show the partial effect of each determinant on the individual probability of taking part, again holding the other causes constant.[2]

With this evidence we begin to elaborate and test the arguments we developed in Chapter 2, which linked citizen participation to resources, interests, and strategic mobilization. We proceed methodically from individual to systemic causes of governmental participation. Primarily using the cross-sectional analysis, the first section examines the resources and social positions that allow and encourage people to take part; the second examines the social involvements through which people enter politics. Then, turning to the time-series analysis, the third section focuses on the efforts of political leaders to mobilize people into politics; the fourth focuses on the issues around which leaders mobilize, and the fifth on the opportunities for leaders to mobilize people to take part.

As the chapter proceeds, the magnitude of the contribution of strategic mobilization to citizen participation in government becomes increasingly clear. Political leaders time their efforts to induce public involvement in government decisions strategically, for maximum political effect. They mobilize participation to gain advantage in their contests over issues. They contact citizens directly as well as through the social networks in which people take part.

---

[2] The entries represent our conversion of the probit coefficients reported in Appendix C into probabilities. Probit coefficients indicate the amount of change on the cumulative normal probability distribution that results from a unit change in the independent variable. Because the cumulative normal is not linear, the effect of a variable on the probability that people participate depends upon the probability that they would otherwise participate—the effect is greatest when people otherwise have a 50 percent chance of taking part and the effect is least when people otherwise are nearly certain to participate or nearly certain not to participate. This nonlinearity makes interpretation of probit coefficients more difficult than interpretation of ordinary least squares regression coefficients. To ease interpretation, we translate each probit coefficient into the effect of each variable on the probability of taking part averaged across all the individuals in the sample. For each variable, we calculate the probability that each individual will participate under two scenarios: first assuming that the variable takes its lowest value, then assuming that the variable takes its highest value, allowing all other variables to take their observed values. The reported effect is the difference between the two probabilities, averaged across the entire sample.

Strategic mobilization, in short, proves to be of paramount importance in solving the puzzle of public participation in government. Citizen participation rises and falls with the efforts of political leaders to bring people into the political process.

Resources

Because of accidents of birth, accomplishment, and plain dumb luck, people possess different quantities of important political resources such as money, skills, and self-confidence. Resources promote participation in governmental politics, we argued earlier, both for what they allow and for what they indicate. Money, time, knowledge, skill, and self-confidence allow people to meet the economic and psychological costs of political activism. At the same time, resources indicate social position and the likelihood that political leaders will attempt to induce people to take part. The effects of resources on political participation derive from both.

Education

Our analysis confirms the contribution of education to participation in governmental politics, a finding well in keeping with previous research.[3] The best educated are 12.0 percent more likely to have written to U.S. senators or representatives than the least educated, and the best educated are 12.5 percent more likely to have attended local meetings than those with less formal education (Table 4-2). On the other hand, taking into account other things that are associated with schooling, the more educated are no more likely to sign a petition than the less educated.

These findings make sense, of course, in terms of both what education allows and what it indicates. On the one hand, education allows people to surmount the barriers to participation. To write a letter, people need to know who the public officials are and where to reach them. To attend a meeting, people need to know when and where it

---

[3] On governmental politics specifically, Robert E. Lane, *Political Life: Why and How People Get Involved in Politics* (New York: Free Press, 1959), chap. 5; Sidney Verba and Norman H. Nie, *Participation in America: Political Democracy and Social Equality* (New York: Harper & Row, 1972), chap. 8.

Table 4-2 Summary: Causes of Participation in Governmental
Politics, 1976

Variable	Form of Participation in Governmental Politics		
	Wrote Congress	Attended Meeting	Signed Petition
Resources			
Education	12.0	12.5	
External efficacy	5.7		9.2
External efficacy (local)		3.2	
Internal efficacy (local)		5.4	
Age	4.4		
Women	−3.7		
Blacks	−7.3		
Mexican-Americans and Puerto Ricans	−14.4		
Social Involvement			
Unemployed	−8.1		
Employed			4.2
Income			18.7
Joined with others to work on national problem	22.7		14.0
Joined with others to work on local problem	12.9	28.7	22.9
Mobilization by Political Leaders			
Contacted by party or candidate	7.8		7.4
New Senator	−4.3		−7.0
New Representative			−4.2
Mobilization around Issues			
School-aged children		12.8	4.0

Note: Entries are the partial effects of independent variables on the probability of
participation (in percentages).
Source: Appendix C.

is to be held and what to do when they get there. None of this information is difficult to come by if one knows where to find it. The more educated usually know, and the less educated often do not. Similarly, correspondence with public officials and participation in meetings require a measure of skill. In Table 3-4 in Chapter 3, we found a greater degree of overlap among activities such as writing a letter to the newspaper, writing an article for a magazine, and making a speech, and for good reason. All of these activities require verbal acuity and facility in composition and argumentation. So do writing to public officials and participating in local meetings. The highly educated usually possess these skills, and the less educated do not.

No particular knowledge or skill is required, of course, to sign a petition: It demands only that people be able to write their names on whatever is put before them.

By this line of reasoning, then, the ability to participate is conditioned by costs associated with the activity at hand. When political participation requires that knowledge and cognitive skills be brought to bear, people with more education are more likely to participate than people with less education. Participation, that is, requires resources that are appropriate to the task.[4]

On the other hand, education also indicates both the likelihood that people will be contacted by political leaders and the likelihood that they will respond. Educated people travel in social circles that make them targets of both direct and indirect mobilization. Politicians and interest groups try to activate people they know personally and professionally, who tend—as do they themselves—to be well educated. Political leaders try to move good speakers to attend public meetings and good writers to contact members of Congress. Political leaders try to inspire people who public officials know and respect to attend meetings and to write letters. Education, then, puts people into contact with the political class.

In addition, because educated people have educated friends, they are likely to come in contact with people who readily pass along and discuss the messages they receive from political leaders, mobilizing indirectly. Socialized to value political involvement, the educated friends

---

[4]See also M. Margaret Conway and Judith Garber, "Stability and Change in Political Participation: A Panel Analysis," paper presented at the annual meeting of the Southern Political Science Association, 1983, pp. 11–12.

and associates of educated people convey expectations that encourage participation, creating selective incentives for political activism.

In sum, then, education promotes political participation in two ways: by giving people the knowledge and skills that facilitate participation and by placing people in social networks that inform them about politics and reward political action.

Experience

There are other ways, besides formal schooling, for people to acquire political resources and attain social position. The longer people live, the more knowledge, skills, and social contacts they acquire. As they go through life, they learn better how to draft competent letters. As they settle down into work and community, they accumulate family, friends, and professional colleagues, some of whom encourage them to write. According to our estimates, a sixty-five-year-old is about 4.4 percent more likely to write a letter to a senator or representative than an eighteen-year-old. Communication with leaders of national government increases with age. Experience gives people the skills they need to participate; experience places people into the social networks through which they are more likely to be contacted and mobilized.

Gender, Race, and Language

The two-sided political effect of resources carries a little further. As Table 4-2 also shows, women, African-Americans, Mexican-Americans, and Puerto Ricans are less likely to write to public officials than other people.

Overall, the disparity owes both to resources and to social position. In 1976, Congress was disproportionately male and overwhelmingly white: Only 20 percent of African-Americans were represented by a U.S. senator or member of the House who was black; only 5 percent of American women were represented by a member of the House who was a woman.[5] Blacks and women

[5]The lone black senator was Republican Edward Brooke of Massachusetts. The sixteen African-American House members, all Democrats, represented mostly northern, urban districts with majority black populations. Only two blacks represented southern constituencies, Andrew Young of Georgia and Barbara Jordan of Texas. The nineteen women House members were mostly Democrats.

encounter an "ascriptive barrier" to communications with predominantly white, male, public officials.[6] The barrier surely has two aspects, one psychological and one systemic. Psychologically, Sidney Verba and Norman Nie argue, African-Americans (and we suspect women) doubt that white politicians will be sympathetic to their views, and they therefore hesitate to offer them. Systemically, we suspect, African-Americans are less likely to be central to the electoral coalitions of white politicians, and office holders are therefore less likely to mobilize them to express their opinions. Richard Fenno recounts a conversation between a white member of Congress and his staff assistant as they drove through a black neighborhood in the district:

> Staffer: I wouldn't want to be out there walking on the sidewalk.
> Member of Congress: It's like some Caribbean country.
> Staffer: It sure is a different country here.

In many cases, African-Americans are outside the primary constituencies of white politicians. Consequently, for African-Americans—and perhaps equally for women—there are few sympathetic outlets for their concerns.[7]

Mexican-Americans and Puerto Ricans, although sharing these problems, are further inhibited from writing public officials by other resource deficiencies. Some are recent immigrants, new to their communities, to public officials, and to the political system, and often lacking the privileges, protections, and resources of citizenship.[8] Moreover, many lack the facility in English possessed by native speakers and therefore may feel less able to make an effective appeal to elected representatives. Consequently, where women are 3.7 percent less likely to convey their views to public officials and blacks

[6]Verba and Nie, *Participation in America*, pp. 160–70, quoted at p. 163.
[7]Richard F. Fenno, Jr., *Home Style: House Members in Their Districts* (Boston: Little, Brown and Co., 1978), pp. 21–24, 68, 122–23, quoted at p. 21. At the local level, of course, leaders mirror their constituents more closely. Hence, blacks face fewer barriers at the local level, and because of this they are just as likely to have attended local meetings as white Americans.
[8]As we will show in Chapter 6, Mexican-Americans and Puerto Ricans are also less likely to vote, even though Puerto Ricans are American citizens from birth.

are 7.3 percent less likely, Mexican-Americans and Puerto Ricans are 14.4 percent less likely to send a letter to Congress. Compared even to those who are equally disadvantaged economically, the barriers to communication with Congress are more difficult for Mexican-Americans and Puerto Ricans to surmount. [9] Because of language and recent migration, they lack the resources to take part in politics. Because of language and often because of recent migration, they are less often in positions where they are encouraged to take part.[10]

Political Efficacy

People differ, too, in the psychological resources they bring to politics. As many analysts have demonstrated, whatever the form of political activity, a sense of efficacy fosters political involvement. It has a modest effect, we find, on the probability of participation in governmental politics. People who feel a sense of personal competence to figure out what is going on in local politics are 5.4 percent more likely to attend local meetings, and people who believe that their actions will affect what local government does are 3.2 percent more likely to attend. Likewise, people who believe that their actions will make the government respond are 5.7 percent more likely to write to public officials and 9.2 percent more likely to sign petitions. The logic behind the findings is straightforward: People who believe, for instance, that a petition is a silly exercise that is not likely to be taken seriously are not inclined to stop to sign one. A psychological sense of political efficacy helps to overcome the very natural suspicion that nothing one can do could possibly make very much difference.

[9]See Maria Antonia Calvo and Steven J. Rosenstone, *Hispanic Political Participation* (San Antonio: Southwest Voter Research Institute, 1989).
[10]See also Carole J. Uhlaner, Bruce E. Cain, and D. Roderick Kiewiet, "Political Participation of Ethnic Minorities in the 1980s," *Political Behavior* 11 (September 1989), pp. 195–321; and Carole Jean Uhlaner, "Political Participation and Discrimination: A Comparative Analysis of Asians, Blacks and Latinos," pp. 139–70 in William Crotty, ed., *Political Participation and American Democracy* (New York: Greenwood Press, 1991). Like Uhlaner, many scholars argue that a sense of group consciousness helps to overcome the effects of resource deficiencies and unfavorable social placement. See Verba and Nie, *Participation in America,* chap. 10; and Arthur H. Miller, Patricia Gurin, Gerald Gurin, and Oksana Malanchuk, "Group Consciousness and Political Participation," *American Journal of Political Science* 25 (August 1981), pp. 494–511.

Summary

In sum, people with more abundant resources participate more in governmental politics than people with less abundant resources. Clearly, one reason is personal. People with ample resources can more easily meet the costs incurred by involvement in politics. The educated and experienced have the knowledge; English speakers have the language skills; the efficacious have self-confidence. Certainly, though, another reason is political. People with ample resources have friends and associates who expose them to political information and reward their participation. Political leaders target for mobilization the people who are like them: the educated, skilled, and politically important.

Social Involvement

Everybody participates in social life, in interactions with family, friends, neighbors, and co-workers. Some people, though, are more extensively involved in social life than others and are thus more likely to be exposed to the information and the social expectations that motivate political action. When people are part of large social networks, they are more likely to be the targets of mobilization efforts, both directly and indirectly. When people have a large number of friends and know many neighbors and co-workers, they are more likely to be exposed to the selective, solidary rewards for participation. For all of these reasons, they are more likely to participate in politics.

The Workplace

One of the most influential social involvements is the workplace. People spend almost half their waking hours there. Socially, people are bound to co-workers by friendship, common interests, and financial necessity. In part because of those strong ties and in part because of the ease of reaching people, political leaders often mobilize through the workplace. Interest groups contact the professions and the industries they represent.[11] Politicians appear at factory gates and office buildings. Employers suggest political action to benefit

---

[11] Jack Walker, for instance, surveyed Washington advocacy groups and found that 76 percent represented interests defined in some way by occupation. Based on a different sampling, Kay Lehman Schlozman and John T. Tierney found an even

the company and to preserve jobs. The purpose is straightforward. "A prudently managed grass roots program can be a team-building exercise," one management consultant writes. "Providing information that will affect . . . company activities will be of interest to many employees at all ranks. . . . Building a grass roots program with employees makes them part of the team."[12] Mobilization through the workplace creates powerful social and professional expectations and, as a consequence, the workplace is a powerful promoter of political activity.

The importance of social contacts in the workplace is apparent in our results. Compared to people who are working or who are retired, in school or otherwise not in the workforce, people who are unemployed are 8.1 percent less likely to have written a letter to a U.S. senator or a representative. Part of the reason, surely, is that unemployed people have better things to do than to fire off angry letters: They are busy finding new jobs and figuring out how to make ends meet. The opportunity costs of political participation are high.[13]

Another part of the reason, though, is that the unemployed have been wrenched from social situations that encourage and reward their participation in politics. Without the daily experiences of work, they are cut off from information about opportunities to participate.

---

greater concentration—over 90 percent—of business and occupational interests. Jack L. Walker, Jr., *Mobilizing Interest Groups in America: Patrons, Professions, and Social Movements* (Ann Arbor: University of Michigan Press, 1991), chap. 4, esp. p. 59; Kay Lehman Schlozman and John T. Tierney, *Organized Interests and American Democracy* (New York: Harper & Row, 1986), pp. 66–71.

[12] Gerry Keim, "Corporate Grass Roots Programs in the 1980s, " *California Management Review* 28 (Fall 1985), p. 117, as quoted in David Vogel, *Fluctuating Fortunes: The Political Power of Business in America* (New York: Basic Books, 1989), p. 205. Bauer, Pool, and Dexter found, correspondingly, that business executives who had discussed trade policy with people inside and outside of their firms—that is, who had been exposed to the social expectations of peers—were more likely to have written a letter to Congress on trade policy. Raymond A. Bauer, Ithiel de Sola Pool, and Lewis Anthony Dexter, *American Business and Public Policy: The Politics of Foreign Trade*, 2nd ed. (Chicago: Aldine-Atherton, 1972), pp. 187–91.

[13] Richard A. Brody and Paul M. Sniderman, "From Life Space to the Polling Place: The Relevance of Personal Concerns for Voting Behavior," *British Journal of Political Science* 7 (July 1977), pp. 337–60; Steven J. Rosenstone, "Economic Adversity and Voter Turnout," *American Journal of Political Science* 26 (February 1982), pp. 25–46; but see Kay Lehman Schlozman and Sidney Verba, *Injury to Insult: Unemployment, Class and Political Response* (Cambridge: Harvard University Press, 1979), chap. 9.

Without the daily contact of co-workers, they are not subject to the social expectations and pressures that foster political activism. Not being present at the office or the factory, they are not available to political leaders for mobilization.

Presentation of Opportunities

Two other findings point in the same direction, toward mobilization through social involvements. Both concern the propensity to sign a petition. Of all of the kinds of participation we examine in this book, putting a signature on a petition is the activity that stems most obviously from mobilization. Petition signing depends less on a person's propensity to act than on a person's likelihood of encountering somebody who is carrying a petition. "Having circulated political petitions myself on many occasions, door-to-door," our colleague Harold Stanley recounted to us, "I am struck by how obliging total strangers are to the mere request for a signature. Petition signing reveals more about an individual's politeness than his politics."[14] People, that is, sign petitions mostly out of simple courtesy, and the key to understanding who signs petitions is to identify who is most likely to encounter the people who circulate them.

In this light, it makes sense, as our estimates in Table 4-2 indicate, that people who are employed are 4.2 percent more likely to sign a petition. Employed people are out and about, in places where they are likely to encounter somebody with a petition, at or on the way to work. The employed are in a position to be mobilized.

In addition, it makes sense that people with the highest incomes are 18.7 percent more likely to sign a petition than people with the lowest incomes. Obviously, signing a petition does not involve much expense; it requires no outlay of money and only a trivial investment of time. There is no reason to believe that income per se facilitates activity. Signing a petition does, however, require opportunity, and the wealthy are more likely to be presented with it than the poor. They are more likely to go to places where people circulate petitions: shopping malls and entertainment districts. They are also more likely to live in safe neighborhoods, the kinds of neighborhoods where political activists, including those carrying petitions,

---

[14]Harold Stanley, personal communication, 1984.

will not hesitate to go door-to-door.[15] They live in neighborhoods where political activists believe influential people live. Finally, they live among other people with wealth and status, among neighbors who more earnestly (and accurately) believe that their political actions are consequential. The wealthy, in short, are more likely to encounter a person carrying a petition than the poor.

In sum, the more involved people are in social life, the more likely they are to be mobilized, the more likely they are to be offered the social incentives toward activism, and the more prone they are to take part in politics.

Voluntary Associations

Social involvement has a second dimension to it, of course—this one voluntary. Political analysts have long known that people who belong to clubs, organizations, and interest groups are more likely to participate in politics than people who do not, even after factoring out the influences that might cause people to do both.[16]

Membership in organizations causes people to be targeted by political leaders for mobilization. First, organizations mobilize their own members, often explicitly. When Congress took up legislation to allow common site picketing in 1977, for example, the U.S. Chamber of Commerce alerted its members to the challenge with "emotional antilabor themes." The result: In a single day 55,000 letters arrived in House Speaker Thomas P. (Tip) O'Neill's office.[17] In other cases, mobilization is more subtle. Members of bridge clubs, for instance, are prone to political activism because they often talk politics over cards.[18]

[15] Even people who are paid to conduct surveys will refuse to go into neighborhoods that they perceive to be unsafe.

[16] Lane, *Political Life*, pp. 74–79; Verba and Nie, *Participation in America*, chap. 11.

[17] Burdett A. Loomis, "A New Era: Groups and the Grass Roots," pp. 169–90 in Allan J. Cigler and Burdett A. Loomis, eds., *Interest Group Politics* (Washington, D.C.: Congressional Quarterly Press, 1983), p. 177; Norman J. Ornstein and Shirley Elder, *Interest Groups, Lobbying and Policymaking* (Washington, D.C.: Congressional Quarterly Press, 1978), chap. 5; *Hearings before a Subcommittee of the Committee on Appropriations, House of Representatives*, "Legislative Branch Appropriations for 1979," 95th Congress, 2d session, 1978, p. 110.

[18] Bonnie H. Erickson and T. A. Nosanchuk, "How an Apolitical Association Politicizes," *Canadian Review of Sociology and Anthropology* 27 (1990), pp. 206–19. See also

(continued)

Second, organizations expose their members to mobilization by sympathetic politicians, activists, and other organizations. In Massachusetts, for example, during a 1988 campaign for a prevailing wage initiative, the Building Trades Council combed friendly churches and ethnic associations, soliciting activists to write letters to newspapers.[19]

Finally, membership in organizations exposes people to social rewards. In voluntary associations, people are among friends, among people who share their interests and reward their participation in politics.

Involvement in associations promotes political activism. In fact, no variable in our cross-sectional analysis has a larger impact on the probability that people will participate.[20] People who have joined with others to work on a national problem are 22.7 percent more likely to write to public officials and 14.0 percent more likely to sign a petition. Likewise, people who have joined with others to work on a local problem are 12.9 percent more likely to write national leaders, 22.9 percent more likely to sign a petition, and 28.7 percent more likely to take part in a local political meeting.

The pattern here makes sense. First, joining with others to work on a national problem has a greater effect on the probability of writing to Congress than it does on signing a petition or attending a local

---

(*continued*)

Philip H. Pollock, III, "Organizations as Agents of Mobilization: How Does Group Activity Affect Political Participation?" *American Journal of Political Science* 26 (August 1982), pp. 485–503.

[19]Clyde W. Barrow, "Unions and Community Mobilization: The 1988 Massachusetts Prevailing Wage Campaign," *Labor Studies Journal* 14 (Winter 1989), pp. 18–39, esp. p. 33.

[20]Some caution must be exercised in interpreting these relationships. The relationship between collective political activity and individual political participation might be inflated by double counting. When people respond that they have joined with others to solve a local problem, for instance, they may have in mind their attendance at a local meeting.

The extent of double counting in the 1976 National Election Study is unknowable to us, but we do have side evidence from the 1989 Detroit Area Study (DAS) indicating that it is less a problem than it might appear. In examining the impact of organizational membership on participation in the local public schools, the DAS researchers found that organizational membership has the same effect on participation even after memberships in school-related organizations are excluded from the analysis.

meeting. Similarly, joining with others to work on a local problem has a larger effect on the probability of attending a local meeting than it does on the other two forms of participation. Involvement with others has quite discerning political effects: People engaged around national issues are more likely to be encouraged to write to Congress—an activity designed to influence national leaders. If they are working with others on local problems, they are encouraged to participate in local meetings—that is, an activity more likely to influence local leaders.

These relationships hold because political leaders mobilize strategically. When issue activists at the national level seek to generate letters to Congress, they are likely to target groups that are interested in national problems, and when issue activists at the local level seek to bolster attendance at local meetings, they target groups that primarily care about local issues.[21]

At the national level, however, there is some spillover effect. People involved in groups concerned with either local problems or national problems are more likely to write their representatives and senators in Washington. Political leaders jockeying for advantage in Congress obviously target citizens who belong to national organizations. Americans for Democratic Action (ADA), for example, lobbies representatives and senators through the grass roots. It contacts ADA members in key constituencies and asks that they communicate their views to their leaders in Washington.[22]

---

[21]For a revealing look at the process by which people came to participate in block organizations, see Abraham Wandersman and Gary A. Giamartino, "Community and Individual Difference Characteristics as Influences on Initial Participation," *American Journal of Community Psychology* 8 (April 1980), pp. 217–28; Abraham Wandersman, John F. Jakubs, and Gary A. Giamartino, "Participation in Block Organizations," *Journal of Community Action* 1 (September/October 1981), pp. 40–47; Donald G. Unger and Abraham Wandersman, "Neighboring and Its Role in Block Organizations: An Exploratory Report," *American Journal of Community Psychology* 11 (June 1983), pp. 291–300; Richard C. Rich and Abraham Wandersman, "Participation in Block Organizations," *Social Policy* 14 (Summer 1983), pp. 45–47. See also Paul J. Lavrakas and Elicia J. Herz, "Citizen Participation in Neighborhood Crime Prevention," *Criminology* 20 (November 1982), pp. 479–98.

[22]James N. Rosenau, *Citizenship between Elections: An Inquiry into the Mobilizable American* (New York: Free Press, 1974); Schlozman and Tierney, *Organized Interests*, pp. 184–97; Linda L. Fowler and Ronald G. Shaiko, "Contact with Congress: A New Attentive Constituency," paper presented at the Conference on Citizen Participation, Tallin, Estonia, U.S.S.R., 1987, pp. 23–30.

But political leaders seeking to influence Congress also mobilize people who are involved in local organizations, and for good reason. Senators and representatives are national office holders, but they represent localities: states and congressional districts. Accordingly, it makes no real difference to them whether mail comes from members of the Chamber of Commerce or from members of the Lion's Club. They are all constituents.[23]

Thus, organizational involvement promotes participation in governmental politics in appropriate ways. Political leaders seeking to mobilize citizens to effect government outcomes target people who share their concerns. They mobilize local organizations when the issues are local, national organizations when the issues are national, and both when elections link national officials to local communities. People who belong to organizations are more likely to participate in politics because they are accessible and susceptible to mobilization.

This argument carries over to an explanation of participation in governmental politics over time. If involvement in organizations promotes political participation, then the higher the level of organizational activity in American society, the more participation we should observe in governmental politics. As shown in Table 4-1, this expectation is confirmed: The higher the level of involvement in organizations, the higher the involvement in governmental politics. As participation in organizations declined, from about 10.9 percent in the early 1970s to about 8.3 percent in the late 1980s, around 1.2 million fewer people wrote letters to Congress (0.8 percent), around 1.3 million fewer people attended local meetings (0.9 percent), and around 2.8 million fewer people put their signatures on petitions (1.8 percent).[24]

In part, this finding suggests the power of direct mobilization. Club presidents, officers, and members are centrally situated in social networks; hence they are more likely to be contacted by activists and are more likely to participate. In part, this finding also rep-

---

[23] In addition, many national interest groups are federations of state and local groups, so that survey respondents may think of the local chamber of commerce as a local organization when in fact it is federated into a national organization.

[24] Unlike the other variables in this analysis, the organizational involvement variables are drawn from the same source as the dependent variables. Consequently, one concern is that the relationship is inflated spuriously by variations in the quality of Roper samples: When Roper inadvertently oversamples well-educated people, for

resents the effect of indirect mobilization. Once contacted, people in organizations contact other people, inside and outside the organization. They ask their friends to write, to attend, and to sign. Organizations, by design, multiply contact. As one how-to guide for community activists recommended,

> Immediately after your organizational meeting, call together the elected leaders and any people you have appointed to key roles and ... go over the attendance list which you circulated [during the meeting]. Review the card file of potential supporters you built up prior to the meeting. But even more importantly, discuss the acquaintances of every member of your leadership group.... Make sure [those] who are personal friends of ... your leadership group are assigned to those [leaders] for recruitment.... Then phone, phone, phone as rapidly as possible.[25]

As in the findings we presented earlier, the effect of organizational involvement is quite discerning. Involvement in organizations generally increased the level of contact with national office holders, the level of involvement in community government meetings, and the number of signatures on petitions. Involvement in expressly local organizations, on the other hand, affected only attendance at local political meetings. The 2.3-percentage-point drop in participation in local organizations between 1973 and 1990 caused a 1.5-percentage-point decline (or about 2.3 million people) in attendance at local meetings.

Involvement in organizations, in short, promotes political participation by making people susceptible to mobilization. Politically, organizations stand between national and local political leaders and ordinary citizens. Accordingly, they are both the subjects and the

---

example, it ends up with larger numbers of all kinds of participants; and when Roper mistakenly oversamples less-educated people, it ends up with smaller numbers of all kinds of participants. It is difficult to judge whether this is a problem. We include the group activity variables in the analysis because there is a theoretical reason to include them. Nevertheless, the findings must be interpreted cautiously.

[25]John Huenefeld, *The Community Activist's Handbook: A Guide to Organizing, Financing, and Publicizing Community Campaigns* (Boston: Beacon Press, 1970), p. 90. Paul Freedman, analyzing data from the 1989 Detroit Area Study, shows that contact concerning one local issue spills over to promote participation around other local issues. See Paul Freedman, "Mobilization and Participation," unpublished manuscript, University of Michigan, 1992.

agents of mobilization: Political leaders mobilize them; they mobilize others. Participation in governmental politics rises and falls with the numbers of citizens who take part in these important mediating institutions.

Summary

In summary, then, involvement in social life encourages participation in governmental politics. Involvement in the workplace and in organizations brings greater exposure to the mobilization efforts of political leaders. Integration into extensive social networks creates selective social incentives for participation.

To this point in our analysis, we have focused on the personal attributes of individuals and their effect on political participation. We have considered the ways in which resources and social positions promote and discourage activism in governmental politics. Starting with the next section, we direct our attention to the political system and its effect on political activism. The change of focus is essential to the solution of the puzzles we posed in Chapter 3. Simply put, individual attributes do not change fast enough to account for much of the variation in citizen involvement over time. The important causes of participation, we argued in Chapter 2, arise outside of individuals, in the strategic calculations of political leaders. Their calculations differ according to the opportunities the political system presents to them.

Mobilization by Political Leaders

Democracy as a political system places a premium on public support. Politicians must win public confidence to attain their offices, but their dependence on the people does not end on election day. Officials make extraordinary efforts to maintain support between elections for a couple of reasons: They need public support to be reelected, and they secure political advantages from appearing to have the people behind them. Politicians do not simply sit around and wait for public backing to come to them, however. Instead, they try to create it. Some of the most far-reaching efforts to mobilize public pressures on the government are made by elected officials themselves.

Political Parties and Candidates

One of the main objects of political leaders in a democracy is to win election to public office. To that end, in some locales politicians build and maintain political parties—organizations devoted to electing whole slates of candidates. In strong party states such as New Jersey, Maryland, and Illinois, party organizations function continuously—before, during, and after the campaign. In other locales politicians build campaign organizations to promote the election of individual candidates. In weak party states such as Alabama, South Dakota, and California, campaign organizations come and go as the need for them arises.[26]

In both kinds of places, though, party and campaign workers are important agents of mobilization of political participation. This is most apparent for participation in electoral politics, as we will discuss in Chapter 6. It is also true of participation in governmental politics.

Party and campaign workers stand between political leaders and ordinary citizens. Their campaign activities give them access to public officials. Their campaign activities also connect them to ordinary citizens. Consequently, party activists, like organization activists, are both the subjects and the agents of mobilization. The political centrality of party and campaign workers makes them important conduits for mobilization efforts, both inside and outside campaigns.[27]

The boost that the efforts of party and campaign workers give to participation in national government is shown in Table 4-2. People who report contact with a political party in 1976 are 7.8 percent more likely to write a letter to Congress and 7.4 percent more likely to sign a petition than people who report no contact. The reasons are straightforward. First, contact with campaign activists communicates information about politics. Party workers inform people about

[26]David R. Mayhew, *Placing Parties in American Politics: Organization, Electoral Settings, and Government Activity in the Twentieth Century* (Princeton: Princeton University Press, 1986), part 1.
[27]For some suggestive evidence, see Alan S. Zuckerman and Darrell M. West, "The Political Bases of Citizen Contacting: A Cross-National Analysis," *American Political Science Review* 79 (March 1979), pp. 117–31.

the issues facing the nation and the steps people can take to influence their resolution. Second, contact with campaign activists presents opportunities to participate. Party workers bring nominating petitions into workplaces and homes. They suggest ways of contacting public officials about important political problems. Campaign mobilization spills over into other kinds of political participation.[28]

Because of the information and expectations that are conveyed in contacts with party activists, involvement in political parties and campaign organizations, like involvement in voluntary organizations, promotes political participation. Indeed, as Table 4-1 shows, the more people are involved in party politics, the higher the level of participation in national governmental politics. As the number of Americans working for political parties declined from about 5.9 percent of the electorate in the early 1970s to about 3.1 percent in the late 1980s, 1.4 million fewer people wrote letters to Congress (0.9 percent of the population) and 4.7 million fewer people signed petitions (3.0 percent). Fewer people participated in national government in the 1980s because fewer party activists mobilized them to do so.[29]

The efforts of political parties to mobilize support in elections, then, spill over into governmental politics. In the course of electoral mobilization, campaign workers convey information and expectations that mobilize participation in government as well. Similarly, in the normal course of national legislative battles, elected officials and issue activists call upon campaign workers to help them mobilize the support of the general public.

Members of Congress

Outside the electoral arena, members of Congress are the government officials who are the most frequent targets of mobilization

---

[28] Freedman, "Mobilization and Participation." In addition, we suspect that survey respondents do not clearly distinguish between mobilizers who work for a political party and those who work for a candidate or other causes.

[29] Like the organizational involvement variables, the party activism variable comes from the same source as the dependent variables. Consequently, for the reasons outlined in note 24, this finding should be interpreted cautiously.

efforts. Together, the House and the Senate receive more than 100 million pieces of mail a year: The typical House member receives 130,000 pieces and the average senator half a million.[30]

Some people write Congress on their own initiative to get help in negotiating the bureaucracy or simply to blow off steam. Some of the mail is inspired by interest groups, issue activists, employers, and organization leaders, who ask people to write Congress. Some of the mail is stimulated by members of Congress themselves. People write Congress because lawmakers at public appearances, in interviews, in newspaper columns, and in newsletters invite them to write.[31]

The motivation to write varies, in part, with how familiar representatives are to their constituents. Familiarity tends to promote citizen contacts and unfamiliarity tends to discourage them. Citizens tend not to have met new members of the Senate or House and have difficulty remembering their names.[32] Interest groups know little about their orientations and the best ways of approaching them. New legislators themselves have not had the time to build up the recognition and contacts that encourage people to write.

Over the period from 1973 to 1990, as Figure 4-1 indicates, turnover in Congress rose and fell. Turnover topped out in 1981 and 1982 at 38 percent and bottomed out in 1985 and 1986 at 16 percent for the House and the Senate together. As Table 4-1 shows, citizen involvement in governmental politics rises and falls

---

[30]Fowler and Shaiko, "Contact with Congress," p. 8.

[31]Stephen E. Frantzich, *Write Your Congressman: Constituent Communications and Representation* (New York: Praeger Publishers, 1986), chap. 2; Fowler and Shaiko, "Contact with Congress," pp. 27–30. Members of Congress encourage constituents to write to them because of the potential electoral payoffs. Voters overwhelmingly report satisfaction with lawmakers' responses to their communications, and voters' satisfaction in turn contributes to the much more favorable impressions that incumbents enjoy relative to challengers. See Gary C. Jacobson, *The Politics of Congressional Elections*, 3rd ed. (New York: Harper Collins Publishers, 1992), pp. 136–41; and Morris P. Fiorina, *Congress: Keystone of the Washington Establishment* (New Haven: Yale University Press, 1977), chap. 5.

[32]Charles H. Franklin, "Incumbent Visibility over the Election Cycle," paper presented at the Stanford/Hoover Conference on Senate Elections, 1991.

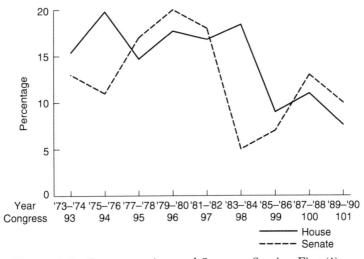

Figure 4-1   Representatives and Senators Serving First Two
Years of Term, 1973–1990.
Source: See Appendix A.

with congressional turnover. Correspondence with Congress was
1.8 percentage points lower and petition signing was 2.2 percentage
points lower when congressional turnover was at its highest point
than when it was at its lowest. High turnover in the 1970s discour-
aged communication with Congress.

Our cross-sectional analysis from 1976 confirms this finding and
enables us to elaborate it. Two results stand out. First, both new
senators and new representatives reduce the likelihood that their
constituents sign petitions: People who live in districts represented
by new representatives are 4.2 percent less likely to sign petitions,
and people who live in states served by new senators are 7.0 percent
less likely to sign. Given, as we argued before, that petition signing is
driven more by mobilization than by self-initiation, these findings
suggest that interest groups and issue advocates are less likely to
mobilize in districts held by new members than in districts held
by members who have served many terms. Lobbyists concentrate
their efforts on lawmakers who have risen to important leadership
positions in Congress.

In contrast, only new senators lower the probability that people will write letters to public officials. People who live in states represented by new senators are 4.3 percent less likely to write, but people who live in districts represented by new representatives are no less likely to do so. The reason is simple: New representatives put a lot more effort into mobilizing political support than first-term senators. Representatives serve two-year terms and start running for reelection the day they are elected. They seek out casework, opinions, and just simple contact. Members of Congress mobilize the demands that constituents make on them.[33] Senators, on the other hand, serve six years and can afford a couple of years of taking it easy.

Members of Congress, David Mayhew reminds us, mobilize electoral support in three distinct ways: by advertising, by position taking, and by credit claiming.[34] Legislators advertise by making their names known to their constituents. They take positions by enunciating policy stands designed to please voters and major constituency groups. They claim credit by passing bills, blocking amendments, and winning favors for their constituents and for friendly interest groups. In doing so, they pursue a variety of activities. Two prominent activities, however, are use of franked mail and issue activism.

Until recently, the amount of mail that congressional offices could send out at public expense was virtually unlimited, and lawmakers exploited their perquisite to maximum advantage. As shown in Figure 4-2, congressional mailings exploded in the early 1970s and rose steadily and rapidly into the 1980s, when the sheer volume of franked mail led to charges of abuse and to more stringent efforts to regulate it. A large proportion of the congressional outflow comprised newsletters printed and mailed at public expense, especially around election time, creating the sawtooth pattern of outgoing mail so evident in the figure. By the late 1980s, Congress

---

[33]Jacobson, *Congressional Elections*, p. 44; Richard F. Fenno, Jr., *The United States Senate: A Bicameral Perspective* (Washington, D.C.: American Enterprise Institute, 1982), chap. 3; Albert D. Cover, "Contacting Congressional Constituents: Some Patterns of Perquisite Use," *American Journal of Political Science* 24 (February 1980), pp. 125–35; Franklin, "Incumbent Visibility."

[34]David R. Mayhew, *Congress: The Electoral Connection* (New Haven: Yale University Press, 1974).

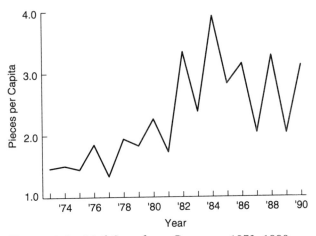

Figure 4-2   Mail Sent from Congress, 1973–1990.
Source: Norman J. Ornstein, Thomas E. Mann, and Michael J. Malbin, *Vital Statistics on Congress, 1989–1990* (Washington, D.C.: Congressional Quarterly Press, 1990); U.S. Bureau of the Census, *Current
Population Reports,* Series P-25, No. 1045, January 1990, pp. 86–87.

mailed out about three franked pieces for every man, woman, and
child in the United States and, by one estimate, only 4 percent of
it was in response to constituent letters.[35]

Although outgoing congressional mail serves the important
political purpose of making incumbents better known, it is less
successful in stimulating people to write to Congress. Certainly, as
Figure 4-2 shows, the increasing *volume* of outgoing congressional
mail parallels the increasing volume of incoming mail, and certainly,
as congressional offices have discovered, congressional mailings al-
ter the *content* of the incoming mail. They do not, however, affect
the *percentage* of the population that writes to their senator or representative. As is clear from reinspection of Figure 3-11, and as is also
clear from our regression estimates, the *biennial* election-year flood

[35] Cover, "Contacting Congressional Constituents," pp. 125–35; Michael J. Robinson,
"Three Faces of Congressional Media," pp. 55–96 in Thomas E. Mann and Norman
J. Ornstein, eds., *The New Congress* (Washington, D.C.: American Enterprise Institute,
1981), pp. 59–62; Tim Miller, "Why Congress Wants Computers," *Washington Post
Magazine,* May 15, 1983, p. 21.

of outgoing franked mail does not match up with the *annual* summertime peaks of citizen letter writing, and the over-time growth of franked mail does not match up with the generally downward trend of citizen contact with Congress.[36]

This is not to say that franked mail has no effect. Its main point, after all, is to advertise incumbent representatives, to increase their visibility and likability, and the evidence indicates that it succeeds at that task quite handsomely.[37] Rather, the findings indicate that franked mail, by itself, does not move more people to participate: Congress bombards people so heavily with mail around election time that their efforts far exceed constituent reactions. In tandem with more substantive efforts, however, franked mail undoubtedly stimulates some constituents to participate. In fact, as we will show later, congressional mail follows the progress of important issues quite closely, and one aspect of the mobilization around issues is lawmakers' own efforts to produce a supportive public response.[38]

Congressional activism on issues is a powerful force for mobilization of public participation, and our evidence bears the idea out. In 1989, for example, an analysis of the mail received by one mid-

---

[36] In the analysis reported in Table 4-1, neither of two indicators of outgoing congressional mail had a coefficient distinguishable from zero. The first was the annual number of pieces mailed by Congress (normalized by population), as reported in Norman J. Ornstein, Thomas E. Mann, and Michael Malbin, *Vital Statistics on Congress, 1989–1990* (Washington, D.C.: American Enterprise Institute, 1990), p. 164. The second, available only through the end of 1978, was the monthly number of pieces mailed (also normalized by population), collected by Common Cause for use in its unsuccessful 1981 lawsuit, *Common Cause* v. *Bolger*, alleging political abuses of the franking privilege. Our efforts to update the Common Cause series came to no avail. Even the aggregated month-to-month totals of mail sent from congressional offices are a closely guarded secret. Congress releases such information, we were told, only after written request to high officials in the congressional post office. See also Frantzich, *Write Your Congressman*, pp. 34–37.

[37] Albert D. Cover and Bruce S. Brumberg, "Baby Books and Ballots: The Impact of Congressional Mail on Constituent Opinion," *American Political Science Review* 76 (June 1982), pp. 347–59.

[38] Fowler and Shaiko find that earlier contacts with members of Congress do in fact promote citizen contacts with lawmakers and other public officials. Fowler and Shaiko, "Contact with Congress," pp. 27–30.

western senator found two peaks in correspondence concerned with the drug problem, one around the time of the senator's television blitz on the subject and another around the time of the senator's series of drug conferences held around the state. Others vouch for similar experiences. "One of the most important and most often overlooked [factors in the growth of mail to Congress] is the activity of Members of Congress themselves," House Postmaster Robert V. Rota reported. "Members today are doing more and working harder than ever before. Because such activity attracts attention and comment,... it is not surprising that the volume of constituent mail reflects this increased activity."[39]

As Rota suggests, congressional activism has varied over the last two decades and public correspondence with Congress has varied with it. In the early 1970s, legislators introduced upward of 15,000 pieces of legislation per year proposing solutions to all manner of political, social, and economic ills. Lawmakers scaled back their activity in the 1980s, introducing as few as 2,700 bills a year. Economic ills, the election of a president, Ronald Reagan, who was ideologically hostile to government intervention, and the mounting federal budget deficit made the introduction of proposals for new government programs less viable.

This decline in legislative activity, Table 4-1 indicates, reduced the number of people writing Congress by almost 1.2 percentage points, accounting for a substantial portion of the decline in participation between 1973 and 1990.[40] The logic underlying this relation-

---

[39] *Hearings before a Subcommittee of the Committee on Appropriations, House of Representatives*, "Legislative Branch Appropriations for 1984," 98th Congress, 1st session, 1983, p. 60; Jim Gimpel, "Year-End Wrap-Up on the Drug Mail from Indiana," report, office of Senator Daniel Coats, January 1990. Indeed, Kingdon points out, lawmakers sometimes inspire mail to use as an argument for their own positions. John W. Kingdon, *Congressmen's Voting Decisions*, 3rd ed. (Ann Arbor: University of Michigan Press, 1989), pp. 56–57.

[40] Congressional activism as well as the other yearly variables that appear in this analysis are not just surrogates for a time trend. To test for that possibility, we included a nonlinear time trend (time and time squared) in the equation. Once the structural elements are included in the equation, the time series shows no remaining trend.

ship is straightforward. Ordinarily, senators and representatives seek to benefit their constituents and to identify themselves with popular positions by introducing legislation and shepherding it through the legislative process.[41] Friendly interest groups support their efforts. A smaller legislative agenda, however, contains fewer issues around which politicians and interest groups might mobilize people. The less mobilization, the less participation.

Public participation in congressional politics, in sum, is often mobilized by members of Congress themselves. Sometimes lawmakers set out to mobilize constituents, as when they invite requests for casework, and sometimes mobilization is a by-product of their work on issues that interest groups and constituents really care about. Either way, their activities induce citizens to take part in government and thereby benefit representatives by enabling them to advertise, to take positions, and to claim credit.

The President

Members of Congress are not the only politicians who find citizen participation politically useful. One of the most familiar instances of efforts made by political leaders to mobilize public involvement is the president's strategy of "going public." Since the turn of the century, presidents have attempted to advance their legislative programs by appealing over the heads of Congress directly to the people. In the 1910s, Woodrow Wilson traveled across the country to plead his case for ratification of the Treaty of Versailles and U.S. entry into the League of Nations. In the 1930s, Franklin D. Roosevelt went on radio to appeal for public support for his New Deal program to combat the Great Depression. And in the 1980s, Ronald Reagan appeared on national television to encourage citizens to convey their support for his economic recovery program to their senators and their representatives.[42]

---

[41] See T. R. Reid's account of New Mexico senator Pete Domenici's efforts to secure an accomplishment: T. R. Reid, *Congressional Odyssey: The Saga of a Senate Bill* (New York: W. H. Freeman, 1980), chap. 2.
[42] Samuel Kernell, *Going Public: New Strategies of Presidential Leadership* (Washington, D.C.: Congressional Quarterly Press, 1986).

With the advent of mass broadcast media, first radio and then television, it became easier for presidents to go public. From the beginning of 1973 to the end of 1990, presidents Nixon, Ford, Carter, Reagan, and Bush spoke on television during prime time on seventy-four separate occasions, addressing topics ranging from the state of the union, to the eighteen-minute gap in the White House tapes, to the Camp David peace accords, to the deficit reduction program, to the deployment of U.S. troops to the Persian Gulf. Usually, presidents left implicit their desire that Americans act to show their support. Occasionally, though, presidents asked citizens explicitly to write to Congress—eleven times in the eighteen-year span from 1973 to 1990.

Presidential efforts to stimulate citizens to pressure Congress by and large are successful. Senator Daniel Patrick Moynihan's staff testifies to a "predictable, generally supportive, surge in mail immediately following a television appearance by any president."[43] After one of Ronald Reagan's appeals in 1981, the Capitol Hill post office received 1,250,000 letters, 800,000 post cards, 800,000 telegrams, and 600,000 pie plates (to protest the proposed cuts in the school lunch program) *in a single day.* Our findings show that the number of Americans writing Congress rises 1.1 percentage points—or about 1.7 million people—in the week following presidential appeals for letters to Congress. The presidency is indeed, as Theodore Roosevelt put it, a "bully pulpit."[44]

Although it is clear that the president has the power to move people to participate, it is not clear from our analysis just why he

---

[43] Elizabeth B. Moynihan, "Mail Call on Capitol Hill," *New York Times Magazine,* November 15, 1981, p. 158. The president on television is not alone in this power. In May 1985, House Ways and Means Committee chairman Dan Rostenkowski invited citizens who wanted tax reform to send a letter to him in Washington: "Just address it to R-O-S-T-Y, Washington, D.C. The post office will get it to me." Seventy-five thousand people wrote Rosty. See Jeffrey H. Birnbaum and Alan S. Murray, *Showdown at Gucci Gulch: Lawmakers, Lobbyists and the Unlikely Triumph of Tax Reform* (New York: Random House, 1987), pp. 99–100.

[44] *Hearings before a Subcommittee of the Committee on Appropriations, House of Representatives,* "Legislative Branch Appropriations for 1984," 98th Congress, 1st session, 1983, part 2, p. 57. In his study of members of Americans for Democratic Action, Rosenau found that the president (who was a liberal Democrat at the time) was the person to whose call for letters the greatest number claimed they would respond. Rosenau, *Citizenship between Elections,* chap. 11.

does. One possibility is that citizens respond to the president personally and derive vicarious pleasure from lending a helping hand to the most important person in America, or perhaps even the world. Another possibility, suggested by James Rosenau, is that citizens respond to what the president stands for, a program of large national importance as distinct from a program of parochial special pleading.[45]

Although both of these interpretations are plausible, both also imply that citizens respond to the office rather than the particular office holder. This does not seem wholly satisfactory. At a minimum, historical experience suggests that Ronald Reagan was much more successful than either Jimmy Carter or George Bush in mobilizing the public. Unfortunately, we are unable to compare the impact of presidential mobilization efforts separately for the five presidents in our period; as it happens, only four presidential calls for letters immediately preceded Roper surveys, and all four were Reagan's.[46]

We do know, however, that Reagan resorted much more frequently than other presidents to the strategy of going public (see Figure 4-3). Reagan appealed for letters to Congress four times in his first term and three times in his second term; Jimmy Carter asked twice, George Bush (in his first two years) and Richard Nixon (in his second term) asked only once, and Gerald Ford never at all. That fact in itself is significant. Presidents use this tactic strategically because there is nothing worse than to ask for public support and to be met with yawning silence. There was something about Reagan, we think, that made his efforts more likely to succeed. One aspect, surely, was his public appeal. People tended to like Reagan more than they liked Nixon, Ford, Carter, or Bush, and their affection for him perhaps brought them greater rewards from responding to his call.[47]

---

[45] Rosenau, *Citizenship between Elections*, pp. 422–28.

[46] An appeal on behalf of his budget in April 1982, on behalf of his tax bill in August 1982, on behalf of his defense budget in March 1983, and on behalf of his plan to aid the rebels in Nicaragua in March 1986.

[47] Lane, *Political Life*, pp. 73–74. As we will show later, favorable affect toward candidates also increases electoral participation.

Another aspect was Reagan's political program. Especially in his first term, Reagan concentrated on feel-good remedies to bread-and-butter issues—tax cuts in particular—that affected people's pocketbooks more directly than Carter's energy program or Bush's complicated budget accord. A third aspect, though, was Reagan's program, which significantly reduced and reallocated federal expenditure. Because Reagan's proposals advanced or threatened the interests of so many people, politicians, groups, and activists took to the field. People responded to Reagan's speeches because interest groups and other advocates had more at stake in the Reagan years than they had had before, and they mobilized the public to support or oppose his program.[48]

Whatever the particular source of the president's appeal, he clearly has the capacity to mobilize large numbers of people directly

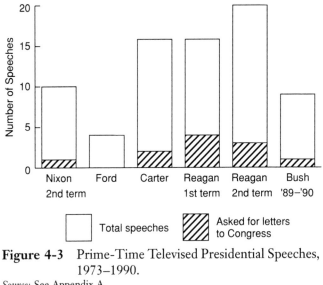

Figure 4-3   Prime-Time Televised Presidential Speeches, 1973–1990.

Source: See Appendix A.

---

[48]Kernell, *Going Public,* p. 117; Mark A. Peterson, *Legislating Together: The White House and Capitol Hill from Eisenhower to Reagan* (Cambridge: Harvard University Press, 1990), chap. 5. We will take up some of the aspects of the mobilization around Reagan's policies later in this chapter.

or to cause large numbers of people to be mobilized indirectly. Few actors in the American system are this effective.

Summary

Political participation is a resource that political leaders use strategically in their battle for political advantage. They attempt to win elections and to enact policies, and in the process they inform citizens about the issues at stake and the courses of action that might be most effective to produce the outcomes they want. In response to their calls, interest groups gear into action, social networks buzz with political discussion, and people respond by participating in governmental politics.

Mobilization Around Issues

Participation in politics serves definite political purposes. Politicians and interest groups urge people to take part in governmental politics because they want to accomplish something: to preserve favorable tax treatment for oil exploration, limit U.S. involvement in Central America, maintain the music curriculum in the high school, lower the speed limit in residential neighborhoods. By mobilizing public support, politicians hope to gain the upper hand in political disputes. Likewise, ordinary people get involved in governmental politics because they want to accomplish something, often the same thing. By participating, they hope to bring about policies that benefit them. Political leaders and ordinary citizens work hand in hand to accomplish their mutual goals. Leaders inform people about the issues they both care about, and people act to the benefit of both.

Local Issues

Mobilization of citizen participation around specific issues is common in local politics. In the 1970s and 1980s, for instance, one of the hottest issues in many school districts around the country was the content of school textbooks. Religious fundamentalists and biologists waged pitched battles over the coverage of evolution in biology texts. Feminist and minority groups fought for inclusion of the historical accomplishments of women, blacks, and Latinos, while Christian activists sought greater recognition of the historical role of religious faith. Under pressure from moral conservatives, school districts banned *The Learning Tree*, by Gordon Parks; under pressure from African-American parents, school boards removed *Huckleberry Finn*, by Mark Twain. In hundreds of communities, neighbors mobilized neighbors, churches mobilized parishioners, and teachers mobilized parents to lobby school boards and school administrators for changes in curriculum. In some communities, most famously in Kanawha County, West Virginia, contending parties even turned to boycotts and threats of violence.[49]

On a more mundane issue, citizens in San Diego, California, mobilized in 1984 around street lights. On one side, scientists from the Mount Palomar Observatory argued that the new low-pressure sodium lamps would create less interference for their telescope. On the other side, neighborhood groups worried that the new lamps would not shine as brightly, increasing the risk of crime, and they complained that the yellow-orange glow of the sodium lamps "made everyone look like cadavers." "After a stormy and controversial meeting," at which the various interests presented their arguments, the San Diego city council opted to purchase the new sodium street lights.[50]

Because of the nature of our data, which are aggregated across communities all over the nation, we cannot discern the separate effects of the thousands of local controversies that move people to participate in local politics. We can only identify the effects of mobilization around issues that consistently have an impact on citizens and local leaders all over the country. Accordingly, we turn our attention here to two of the issues that have dominated local politics: education and taxes.

Primary and secondary education is one of the most important public policies financed and controlled primarily at the local level.

---

[49] Caroline Cody, "The Politics of Textbook Publishing, Adoption, and Use," pp. 127–45 in David L. Elliot and Arthur Woodward, eds., *Textbooks and Schooling in the United States* (Chicago: National Society for the Study of Education, 1990); James Moffett, *Storm in the Mountains* (Carbondale: Southern Illinois University Press, 1988).

[50] Richard J. Waste, *The Ecology of City Policymaking* (New York: Oxford University Press, 1989), pp. 98–99.

In 1980, 45 million children enrolled in elementary and secondary schools in the United States, 89 percent of them in public schools. Spending on the schools in fiscal 1980 amounted to $96 billion, or about 40 percent of local government budgets, making education their largest single expenditure. Across the United States, more than 15,000 school districts govern 62,000 elementary schools and 24,000 secondary schools.

The major constituency for the public schools, of course, is parents. Three-quarters of the calls that school board members receive come from parents, the rest from the general public. The greater attention of parents to school politics is plain in Table 4-2: People who have school-age children are 12.8 percent more likely to attend local meetings and 4.0 percent more likely to sign petitions than people who do not.

Parents' specific concerns are often quite narrow, focusing on the educational needs of their own children. Half of the nation's school boards report being contacted by parents about their children's academic performance, two-thirds are contacted about school discipline, and 69 percent are contacted with reports about teacher performance. A large fraction of the attendance at school meetings and the signatures on petitions is surely motivated by the particular concerns that parents have about their own children's education.[51]

At the same time, a large fraction of the attendance at school meetings and a large number of the signatures on petitions are also mobilized by administrators, teachers, parent-teacher associations, and other parents. As any parent can attest, having children in school means involvement in new social networks that revolve quite specifically around the schools. Naturally, parents become acquainted with their children's teachers and with the parents of their children's classmates and friends. They become acquainted with other teachers and parents through the parent-teacher associations they join.

[51] National School Boards Association, "School–Community Communication: School Board Members and Their Constituents," Research Report 1980-1, National School Boards Association, 1980, pp. 8–9; Robert H. Salisbury, *Citizen Participation in the Public Schools* (Lexington, Mass.: Lexington Books, 1980), chaps. 3–4. Bauer, Pool, and Dexter found similar relationships between the extent to which trade policy affected the business of firms and the likelihood that their executives would write a letter to Congress. Bauer, Pool, and Dexter, *American Business and Public Policy*, pp. 202–7.

In their dealings with other people they know through their children's school, citizens learn about what is happening in the schools and they are mobilized to do something about it. Not surprisingly, then, parents take actions not only to look after the particular interests of their own children but also to advance more general public policy positions. Over half the nation's school boards report being contacted by parents about issues discussed at school board meetings, and 70 percent are contacted with "criticism of something in the district." Significant portions of activist parents get started in school activities because of an issue or an event or because they were asked to help. The social contacts that arise from having children in school become the basis for mobilization to support or to oppose broad school policies.[52]

The greater propensity of parents to take part in school politics has an important implication for the ebb and flow of involvement in community affairs over time, as Table 4-1 shows. In the 1970s, when the tail end of the "baby boom" generation was still in secondary school, there were 320 children in school for every thousand adults. In the late 1980s, there were only 220. Between 1973 and 1990, the declining numbers of children in school lowered attendance at local meetings by almost 2.6 percentage points, or by about 3.9 million people, accounting for more than half of the seventeen-year drop in participation.[53] Thus, as the baby boom generation graduated from the public schools, fewer and fewer people had a personal stake in school issues; fewer and fewer people were susceptible to being mobilized to take part.

Another important issue of local concern waxed and waned in importance over the 1970s and 1980s with enormous political consequences: local taxes. Historically, local governments in the United States have derived the lion's share of their revenues from property

---

[52] National School Boards Association, "School–Community Communication," pp. 8–9; Salisbury, *Citizen Participation*, chap. 4. See also Norman I. Fainstein and Susan S. Fainstein, *Urban Political Movements: The Search for Power by Minority Groups in American Cities* (Englewood Cliffs, N.J.: Prentice-Hall, 1974), chap. 6.

[53] School attendance is highly associated with the time trend in participation in local meetings, to the extent that when both are included in the equation both have coefficients that are statistically indistinguishable from zero.

taxes. Lately, transfers of funds from state and federal governments have been their largest single revenue source, but property taxes still account for about 25 percent of local funding and about 75 percent of local taxes.

In the late 1970s and throughout the 1980s, two circumstances conspired to make property taxes an important issue across the nation. First, powerful demand for housing drove home prices rapidly upward, especially in urban areas on the East and West coasts. Between 1976 and 1980, the median home sales price increased by an average of 12 percent a year nationally, and in the West, the median price of a home increased by an average of 18 percent a year. Prices doubled in five years. Then, in the early 1980s, a reduction of federal aid to local governments forced counties, cities, and school districts to raise property taxes to maintain local services. Rising home values and revenue-strapped local governments combined to force up per capita property taxes (see Figure 4-4).

Across the nation, rising property taxes touched off tax revolts, and one effect of the resulting furor is visible in Table 4-1. The large tax increases of the 1980s, contrasted to the real decreases of the late 1970s, drove up participation in local meetings and signatures

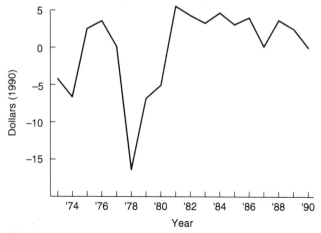

Figure 4-4 Average Per Capita Changes in Property Taxes Paid, 1973–1990.
Source: See Appendix A.

on petitions by about 0.6 to 0.7 percentage points—or 900,000 to 1.1 million people.

Rapidly escalating property tax bills sent many homeowners to county commissions and city councils to demand tax relief. Although some of the protest was surely spontaneous, in many parts of the country the political movement for tax relief was carefully orchestrated. The effort to pass Proposition 13 in California, for instance, was led by two veteran antitax activists, Howard Jarvis and Paul Gann. Jarvis and Gann pleaded on radio talk shows for people to sign petitions to place their tax relief initiative on the ballot. They built their organization by "graft[ing] their campaign onto local taxpayer and homeowner associations." Their lobbying group, the United Organization of Taxpayers, mobilized thousands of people in support of Proposition 13. The opposition, led by teachers' associations and municipal employees' unions, mobilized thousands of people against the initiative. In June 1978, the antitax activists triumphed when Californians endorsed Proposition 13 by a margin of two to one.[54]

At the local level, then, issues motivate political action both directly and indirectly. Except in the largest cities, local governments are still relatively accessible to ordinary citizens, and it makes sense that people who have a stake in a particular issue might act on their own initiative to defend it. At the same time, local governments are undoubtedly more responsive to arguments made by the many than to those made by the few. Consequently, even in local politics, political leaders have incentives to mobilize other citizens to induce them to participate. In local politics, issues provoke some people to action. These people, in turn, contact others—friends, neighbors, co-workers, homeowners, and parents—who share their interest in the issue. Participation in local government may begin spontaneously in response to issues but it nonetheless spreads through mobilization.

National Issues

Participation in national government revolves just as plainly around issues as participation in local government does. Of the 100 million

---

[54]David O. Sears and Jack Citrin, *Tax Revolt: Something for Nothing in California* (Cambridge: Harvard University Press, 1982), chaps. 2 and 6–7, quoted at p. 26.

pieces of mail Congress receives annually, the largest share deals with pending legislation. About a quarter of the letters request information, and a few more ask for help in dealing with government agencies. Half, though, express an opinion about current issues.[55]

Mobilization of citizen participation in governmental politics is even more important at the national than at the local level. National government is so remote from the experience of most Americans that they would be nearly clueless about its functionings were it not for the efforts of political leaders to keep them informed. Equally, national policymaking is so immense an undertaking that few people would be able to overcome the paradox of participation were it not for the efforts of political leaders to motivate them to participate.

In some cases, the media play the leadership role, informing people and generating social discourse. "Senators from states large and small," the staff of Senator Daniel Patrick Moynihan (D–N.Y.) reports, "experience a dramatic increase in volume [of mail] whenever matters of national concern, such as the Federal budget, dominate the news."[56] Through television, political leaders present information and arguments about issues and mobilize people into politics.

In most cases, though, the issue mail Congress receives is "inspired"—mobilized by political interest groups. This practice has a long history. In 1950, for instance, the American Medical Association (AMA) launched an aggressive grass-roots lobbying campaign against President Harry S Truman's national health insurance plan. At first, congressional mail ran five to two in favor of national health coverage. Then the AMA intervened, and it ran four to one against.[57]

If anything, inspired mail is even more prevalent today. Technological advances of the late 1970s and 1980s—especially desk-top

[55] Frantzich, *Write Your Congressman*, p. 13.

[56] Moynihan, "Mail Call," p. 138.

[57] V. O. Key, Jr., *Politics, Parties, and Pressure Groups*, 5th ed. (New York: Thomas Y. Crowell Co., 1964), pp. 131–32, and more generally pp. 130–42; Bauer, Pool, and Dexter, *American Business and Public Policy*, passim; Lewis Anthony Dexter, "What Do Congressmen Hear: The Mail," *Public Opinion Quarterly* 20 (Spring 1956), pp. 19–20; Schlozman and Tierney, *Organized Interests*, pp. 196–97.

computers, inexpensive WATS lines, overnight mail, and FAX machines—make it easier and cheaper than ever before to mobilize grass-roots lobbying. More than anything else, the new technologies are responsible for the recent explosion in the volume of congressional mail:

> Representative David R. Obey (D–Wisc.): When [I first] came here [in 1971], I actually used to be able to basically figure out what it was that people really cared about. Today, individual mail is being buried by lobby operations. Do you have any idea what percentage of mail comes into this place from organized groups with an axe to grind as opposed to family members on Main Street?
>
> House Postmaster Robert V. Rota: Special interest group mailings represent 62% of our total volume of mail.... They can send in millions at a time.... Social Security represents the largest portion. If you look at the chart in 1972, you see they were inactive. They only began after the computers started to get popular, in the 1980s. You see what happened to mail volume in the 1980s.[58]

The House Post Office handled 40 million letters in 1981, 11 million more than in 1980.[59]

Observers frequently question the effectiveness of inspired mail, as well they might. "Given enough lead time," one House staffer

---

[58] *Hearings before a Subcommittee of the Committee on Appropriations, House of Representatives*, "Legislative Branch Appropriations for 1991," 101st Congress, 2d session, 1990, part 2, p. 107. The other thing that happened to mail volume in the 1980s, it now appears, was that House Postmaster Rota cooked the estimates. According to a House Administration Committee report, Rota overstated the volume of congressional mail by as much as 350 percent in an effort to win funding for more patronage employment. The incident is an interesting reminder that survey estimates are sometimes more accurate than ostensibly more "objective" figures. See U.S. House of Representatives, Committee on House Administration, "Report of the Committee on House Administration Task Force to Investigate the Operation and Management of the Office of the Postmaster," 102d Congress, 2d session, July 21, 1992, pp. 31–34.

[59] Loomis, "A New Era," pp. 169–90; Schlozman and Tierney, *Organized Interests*, pp. 184–96; Frantzich, *Write Your Congressman*, pp. 10–11, 66–70; R. Kenneth Godwin, "Money, Technology, and Political Interests: The Direct Marketing of Politics," pp. 308–25 in Mark P. Petracca, *The Politics of Interests: Interest Group Politics Transformed* (Boulder: Westview Press, 1992), pp. 319–21.

noted, "lobbyists will use computers to generate letters of concern from constituents which will be answered by Hill computers generating letters of placation. This process is called 'direct-mail lobbying.' It closely resembles the communication achieved by turning on two television sets facing each other." It is easy to discount the level of personal commitment that underlies inspired mail.[60]

Nevertheless, there must be some good reason for lobbying groups to spend millions of dollars a year on efforts to mobilize letters. Even if direct mail lobbying achieves nothing else, it does give lawmakers pause. One member of Congress, the story goes, was beset by a lobbyist who urged him to support the lobby's position. "I'd love to help you," he replied, "but my mail is running three-to-one against you." "But surely you know that all that mail is inspired by interest groups," the lobbyist objected. "That's true," he acknowledged, "but it's there." Members of Congress may discount inspired mail, but they cannot ignore it. If lobbies can mobilize people once, perhaps they can do it again on election day.[61]

One of the most celebrated of the recent campaigns to mobilize citizen participation in national politics was the battle over Judge Robert Bork's nomination to the United States Supreme Court in 1987. Bork was a well-known conservative legal theorist who had authored attacks on many of the most cherished liberal legal precedents, including Court decisions that restricted state regulation of abortion and legislative statutes that remedied discrimination in employment, housing, and the exercise of political rights. Ronald Reagan's proposal to elevate Bork to the Supreme Court created a firestorm. A broad coalition of abortion rights groups, civil rights groups, women's rights groups, and unions lobbied hard against Bork's confirmation, and a coalition of conservative, religious, and law enforcement groups lobbied hard for it. As a major part of their strategies, both sides mobilized grass-roots pressures on Congress, asking their members and sympathizers to write or to

---

[60] Skip Stiles, "A Field Guide to Capitol Hill: Recognize Strange Inhabitants, Learn the Jargon," *Roll Call*, May 18, 1987, p. 20.
[61] Frantzich, *Write Your Congressman*, chap. 5; Schlozman and Tierney, *Organized Interests*, pp. 194–96; Kingdon, *Congressmen's Voting Decisions*, pp. 54–60.

telephone their senators. Black churches in Georgia, for instance, sponsored "Bork Sundays," which filled collection plates with hundreds of handwritten letters and notes that opposed the nomination. A conservative group in Alabama provided its members with hastily edited form letters urging senators to "Vote for Bark [*sic*]." Hundreds of thousands of letters and phone calls poured into Washington, and the battle ended with the Senate's rejection of Bork's nomination.[62]

Although not as dramatic as the mobilization effort around the Bork nomination, mobilization around particular national issues happens all the time. In 1983, for example, Senator Bob Dole (R–Kan.) proposed to require banks and other financial institutions to withhold federal income tax on interest and dividends. The American Bankers Association and the U.S. League of Savings Institutions swung into action to oppose it. They placed advertisements in newspapers and posted placards in member banks and savings and loans. They placed inserts in almost 80 million monthly bank account statements outlining the danger posed by interest withholding, and supplied a handy postcard with which bank customers could express their displeasure to their representatives. The gambit worked. As V. O. Key, Jr., observed of a strikingly similar campaign some twenty years earlier, "never have so many persons been brought so effectively to the aid of tax evasion." Reportedly, 22 million people sent a postcard or a letter to Congress, and Congress dropped Dole's proposal like a hot potato.[63]

---

[62] Ethan Bonner, *Battle for Justice: How the Bork Nomination Shook America* (New York: W. W. Norton and Co., 1989); Michael Pertschuk and Wendy Schaetzel, *The People Rising: The Campaign Against the Bork Nomination* (New York: Thunder's Mouth Press, 1989); Patrick B. McGuigan and Dawn H. Weyrich, *Ninth Justice: The Fight for Bork* (Washington, D.C.: Free Congress Foundation, 1990). On group strategies in the battle, see Christine DeGregorio and Jack E. Rossotti, "The Nomination of Judge Robert H. Bork to the United States Supreme Court: A Case Study in Contemporary Interest Group Politics," paper presented at the annual meeting of the American Political Science Association, 1990.

[63] Key, *Politics, Parties, and Pressure Groups*, p. 136; Jeffrey M. Berry, *The Interest Group Society* (New York: Scott, Foresman, 1989), p. 114; Paul Taylor, "The Death of Withholding, or How Bankers Won Big," *Washington Post*, July 31, 1983, p. A12.

It is not within the power of our statistical analysis to capture the effects of each of the hundreds of separate grass-roots mobilization efforts that occur at any given time. Many may have a big impact, but on only a few people and at only one moment in time. Instead, we again identify a handful of issues that regularly affect the interests of large numbers of people and hundreds of interest groups.

One of the most salient political events of the last twenty-five years was the investigation of President Richard M. Nixon's involvement in the planning and cover-up of the burglary of Democratic National Committee headquarters at the Watergate complex in June 1972. Soon after the incident came to light, investigators linked the burglars to the White House, and in February 1973 Congress stepped in. The Senate Select Committee on Presidential Campaign Activities, chaired by North Carolina senator Sam Ervin, conducted lengthy and detailed hearings that were televised nationally, day after day. The hearings produced sensational evidence that President Nixon and his aides were deeply implicated in a conspiracy to obstruct the investigation of the burglary and other campaign improprieties, prompting the House Judiciary Committee to open hearings on articles of impeachment. In July 1974, the Judiciary Committee voted to report three articles of impeachment to the full House, and on August 8, Richard Nixon announced his resignation. The next day, Gerald R. Ford assumed the presidency. The full and unconditional pardon Ford granted to Nixon brought the affair to a close in September 1974.

The daily revelations of scandal and malfeasance in the Nixon White House, played out daily on national television, stimulated a flood of constituent mail to Congress. "During July [1974]," House Postmaster Robert V. Rota reported, "the hearings of the Judiciary Committee were televised nationally and we received about 3.5 million letters compared to 1,780,000 in [July] 1973." All in all, the volume of mail in 1974 exceeded the volume in 1973 by almost 25 percent.[64] We find, likewise, from our analysis that about 2.2 million

---

[64]*Hearings before a Subcommittee of the Committee on Appropriations of the House of Representatives,* "Legislative Branch Appropriations for 1976," 94th Congress, 1st session, 1975, p. 854.

more people (1.4 percent of the population) wrote Congress in the period leading up to President Nixon's resignation and pardon than in the period following (see Table 4-1).

Some of the Watergate mail, clearly, was mobilized directly by politicians and interest groups. Nixon attempted to generate public sympathy for himself with three prime-time televised speeches giving his side of the Watergate story—in April 1973, August 1973, and April 1974.[65] On the other side, interest groups anxious to see Nixon impeached focused grass-roots lobbying efforts on members of the Judiciary Committee who would face difficult reelection campaigns.[66]

Much of the Watergate mail, though—indeed, probably most of it—was mobilized by the television coverage. "Day after day, week after week, we watched the drama played out in one disclosure after another," a PBS documentary later noted. "It was all on television." The sordid dealings of the Nixon White House, laid bare in the hearings of the Senate Watergate Committee and the House Judiciary Committee, angered and dismayed the American public. The intense media scrutiny fueled discussions in homes, offices, and factories all over the country and moved millions of citizens to action.[67]

Beyond Watergate, the other issues that were salient to large numbers of people were primarily economic. A 5 percent upswing in unemployment boosts correspondence with Congress about a percentage point and a half, as reported in Table 4-1. As we saw earlier

[65]Nixon's most memorable pronouncement on the Watergate affair—"People have got to know whether or not their President is a crook. Well, I'm not a crook"—occurred not in a speech but in a press conference, on November 17, 1973, soon after the famous Saturday Night Massacre.

[66]Frantzich, *Write Your Congressman*, p. 79; "The Impeachment Lobby: Emphasis on Grass Roots Pressure," *Congressional Quarterly Weekly Report*, May 25, 1974, pp. 1368–74.

[67]Public Broadcasting Service, "Summer of Judgment: The Watergate Hearings," July 27, 1983. Media coverage appears most likely to mobilize mail when the issue strikes an emotional chord with the electorate. News of scandals of any sort seems to mobilize letters, and congressional pay raises are always good for thousands of letters. See Kingdon, *Congressmen's Voting Decisions*, pp. 220–21.

in this chapter, it is not personal unemployment that drives people to write letters.[68] Unemployed people are busy trying to hold body and soul together—they have better things to do with their time than to get involved in politics. Instead, high unemployment scares many people as it spills over to neighbors, local businesses, local governments, churches, and schools. Business fears losses of sales, governments fear losses of revenues, labor fears losses of jobs. Accordingly, businesses, unions, community leaders, and politicians mobilize demands for relief. Economic hardship is a promising issue around which to mobilize people: Citizens respond more readily when conditions threaten their well-being, and politicians understand that voters typically punish them for hard times. The major recessions of the mid-1970s and early 1980s were a rallying point for public discontent. As Stephen Frantzich observed, "more people ... tend to write out of fear than out of hope."[69]

The other matter of sustained political salience in the 1970s and 1980s was the federal budget. During the early 1970s, a period of growth, detente, and political optimism, presidents proposed budget increases on the order of a percentage point and a half above the previous year's budget, adjusted for inflation, and moved expenditures from defense to domestic needs (see Figure 4-5). In contrast, as the United States entered a period of stagnation, tension, and political pessimism in the early 1980s, proposed budgets fell nearly 5 percent below the previous year's and reallocated monies from domestic to defense programs. Our estimates reported in Table 4-1 indicate that big budgetary swings, in either the positive or negative direction, mobilize letters to Congress. Politicians and interest groups solicit public pressures during periods when the government reorders its priorities.

Much of this effect stems from the heightened salience of the budgetary process in the Reagan years. As Postmaster Rota put it,

---

[68]Donald R. Kinder and D. Roderick Kiewiet, "Economic Discontent and Political Behavior: The Role of Personal Grievances and Collective Economic Judgments in Congressional Voting," *American Journal of Political Science* 33 (May 1979), pp. 495–527; Donald R. Kinder and D. Roderick Kiewiet, "Sociotropic Politics: The American Case," *British Journal of Political Science* 11 (February 1981), pp. 129–61.
[69]Frantzich, *Write Your Congressman*, p. 66.

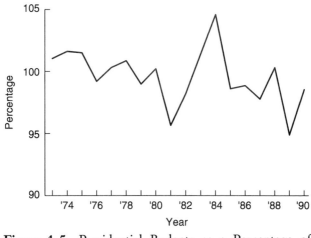

Figure 4-5   Presidential Budgets as a Percentage of
Current Budget, 1973–1990.
Source: See Appendix A.

"congressional consideration of tax and budget legislation" brought
forth a "deluge of citizen mail." "Calendar year 1981 was a highly
unusual year," he noted, "in which we experienced an unprecedented
wave of citizen interest as the new administration took office and
initiated a number of budget and tax proposals that provoked many
more Americans than usual to write their congressmen."[70]

The proposals themselves were not the only provocation. Ronald
Reagan himself appeared on national television to mobilize public support for his budget, and direct mail specialists like Richard
Viguerie churned their lists to find constituents to write in approval
of Reagan's priorities. In opposition, beneficiary groups, service
providers, unions, and Democrats sent out special alerts, warning
people of the dire consequences should the Reagan cuts be enacted,
and urging them to act.[71]

---

[70]*Hearings before a Subcommittee of the Committee on Appropriations, House of Representatives,* "Legislative Branch Appropriations for 1983," 97th Congress, 2d session,
1982, part 2, p. 59; and *idem,* "Legislative Branch Appropriations for 1984," 98th
Congress, 2d session, 1983, part 2, p. 57.
[71]See Frantzich, *Write Your Congressman,* pp. 66–67.

By all accounts, one of the most successful mobilization efforts was the campaign to shield Social Security from the Reagan administration's budget knife. At several points during Reagan's term, the administration proposed to reduce Social Security benefits and to require the elderly to assume a larger share of the cost of Medicare. Organizations representing Social Security recipients mobilized to oppose the plan. Starting in 1981 and continuing throughout Reagan's term, Democratic representatives, labor unions, and the fifteen-million-member American Association of Retired Persons (AARP) sponsored grass-roots lobbying campaigns, asking members to write to Congress in defense of Social Security. The National Committee to Preserve Social Security and Medicare, founded in 1982 by former California congressman James Roosevelt, mobilized the elderly with aggressive "scare" tactics that drew criticism even from Democrats in Congress. "Never in the 45 years since my father, Franklin Delano Roosevelt, started the Social Security system," Roosevelt wrote in a direct mail appeal, "has there been such a severe threat to Social Security and Medicare benefits."[72]

By all indications, the mobilization of the elderly was an outstanding success. In a ten-day period in 1982, New York senator Daniel Patrick Moynihan, for example, received nearly 37,000 letters, most of them protesting the proposed cuts in Social Security. Florida senator Lawton Chiles received 500 to 1,000 letters a day during another ten-day period in 1982, all in response to an alert from the AARP to its members. The effects show up in our data as well. Table 4-3 shows the percentages of the population—broken down by age—that wrote to Congress, signed petitions, and

[72] Valerie J. Martinez, "Old-Age Interest Groups and Grassroots Mobilization," paper presented at the annual meeting of the American Political Science Association, 1991; Pamela Fessler, "Compromise Explored on Social Security," *Congressional Quarterly Weekly Report*, May 30, 1981, pp. 936–37; Neil R. Peirce and Peter C. Choharis, "The Elderly as a Political Force—26 Million Strong and Well Organized," *National Journal*, September 11, 1982, pp. 1559–62; Pamela Fessler, "Tactics of New Elderly Lobby Ruffle Congressional Feathers," *Congressional Quarterly Weekly Report*, June 2, 1984, pp. 1310–13, quoted at p. 1311; Jonathan Rauch, "Interest Groups Preparing for Worst as They Lobby against Budget Cuts," *National Journal*, December 15, 1984, pp. 2380–85; Michelle M. Murphy, "Elderly Lobby Group Continues to Thrive but Image on Capitol Hill Still Tarnished," *Congressional Quarterly Weekly Report*, March 26, 1988, pp. 778–79.

Table 4-3   Age and Participation in Governmental
Politics, 1976–1988

Wrote Congress
Percentage of Age Group Taking Part

Year	18–21	22–29	30–44	45–59	60 and over
1976	8.6	15.1	16.3	18.1	14.2
1980	6.6	10.9	15.9	16.3	13.3
1984	6.7	10.5	16.4	18.6	18.1
1988	6.7	7.7	15.8	14.4	15.9

Attended Meeting
Percentage of Age Group Taking Part

Year	18–21	22–29	30–44	45–59	60 and over
1976	16.3	20.7	27.9	20.7	10.4
1980	12.9	15.8	26.0	16.8	9.0
1884	12.2	14.5	25.3	17.7	9.2
1988	12.2	13.0	24.1	18.0	8.5

Signed Petition
Percentage of Age Group Taking Part

Year	18–21	22–29	30–44	45–59	60 and over
1976	36.2	42.7	41.8	36.7	24.2
1980	29.5	38.8	40.6	33.8	23.8
1984	30.3	39.4	43.2	39.5	28.4
1988	23.4	33.5	39.4	35.7	26.7

Source: Roper Surveys, 1976, Nos. 76-1, 76-2, 76-6, 76-7; 1980,
Nos. 80-1, 80-2, 80-6, 80-7; 1984, Nos. 84-1, 84-2, 84-6, 84-7; 1988,
Nos. 88-1, 88-2, 88-6, 88-7.

attended local meetings. The figures show an extraordinary influx
of elderly Americans into activities aimed at influencing Congress.
In 1976 and 1980, older citizens were less likely than middle-aged
citizens to write to Congress; in 1984 and 1988, older citizens were

as likely or more likely to write. Between 1976 and 1984, younger Americans grew less likely to write; over the same period, older Americans grew more likely to write. Appropriately, petition signing shows the same pattern, and, also appropriately, attendance at local meetings does not. Plainly, groups intent on defending Social Security mobilized thousands of elderly citizens into national politics in the mid-1980s.[73]

Summary

In sum, at both the local and national level political leaders mobilize citizen participation around especially salient issues. In the course of their constant struggles for influence, politicians, interest groups, and activists mobilize when conditions—such as widespread anger over rising property taxes and widespread anxiety over proposed cuts in Social Security—make it possible for them to muster public support. Political leaders identify opportunities for citizens to influence governmental decisions and propagate information through organizations such as homeowner associations and senior citizens' groups. Their activities inform and direct people and give them causes to rally around. They generate political discussions and occasion the creation of social rewards for political involvement. By their efforts, political leaders turn public grievances into political action.

Mobilization Around Political Opportunities

The institutions of American government work on distinctive calendars that set the rhythm for the production of policy decisions. Governing bodies meet and adjourn. Decisions pass from one stage of the process to another. As a result, the strategic value of citizen participation varies with the political cycle. At some moments in the cycle, decisions are imminent, many public officials are involved, and thus the incentives that leaders have to mobilize citizens to participate are higher than at other times of the year.

---

[73] Fowler and Shaiko, "Contact with Congress," pp. 13–30; Moynihan, "Mail Call," p. 138; Peirce and Choharis, "The Elderly as a Political Force," p. 1560.

Local Calendars

The opportunities to influence the decisions of local governments come and go. We find, for instance (Table 4-1), that attendance at local meetings drops by 0.2 percent (nearly 300,000 people) in the weeks following a holiday, and by nearly twice that in the weeks after Christmas and New Year's Day. One reason, certainly, is that people understandably prefer to spend their holidays in the company of family and friends rather than in the company of local politicians. A more likely reason, we suspect, is that people can attend meetings only if somebody holds them and, typically, city councils and school boards do not schedule meetings during holidays. Political elites, like the rest of us, are busy with other things. Local governments do not present many opportunities to participate during the holiday season, and so participation drops.

The Congressional Calendar

At the national level, too, the opportunities to influence government vary throughout the year. The U.S. Congress alternates between periods of intense legislative activity and periods of recess (or, as the House calls them, "district work periods"). The 101st Congress, in 1989 and 1990, was typical. (See Figure 4-6.) Congress convened early in January 1989 and worked on and off until the end of July, going into recess for Inauguration Day, Presidents' Day, Easter, Passover, Memorial Day, and Independence Day, during which most members went home to their districts. Congress recessed for the whole month of August, in deference to Washington's spongy summer heat, then worked intensely up until adjournment just before Thanksgiving. The second session, which convened late in January 1990, followed the same rhythm but for one significant detail: Because of the election, it adjourned in October, in time for anxious members to get home for last-minute campaigning.

The seasonal rhythm of congressional activity accounts for a substantial portion of the seasonal pattern of congressional mail. As we report in Table 4-1, Congress hears from about 1.1 million more people (0.7 percent of the population) when it is hardest at work, between June and September, than when it is on vacation in

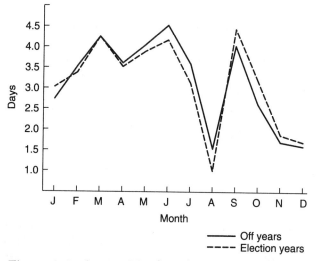

Figure 4-6 Average Number of Days Per Week Congress was in Session, 1973–1990.
Source: See Appendix A.

December. The month-to-month variations in congressional activity explain about a quarter of the total difference between the peaks of citizen participation in congressional politics in the summer and the troughs of participation in the winter.[74]

The reason citizen mail follows the congressional calendar derives from the calculations of the politicians and interest groups who inspire congressional mail. Requests for information or for assistance, the kinds of letters citizens write on their own initiative, have the same effect when Congress is in session as when it is not. Representatives may leave Washington to work in the district, but their staffs stay behind, in part to answer the mail and do the casework.

[74]To guard against the possibility that congressional calendars and other seasonal variables are spuriously associated with the seasonal pattern of congressional mail, we examined the robustness of the results by including one-period and ten-period (one-year) lags of the dependent variable in the equation. If the seasonal variables are merely picking up the seasonality, then including the dependent variables lagged one year should send their coefficients to zero. No such change in the coefficients occurred.

Issue mail, though, accomplishes much more when Congress is in session than when members are on the road. For politicians, interest groups, and activists, efforts to mobilize constituent letters to Congress promise a payoff only during the time Congress deliberates on issues, not sooner and not later. When Congress goes out of town, then, legislative work—and with it mobilization—ceases. Political leaders inspire no special inducements for participation, and citizens receive none. Participation follows the congressional calendar because mobilizers pace their efforts by the congressional calendar.[75]

Congressional Work

The idea that political leaders provide the connection between what government does and what citizens want gains even greater credence from another set of findings. Legislation in Congress progresses through a regular decision-making cycle. (See Figure 4-7.) In the first session of each Congress (that is, in years without elections), lawmakers spend most of the spring at work in committees, holding hearings and drafting and amending legislative proposals. Bills reach the floor in the summer, and into the late part of odd-numbered years legislators debate them and decide their fates. In the second session (in election years), the level of activity on the House and Senate floors is typically higher, as Congress rushes to finish its business in time for the November elections. But the seasonal pattern is similar overall: Lawmakers spend the spring doing committee work and the summer and fall debating and voting on legislation.

The seasonal pattern of debate and decision leads to a seasonal pattern of letter writing to Congress. As Postmaster Rota noted, "You find out the legislation on the floor really has a lot to do . . . with

[75]An alternative explanation for the relationship between the congressional calendar and political participation is that citizens write to Congress when media coverage mobilizes them to do so. When Congress goes out of session, media attention turns elsewhere, and the public does not receive any information that leads people to write letters. We could find little support for this proposition. The media's attention to Congress has no effect on congressional mail once the congressional calendar has been taken into account. From the *Vanderbilt Television News Index and Abstracts*, we coded the total number of stories and the number of lead stories on Congress on the CBS Evening News for each week between 1973 and 1990. We calculated several measures of attention, but none had an independent effect on letter writing to Congress.

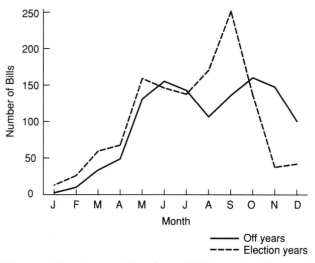

Figure 4-7 Average Number of Bills on the Floor of Congress, 1973–1990.

Source: See Appendix A.

[the] amount of mail that is coming in."[76] According to our estimates reported in Table 4-1, 2 million more Americans (1.3 percent of the population) write during the peak season for legislative debate and decision, June through September, than in December and January, when few bills come to the floor for a vote.[77] Variations in the timing of congressional decisions account for about half of the seasonal variation in correspondence with Congress.

It is possible, of course, that people react to news of congressional debate spontaneously, that they see the debate on television and fire off letters. But, as many studies make clear, television news rarely covers congressional deliberations, and in our analysis TV coverage of the Congress has no independent effect on participation.[78] This interpretation does not take us very far.

[76] *Hearings before a House Appropriations Subcommittee*, "Legislative Branch Appropriations for 1982," 1981, p. 314.

[77] The number of bills on the floor is logged because of extreme values in its distribution—it ranges from 0 to 363 with a mean of 94.

[78] See note 75, and Robinson, "Three Faces of Congressional Media," pp. 72–96; Norman Ornstein and Michael Robinson, "The Case of Our Disappearing Congress," *TV Guide*, January 11, 1986, pp. 4–10.

Instead, it is more likely that interest groups time their mobilization efforts to coincide with legislation reaching the floor. At any point in the legislative cycle, groups mobilize only as much citizen participation as they need to influence decisions. When a bill is in committee, in the spring, relatively few legislators are involved in the deliberations. When the bill reaches the floor, however, in the summer and the fall, interest groups must expand the coalition of support if the bill is to become public law. With more members of Congress to persuade, politicians and interest groups mobilize more broadly—the result being that more citizens contact their members of Congress.

Local Budgeting

Interest groups and community activists ensure that participation in local politics is timed just as strategically. Most issues that fill the agendas of city councils, county commissions, and school boards, such as the placement of stop signs or the design of school dress codes, fire the enthusiasm of only a few citizens. As in national politics, the budget is an issue that both affects large numbers of citizens and dominates local agendas. Taxpayers, homeowners, government employees, and recipients of government services all find their interests directly at stake in local budgetary decisions. Indeed, one study of school boards found school expenditures and taxes far and away the matters of greatest importance to the general public.[79]

Most local governments make their budgetary decisions in early summer. About 80 percent of Americans live in communities that finalize budgets in June. About 10 percent live in communities where the budget showdown occurs in August, 8 percent in September, and 2 percent in December. The seasonal pattern of attention to budgets, we suspect, carries over to local governments other than school boards.[80]

---

[79]National School Boards Association, "School–Community Communication," pp. 8–9; Harmon Zeigler, Harvey J. Tucker, and L. A. Wilson, II, "Communication and Decision Making in American Public Education: A Longitudinal and Comparative Study," pp. 218–54 in Jay N. Scribner, ed., *The Politics of Education* (Chicago: National Society for the Study of Education, 1977), pp. 244–49, esp. p. 247.

[80]School fiscal years are almost perfectly uniform within states, suggesting that state law determines them. Other local governments, we think, fall under the terms of the same state legislation.

The local budget cycle, Table 4-1 shows, is consequential for citizen participation. In the summer, the concentration of local budgeting decisions raises attendance at local meetings by about 1.7 percentage points, the equivalent of about 2.7 million people, accounting for over half of the total seasonal increase in attendance at local meetings. Likewise, the summertime attention to the budget raises petition signing by about 2.7 percentage points, or about 4.2 million people, accounting also for about half of the summertime rise in petition signing.[81]

Again, it is possible that citizen participation in local budgeting is spontaneous, that citizens get wind of impending decisions that might benefit or harm them and head off to meetings and seek out petitioners. More probably, however, parent-teacher associations, public employees' unions, chambers of commerce, merchants' associations, neighborhood groups, service clubs, and cranky neighbors mobilize ordinary citizens into involvement in pending budget fights. An advisory guide for public agencies, in fact, counsels officials to expect a deluge of public participation as the deadlines for vital decisions near. "As you approach a final decision," it points out, "the jockeying for power among interests will increase the likelihood of efforts to enlist the support of the unorganized public."[82]

Ballot Access Petitions

Finally, the relationship between the strategic needs of political leaders and the participation of ordinary citizens is most transparent for petition signing, the most obviously mobilized of the three governmental activities we examine.

To qualify for the ballot as an independent or third party candidate, most states require submission of petitions signed by some number of eligible voters. Many states also allow or require can-

---

[81]The seasonal budgeting variable seems not to be associated spuriously with attendance at meetings. To test the robustness of the findings, we included both one-period and ten-period (one-year) lagged dependent variables in the equation. Nothing changed.

[82]James L. Creighton, *The Public Involvement Manual* (Cambridge: Abt Books, 1981), p. 45. See also Patty Lamiel, "The People's Lobby," pp. 188–97 in Lee Staples, *Roots to Power: A Manual for Grassroots Lobbying* (New York: Praeger Publishers, 1984).

didates for party nominations to file nominating petitions in lieu
of paying filing fees. The petitioning requirements vary from state
to state and from office to office. To make the ballot as an independent in 1992, for instance, on-and-off presidential-candidate H.
Ross Perot had to collect only 200 signatures in Washington state
but over 70,000 in North Carolina. To qualify as an independent
candidate for the House of Representatives, aspirants in Wiscon-
sin need between one and two thousand signatures, but hopefuls in
North Carolina need around ten thousand.[83]
    The deadlines for filing ballot access petitions vary from state
to state as well. In 1976, Pennsylvania required petitions for independent candidates for the House to be submitted by March 1,
eight months before the general election, whereas North Dakota allowed them to be submitted as late as September 23, only six weeks
before. As the result of legal challenges to state ballot access laws
brought by independent presidential contenders Eugene McCarthy
and John Anderson, however, the petition filing dates have been
bunched much more closely together. In 1992, the earliest deadlines were in April, the latest in September, with most in August.
    The regularity of ballot petition calendars imparts a biennial sea-
sonality to petition signing.[84] The clustering of filing deadlines in
the summer of even-numbered years causes 2.5 million more Americans (1.6 percent of the electorate) to sign petitions in election-year
summers than at other times.[85]

---

[83]Stephen A. Holmes, "Perot Encounters a Maze of Ballot Rules," *New York Times*,
May 14, 1992, p. A10; Steven J. Rosenstone, Roy L. Behr, and Edward H. Lazarus,
Third Parties in America: Citizen Response to Major Party Failure (Princeton: Princeton
University Press, 1984), pp. 19–25; U.S. House of Representatives, Committee on
House Administration, "U.S. House of Representatives Election Law Guidebook
1988," House Document 100-208, 100th Congress, 2d session, 1988.

[84]Another possible reason for the seasonal pattern of petition signing is the weather.
It may be that people who carry petitions are not as hardy as Salvation Army bell
ringers. To test for this possibility, we painstakingly calculated an average monthly
temperature for the twenty-five largest cities in the United States, weighted by their
populations. The coefficient for this variable did not approach significance, suggesting that it is not warm weather that underlies the seasonality.

[85]The ballot access variable is the one variable in the petition equation that is not
robust against the inclusion of one-period and ten-period (one-year) lagged dependent variables. This is not too surprising, given that it is coded to zero for the entire
year every other year.

Petition signing, of course, is essentially a passive form of participation that depends more on the availability of an opportunity to sign than on individuals' inclinations to participate. Here, too, citizen participation responds to the rhythms of the calendar because political leaders mobilize around the needs of the moment.

Summary

Participation in governmental politics occurs at strategically important moments. Citizens write letters, attend meetings, and sign petitions when their actions are likely to have their largest impact on some governmental decision. The strategic timing of political participation arises from the strategic efforts of politicians, interest groups, and issue activists. As a normal part of their business, political leaders keep close track of issues as they work their way through the legislative process. As the moment of decision nears, leaders seek ways to influence the outcome. One strategy is to try to mobilize public support. Through the mail and over the phone and FAX machines, they put out the word that a decision that people care about looms imminent. People who belong to groups or social networks learn about the call to arms either directly from their leaders or indirectly from the friends and associates who create the social rewards for political activism. In response, people participate. People act at the right moments because politicians, interest groups, and activists act strategically.

Conclusion: Solving the Puzzle of Governmental Participation

Our theory of political participation, outlined in Chapter 2, does an impressive job of making sense of participation in governmental politics. Interests and social positions tell half the story, distinguishing people who participate in governmental politics from those who do not. People who are educated, efficacious, and socially involved take part in the activities of government more often than others. They possess the resources that participation requires. They occupy social positions that expose them more regularly to the messages and inducements of mobilization.

The strategic opportunities facing political leaders tell the other half of the story, distinguishing times when large numbers of people participate in governmental politics from times when they do not. Involvement rises when salient issues reach the public agenda and falls when they leave it; it rises when governments near decisions and falls after decisions are made. The imminence of important issues gives political leaders incentives to muster ordinary citizens into national politics.

These findings take us a long way toward solving the puzzles of citizen participation in governmental politics that we posed in Chapter 3. As we have seen, political leaders often mobilize citizens into politics through intermediate associations, through clubs, organizations, and political parties. They mobilize citizens into politics around especially salient issues, and around the periodic opportunities for influence.

These three basic elements clarify the sources of the trends of citizen activism in governmental politics over the last two decades. The first suggests that the general downturn of citizen participation in all three kinds of activities has a common cause: the decline of citizen involvement in organizations, clubs, and political parties. As we have argued, associations mediate the contacts between the political system and ordinary citizens. Politicians, interest groups, and activists mobilize groups, and mobilize others through groups. Thus, decreasing public involvement in voluntary organizations weakens an important link in the process by which citizens are moved to participate in government. Participation in governmental politics declines as participation in associational activity declines.

Moreover, against the backdrop of associational atrophy, the second element suggests that citizen participation in governmental politics rises and falls with the advance and retreat of salient issues. Citizen participation in local politics fell off rapidly in the mid-1970s and never really recovered. As the baby boom generation graduated from high school in the late 1970s, parents lost many of the concerns and social involvements that had motivated their participation in meetings at the local level. The removal of education issues from citizens' personal agendas caused participation in local politics to decline. By contrast, citizen participation in national politics peaked and declined once in the 1970s and again in the 1980s. In the early

1980s, the scramble to support or oppose the Reagan administration's attempts to dismantle the federal government drove public involvement in national politics back to the heights of the Watergate era. Politicians, interest groups, and issue activists encouraged ordinary Americans by the millions to write their representatives and to sign petitions. The advent of important and salient issues caused public participation in national politics to revive.

These same ingredients also produce seasonal variation in citizen participation within the year. The third element suggests that the seasonality of participation in different kinds of governmental politics has a common source. More people write letters, attend meetings, and sign petitions in early summer because that is when public institutions conduct most of their business. As issues reach the moment of resolution, politicians and interest groups mobilize public pressure in hopes of influencing the outcome. They inspire pressures on Congress as bills come to the floor. They stimulate pressures on city councils, county commissions, and school boards as budgets take final form. And, when government institutions recess, politicians and interest groups also take a break. They suspend efforts to influence Congress when Congress is out of session. They suspend efforts to influence local governments when local governments are off for the holidays. The activities of political leaders impart a distinctly strategic rhythm to political participation. Citizens time their participation in governmental politics strategically because political leaders time efforts to mobilize them strategically.

The puzzles of citizen participation in governmental politics, then, find their solution in the opportunities for influence that popular issues and government agendas present to politicians, political parties, interest groups and issue activists. Citizen participation in government follows the efforts of political leaders to mobilize the public into politics.

C H A P T E R   5

Participation in Electoral Politics

In many ways, elections are the most conspicuous events in American politics. Campaigns for president, Congress, governor, and mayor bombard citizens with competing themes, personalities, slogans, and promises. Candidates and political parties raise and spend huge sums of money, build campaign organizations, mount media blitzes, gather political intelligence, register voters, recruit campaign workers, hire pollsters and media consultants, canvass the electorate, and strive to get supporters to the polls on election day. The transcendent purpose of their colossal efforts is to win more votes than the other side. Those who prevail earn the right to govern the cities, counties, states, and nation.

The citizen's role in American elections varies, as we have already seen, from person to person and from election to election. Many Americans are spectators who take no part at all in the selection of their leaders. Most others are voters who take part only in the balloting. A handful, finally, are activists who campaign, contribute money, attend meetings, or try to influence the choices of their families and friends. Many fewer Americans volunteer, give, attend, influence, and vote in elections now than thirty years ago, and many more sit elections out.

In this chapter and the next, we identify the causes of participation in electoral politics: the reasons for the activity of some and the passivity of others, the reasons for engagement in some elections and disengagement in others. Our analysis in this chapter focuses on the personal determinants of participation in elections, on individuals' resources, their evaluations of the political system, their assessments of the political parties and candidates, and their social involvements.

128

Our analysis in the next chapter, on the other hand, centers on the political determinants of participation in elections, on the mobilization efforts of political parties, the mobilization activities of political campaigns, the mobilization effects of social movements, and the institutional regulation of mobilization and participation by electoral laws. Chapter 7, finally, pulls our findings together to account for the overall decline of popular involvement in American elections since the 1960s.

In these three chapters, we move beyond descriptions of who participates and who does not. Our goal is to isolate the partial effect that each of the causes has on electoral participation—that is, its impact once the other determinants of participation have been taken into account. We base our conclusions on estimates from four probit equations, one for each of four kinds of participation in elections: voting, attempting to influence the votes of others, contributing money to a party or candidate, and working for a campaign. As we indicated in Chapter 4, probit is a statistical method that estimates the effect of each independent variable on a dichotomous dependent variable (such as participation), holding the other variables in the analysis statistically constant.

In each of the analyses, we consider participation in presidential and midterm election years separately. The four equations for involvement in presidential years analyze the responses of the 16,935 people survey interviewers questioned in the quadrennial National Election Studies from 1956 through 1988; the four equations for involvement in midterm years utilize the responses of 7,473 people interviewed in the midterm National Election Studies (NES) from 1974 through 1986.[1] Tables 5-1 and 5-2 summarize the results, converting the probit coefficients into probabilities, for presidential and midterm years, respectively. [2] We refer to these tables repeatedly in this chapter and the next.

The story that emerges from the analysis of electoral participation bears more than passing resemblance to the conclusions that

---

[1] The analyses begin in 1956 and in 1974 because each is the first year in which NES asked respondents whether they had been contacted by parties or candidates. Appendix B describes the source of the data and the coding of variables.

[2] Appendix D provides the probit equations.

Table 5-1   Summary: Causes of Participation in Electoral
Politics, 1956–1988 Presidential Election Years

Variable	Form of Electoral Participation			
	Vote	Try to Persuade	Do Work	Donate Money
Resources				
Income	15.8	5.7	1.8	14.8
Education	16.6	13.9	2.9	9.8
Unemployed	−2.7			
Age	29.0	−10.9	1.6	9.0
Internal efficacy	2.9	5.6	1.7	2.5
External efficacy	10.6	4.8	1.4	2.8
Evaluation of Parties and Candidates				
Strength of party identification	10.6	7.8	3.0	5.1
Affect for a party	11.4	13.3	3.4	7.0
Care which party wins presidential election	6.4	10.7	1.7	3.5
Affect for presidential candidate	5.6	22.9	4.0	3.3
Social Involvement				
Years in community, logarithm	10.7			
Church attendance	15.1		1.2	
Homeowners	7.5			
Currently employed	2.1	1.8		1.9
Mobilization by Parties				
Contacted by a party	7.8	11.8	4.8	6.7

Table 5-1 *(continued)*

Variable	Form of Electoral Participation			
	Vote	Try to Persuade	Do Work	Donate Money
Mobilization by Campaigns				
Close presidential election	3.0	7.8	1.0	3.2
Perceived closeness of election	1.6	1.4	.8	1.2
Gubernatorial election	5.0			
Presidential primary election	−3.7			
Mobilization by Social Movements				
Civil rights movement actions	7.3		1.8	3.1
Legal Organization of Elections				
Literacy tests × blacks	−16.0			
Poll tax × blacks	−10.2			
Periodic registration × blacks	−11.6			
Voting Rights Act × blacks	26.4			
Voting Rights Act × whites	19.5			
Voter registration closing date	−5.6			
Other Demographic Variables				
Women		−6.5		
Live in southern state	−16.3			−3.2
Live in border state	−6.1			−4.3
Blacks	−4.4			
Mexican-Americans and Puerto Ricans	−5.7			

Note: Entries are partial effects of independent variables on the probability of participation (in percentages).
Source: Appendix D.

Table 5-2 Summary: Causes of Participation in Electoral Politics, 1974–1986 Midterm Election Years

Variable	Vote	Try to Persuade	Do Work	Donate Money

Form of Electoral Participation

Variable	Vote	Try to Persuade	Do Work	Donate Money
Resources				
Income	4.6	3.5		15.5
Education	27.0	19.6	4.3	10.9
Unemployed	−8.5			
Age	25.7	−9.2	2.2	10.4
External Efficacy	8.2		1.1	2.5
Evaluation of Parties and Candidates				
Strength of party identification	17.5	13.7	4.3	6.9
Care which party wins Congressional election	20.7	14.1	3.7	3.7
Social Involvement				
Years in community, logarithm	23.3	3.9	2.6	
Church attendance	10.2		1.0	
Home owners	5.5			
Mobilization by Parties				
Contacted by a party	10.4	11.8	6.1	4.6
Mobilization by Campaigns				
Gubernatorial election		3.7		
Open House seat	3.7		1.7	
Unopposed House seat	−4.0			
Toss-up Senate election				3.7
Toss-up House election	6.0			2.5

Table 5-2   (*continued*)

	Form of Electoral Participation			
Variable	Vote	Try to Persuade	Do Work	Donate Money
Other Demographic Variables				
Women		−5.8		−2.6
Live in southern state	−9.8			−1.9
Live in border state	−8.4			−2.3
Blacks	−8.5			
Mexican Americans and Puerto Ricans	−9.3			

Note: Entries are the partial effects of the independent variables on the probability of participation (in percentages).
Source: Appendix D.

emerged from the investigation of governmental participation. In fact, because the pooled NES data enable us to assess causes that vary both across individuals and over time, the analysis of electoral participation permits us to embellish and elaborate some of the findings of Chapter 4. It weighs the contributions of resources, interests, identities, and attitudes. It bares the logic of party mobilization and reveals the effect of direct contacts. It demonstrates the influence of political parties, social movements, and electoral campaigns. It shows, in short, the decisive contribution of strategic mobilization.

Resources

Participation in electoral politics is costly. Without money, it is impossible to contribute financially to a campaign. Without time, energy, transportation, and child care, it is difficult, even impossible, to volunteer to work for a candidate. Even the simple act of voting requires people to register, to gather and digest a mass of information about the candidates, to make choices, and to get to the polls come election day. Participation in electoral campaigns puts many strains on people's resources, and people with ample resources are better able to participate than people with meager resources. Here we consider four kinds of resources: income, education, experience, and feelings of efficacy.

Income

As we saw in Chapter 3, the wealthy have participated more than the poor in every kind of electoral activity over the last four decades, and by substantial margins.[3] The relationship between income and participation persists even after we take the other causes of participation into account, as reported in Table 5-1. The wealthiest Americans are 15.8 percent more likely to vote in presidential elections, 5.7 percent more likely to try to convince others how to vote, 1.8 percent more likely to work for a party or candidate, and 14.8 percent more likely to make a campaign contribution than the poorest Americans. Income has comparable effects in midterm years, as seen in Table 5-2.

As argued in Chapter 4, income facilitates participation in politics both by what it indicates and by what it allows. Income indicates social position. The wealthy are much more likely than the poor to share the social circles of the candidates, the fundraisers, and the organized supporters. The wealthy, likewise, are much more likely than the poor to be part of social networks that expose them to indirect mobilization and provide them with social rewards if they take part.

More obviously, income allows people directly to bear the material costs of involvement in politics. The wealthy have the money to contribute to political parties, candidates, political action committees, and other causes; the poor do not. No surprise, then, that income has its most substantial effect on campaign giving, the activity that most transparently requires a direct outlay of cash. Money is also, however, the most fungible political resource, the asset most easily converted into other political resources. Money, for

[3] Lester W. Milbrath and M. L. Goel, *Political Participation: How and Why Do People Get Involved in Politics?* (Chicago: Rand McNally, 1977), pp. 96–97; Raymond E. Wolfinger and Steven J. Rosenstone, *Who Votes?* (New Haven: Yale University Press, 1980), pp. 20–22.

instance, allows people to purchase the leisure to work on a political campaign and the transportation to get themselves to campaign events.

Finally, people whose incomes are ample can more easily meet the opportunity costs of participation. The wealthy are less preoccupied than the poor with putting food on the table and meeting the monthly rent. This same line of reasoning explains why the unemployed who, after everything else has been taken into account, are 2.7 percent less likely than other Americans to vote in presidential contests and 8.5 percent less likely to do so in midterm years (see Tables 5-1 and 5-2). The money, time, and energy spent combatting extreme economic adversity provide payoffs that are more immediate and valuable than the benefits that might be gained from investing in electoral politics.[4]

Education

As we reported earlier, participation increases steadily with schooling, and as we report in Tables 5-1 and 5-2 the well educated are still more likely to take part even after taking other causes of participation into account.[5] Compared to those with no more than an eighth-grade education, college graduates are 16.6 percent more likely to vote in presidential elections, 13.9 percent more likely to try to convince others how to vote, 2.9 percent more likely to work for a party or candidate, and 9.8 percent more likely to make a campaign contribution.

Once again, the impact of education derives both from its indication of social position and from its role as a resource. Education imparts citizenship values, and so the educated, like the wealthy, inhabit social circles composed of people who, like themselves, have

[4]Wolfinger and Rosenstone, *Who Votes?*, p. 20; Steven J. Rosenstone, "Economic Adversity and Voter Turnout," *American Journal of Political Science* 26 (February 1982), pp. 25–46; Benjamin Radcliff, "The Welfare State, Turnout, and the Economy: A Comparative Analysis," paper presented at the annual meeting of the Midwest Political Science Association, 1991.

[5]Angus Campbell, Philip E. Converse, Warren E. Miller, and Donald E. Stokes, *The American Voter* (New York: Wiley, 1960), pp. 476–78; Milbrath and Goel, *Political Participation*, pp. 98–102; Wolfinger and Rosenstone, *Who Votes?*, pp. 17–20.

been socialized to follow politics and to value and reward political involvement.

Education, likewise, imparts the knowledge and the skills most essential to the citizen's task. As the estimates show, the impact of education on participation is slightly larger than the impact of income, with one obvious exception: Income—not education—is the most crucial resource for donations of money to political campaigns, as we have already noted.[6] Because of their schooling, the well educated have the skills people need to understand the abstract subject of politics, to follow the political campaign, and to research and evaluate the issues and the candidates.[7] In addition, because of their schooling the well educated are better able to handle the bureaucratic requirements of registration and voting. As we will see in Chapter 6, registering to vote is often much more difficult than voting itself, requiring a longer journey at a less convenient hour to complete a more complicated procedure long before the peak of the electoral campaign.[8] Better educated people are more likely to know they have to register, how and where to register, and where to go to cast their ballots on election day. Even if they do not know, these people can more easily come up with the information and complete the necessary tasks than people who have fewer skills in negotiating bureaucracies. Education has a greater impact on voter turnout than on any other form of electoral participation, largely because the bureaucratic barriers of voter registration are substantially higher than the barriers to participation in campaign work, campaign donations, and campaign persuasion. The greater their relevance to the demands of the task, the greater the impact of resources on participation.

Experience

Experience, like income and education, facilitates participation in electoral politics. In general, as people grow older, their involvement

---

[6]The same pattern holds in midterm years: Education has a bigger impact on participation than income, except when it comes to campaign contributions, where income again dominates.

[7]Wolfinger and Rosenstone, *Who Votes?*, pp. 18–19.

[8]Steven J. Rosenstone and Raymond E. Wolfinger, "The Effect of Registration Laws on Voter Turnout," *American Political Science Review* 72 (March 1978), pp. 22–45.

in American politics deepens. Between 1952 and 1988, Figure 5-1 shows, voter turnout ranged from 42 percent among the youngest Americans, to 60 percent among young adults, to 70 percent among middle-aged Americans, to 75 percent among older adults, before dropping back to 63 percent among the most elderly Americans. Age shows the same relationship with both volunteer work in campaigns and financial contributions to campaigns, rising steadily to plateaus at ages 45 to 65, then tapering off through the retirement years.[9]

There are three ways we might account for the relationship between participation and age. The *life-experience* hypothesis, which we favor, holds that people acquire resources that promote participation as they grow older. They become familiar with the political process, the political parties, and the candidates.[10] They grow more attached to the parties and their candidates. They acquire political knowledge and political skills. Finally, they acquire social contacts; their social ties become denser, increasing their exposure to mobilization and their susceptibility to the social rewards of taking part. As people grow older, in short, they accumulate information, skills, and attachments that help them to overcome the costs of political involvement.

The *life-cycle* hypothesis, in contrast, attributes the relationship between age and participation to the social and psychological involvements of the young and the aged. Young adults are less likely to take part, it contends, not because they lack experience but be-

[9]The relationship between age and attempts to influence others' votes is the clear exception to this pattern. The citizens who are most likely to try to persuade others are those in their mid-thirties, not those in middle-age. We suspect that the peak of persuasion much earlier in the life cycle arises from two factors. First, younger people, unburdened by the responsibilities of established occupations and families, encounter more people in their daily lives. Second, younger people, who have acquaintances of shorter standing, have less prior information about the biases and beliefs of their associates and consequently have more faith in their ability to influence them and more comfort in trying.

[10]Philip E. Converse, *The Dynamics of Party Support: Cohort-Analysing Party Identification* (Beverly Hills: Sage 1976); John M. Strate, Charles J. Parrish, Charles D. Elder, and Coit Ford III, "Life Span Civic Development and Voting Participation," *American Political Science Review* 83 (June 1989), pp. 444–64; John M. Strate, Charles J. Parrish, Charles D. Elder, and Thomas Jankowski, "Life Span Civic Development and Campaign Participation," paper presented at the annual meeting of the American Political Science Association, 1990.

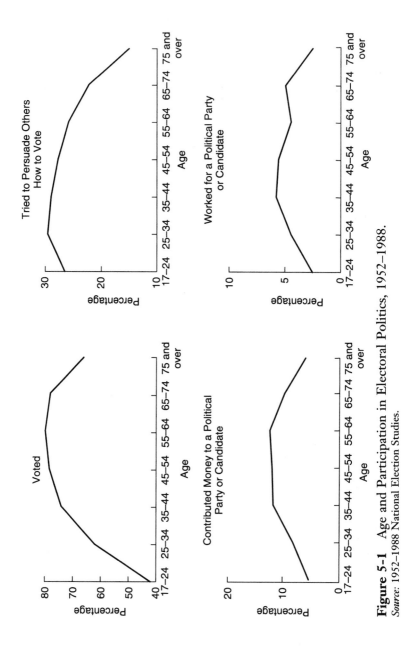

Figure 5-1 Age and Participation in Electoral Politics, 1952–1988.

Source: 1952–1988 National Election Studies.

cause they are not well integrated into communities. Participation declines among the elderly, correspondingly, because of the "onset of physical infirmities and a narrowing of psychological participation in the broader life of the society."[11]

The *generational* hypothesis, finally, contends that differences in participation across age groups are artifacts of the socializing experiences of each generation. Cohorts share unique experiences that determine their orientation toward politics. Older women vote less, for example, because they came of age before 1920, before the Nineteenth Amendment allowed women to vote, when politics was men's business. The young participate less because they missed out on the political experiences that motivated their elders. Their parents reached maturity during the Depression and the New Deal, during events that defined the terms of the political debate and breathed meaning into partisan identities. The young, consequently, entered a political system constructed by and for their parents, strangers to the issues, identities, and commitments that arose from an earlier era. According to the generational explanation, then, the experiences of the first years in politics permanently shape the orientations of that generation. People who come of age at critical turning points that define political allegiances participate more in electoral politics than people who reach maturity in more ordinary times.[12]

---

[11]Philip E. Converse and Richard Niemi, "Non-Voting Among Young Adults in the United States," pp. 443–66 in William J. Crotty et al., eds., *Political Parties and Political Behavior*, 2nd ed. (Boston: Allyn and Bacon, 1971), p. 445; Milbrath and Goel, *Political Participation*, pp. 114–16; Sidney Verba and Norman H. Nie, *Participation in America: Political Democracy and Social Equality* (New York: Harper & Row, 1972), p. 139. Also see Elaine Cumming and William E. Henry, *Growing Old: The Process of Disengagement* (New York: Basic Books, 1961).

[12]Paul Allen Beck, "A Socialization Theory of Partisan Realignment," pp. 199–219 in Richard G. Niemi et al., eds., *The Politics of Future Citizens* (San Francisco: Jossey-Bass, 1974); Robert E. Lane, *Political Life* (New York: Free Press of Glencoe, 1959), p. 125; Jerome M. Clubb, William H. Flanigan, and Nancy H. Zingale, *Partisan Realignment* (Beverly Hills: Sage, 1980), p. 121; Steven J. Rosenstone, Roy L. Behr, and Edward H. Lazarus, *Third Parties in America: Citizen Response to Major Party Failure* (Princeton: Princeton University Press, 1984), chap. 6; Warren E. Miller, "The Puzzle Transformed: Explaining Declining Turnout," unpublished manuscript, Arizona State University, April 1991. See also V. O. Key, Jr., "A Theory of Critical Elections," *Journal of Politics* 17 (February 1955), pp. 3–18; James L. Sundquist, *Dynamics of the Party System* (Washington D.C.: Brookings Institution, 1973).

Choosing between the life experience, life cycle, and generational explanations requires each to be assessed while holding the
others constant. By taking into account respondents' ages, characteristics, mobility, integration, and cohorts, as well as political periods, our analysis enables us to sort out the claims.[13] Figure 5-2
presents the relationships between age and electoral participation,
controlling for all the other causes of political activism.
The evidence strongly favors the life-experience hypothesis. As
Figure 5-2 shows, the relationship between age and electoral participation definitely persists even when life-cycle and cohort effects
have been taken into account. Sixty-five-year-olds are 29.0 percent more likely to vote in presidential elections than eighteen-
year-olds, and the probability of voting does not begin to fall until
after about age sixty-seven, and then by only about 1 percentage
point.[14] The middle-aged are nearly twice as likely as the young
to work for a party or candidate; eighty-year-olds are over twice as
likely as eighteen-year-olds to contribute money to a party or candidate. Consistent with the life-experience explanation, participation
in electoral politics increases throughout life.
Correspondingly, the findings offer little support for either the
generational or the life-cycle hypothesis. Although educational and
income disparities across age groups account for some of the relationship between aging and participation, the effects of generational
cohorts are uniformly insignificant. Common socialization experiences explain neither the lesser involvement of the young nor the
greater involvement of the aged.[15]

---

[13] Age, cohort, and period are collinear, of course, unless one makes some simplifying
assumptions. We defined three cohorts: people who entered the electorate by 1936;
people who entered the electorate between 1937 and 1964; and people who entered
the electorate after 1964. The periods are represented by dummy variables for each
presidential election year (except one).
[14] Our findings about turnout parallel the findings of Wolfinger and Rosenstone, *Who
Votes?*, chap. 3, but differ from the findings of M. Kent Jennings and Gregory B.
Markus, "Political Involvement in the Later Years: A Longitudinal Survey," *American
Journal of Political Science* 32 (May 1988), pp. 302–16.
[15] The coefficients for the cohort effects fail to achieve substantive or statistical significance and were dropped from the equations reported in Appendix D. We also
find no support for the claim that the era of disenfranchisement had a lingering

Also, once demographic differences across generations have been taken into account, voter turnout and campaign work decrease only slightly in old age, and financial contributions to campaigns do not diminish at all. In contradiction to the life-cycle explanation, people do not in fact disengage in their "twilight years."[16]

Over their lifetimes, then, people acquire the knowledge, skills, and attachments that enable them to participate in elections. Except where participation taxes physical stamina, except where infirmity defeats experience,[17] participation rises consistently with age.

Political Efficacy

A mountain of empirical evidence links political efficacy to electoral involvement.[18] Confidence in one's ability to understand politics

---

psychological effect on women who were socialized during a time when politics was literally men's business. Women who reached voting age before ratification of the Nineteenth Amendment were no less likely than others to engage in any of the four electoral activities we examined. There was no lingering socialization effect on the propensity of this generation of women to vote, to try to persuade others how to vote, or to contribute their time or money to a political party or candidate. As we will see in Chapter 6, however, women who reached voting age before suffrage were less likely to be mobilized by a political party, and the failure of mobilization, not lingering perceptions that politics was men's business, reduced their participation rates.

Gender differences in social and political roles, of course, did not evaporate with the adoption of women's suffrage and continue to manifest themselves in two forms of political participation. In both presidential and midterm years, women are about 6 percent less likely than men to try to instruct others how to vote. In midterm years, women are about 3 percent less likely than men to contribute money to a political party or candidate. In every other respect, women participate in electoral politics at rates comparable to those of men.

[16]Exactly the same pattern emerges from our analysis of turnout in 1974–1986 midterm elections: The relationship between age and participation is strong; there is little decline in turnout or working for a party or candidate among the elderly; and there is no decline whatsoever in the propensity of the elderly to donate money to a party or candidate.

[17]Jennings and Markus, "Political Involvement."

[18]Angus Campbell, Philip E. Converse, Warren E. Miller, and Donald E. Stokes, *The American Voter* (New York: John Wiley and Sons, 1960); Gabriel A. Almond and Sidney Verba, *The Civic Culture* (Princeton: Princeton University Press, 1963); Verba and Nie, *Participation in America*, pp. 133–36; Milbrath and Goel, *Political Participation*, pp. 58–59.

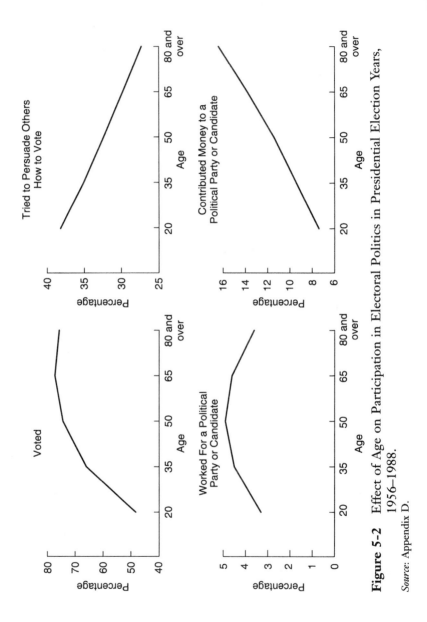

Figure 5-2 Effect of Age on Participation in Electoral Politics in Presidential Election Years, 1956–1988.

Source: Appendix D.

and faith in one's capability to practice politics—internal efficacy—
and belief in the influence of one's actions on the decisions of the
government—external efficacy—help to overcome the constant suspicion that participation is hopeless.[19]

The public's waning sense of political efficacy, many observers
believe, has caused citizens to disengage massively from politics and
elections.[20] After three decades of strife, impasse, scandal, and "a
more generalized feeling that government has failed to solve social
and economic problems," Americans' confidence in the productive-
ness of their political efforts has declined steadily (see Figure 5-3).[21]
In 1960, 75 percent of the electorate rejected the idea that public officials "don't ... care much what people like me think." In 1988,

---

[19]For a discussion of the distinction between internal and external efficacy see Lane,
Political Life; George I. Balch, "Multiple Indicators in Survey Research: The Concept
of 'Sense of Political Efficacy,'" *Political Methodology* 1 (1974), pp. 1–43; Stephen C.
Craig, "Efficacy, Trust, and Political Behavior: An Attempt to Resolve a Lingering
Conceptual Dilemma," *American Politics Quarterly* 7 (April 1979), pp. 225–39; and
Stephen C. Craig and Michael A. Maggiotto, "Measuring Political Efficacy," *Political
Methodology* 8 (1982), pp. 85–109.

[20]The assessments of the contribution of declining efficacy to declining participation
are all over the map. Some assert that the weaker sense of efficacy is the primary
cause of Americans' withdrawal from electoral politics. See Curtis B. Gans, on the
"MacNeil/Lehrer Report," Public Broadcasting Service, November 7, 1978; Curtis B. Gans, "The Empty Ballot Box: Reflections on Nonvoters in America," *Public
Opinion* (September/October 1978), pp. 54–57. Others hold that it is a substantial
but far from primary contributor. See Stephen D. Shaffer, "A Multivariate Explanation of Decreasing Turnout in Presidential Elections, 1960–1976," *American Journal
of Political Science* 25 (February 1981), pp. 68–95; Paul R. Abramson and John H.
Aldrich, "The Decline of Participation in America," *American Political Science Review*
76 (September 1982), pp. 502–21. Finally, some analysts question whether it has
anything at all to do with the decline in turnout. See Orley Ashenfelter and Stanley
Kelley, Jr., "Determinants of Participation in Presidential Elections," *Journal of Law
and Economics* 18 (December 1976), pp. 695–731; Thomas E. Cavanagh, "Research on
American Voter Turnout: The State of the Evidence," paper presented at the Conference on Voter Participation, Carnegie Endowment for International Peace, 1981;
M. Margaret Conway and Judith Garber, "Stability and Change in Political Participation: A Panel Analysis," paper presented at the annual meeting of the Southern
Political Science Association, 1981.

[21]Paul R. Abramson, *Political Attitudes in America* (San Francisco: W. H. Freeman,
1983), pp. 181–82.

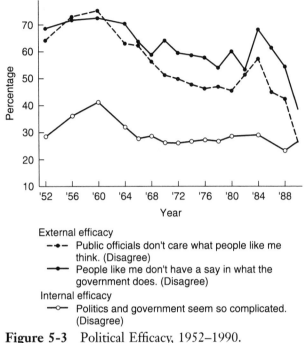

External efficacy
- –•– Public officials don't care what people like me think. (Disagree)
- –•– People like me don't have a say in what the government does. (Disagree)

Internal efficacy
- –○– Politics and government seem so complicated. (Disagree)

Figure 5-3 Political Efficacy, 1952–1990.
Source: 1952–1990 National Election Studies.

only 43 percent disagreed. In 1960, 73 percent of the electorate rejected the idea that "people like me don't have any say in what the government does." In 1988, only 55 percent disagreed. In 1960, finally, 41 percent of the electorate rejected the idea that "politics and government seem so complicated that a person like me can't really understand what's going on." In 1988, only 22 percent disagreed.

Taking into account all the other causes of political involvement, we find a modest to substantial effect (as shown in Tables 5-1 and 5-2). The citizens with the greatest sense of internal efficacy are about 2.9 percent more likely to vote, about 5.6 percent more likely to persuade, about 1.7 percent more likely to volunteer in campaigns, and about 2.5 percent more likely to contribute money than citizens with the least sense of their own competence. Similarly, people with the greatest sense of external efficacy were 10.6 percent more likely to turn out, 4.8 percent more likely to try to influence, 1.4 percent more likely to work for a party, and 2.8 percent more likely to give money than people with the greatest doubts about the government's concern with their opinions.[22]

Thus, political efficacy is in fact an important resource in electoral politics, and as Americans have lost their confidence in the effectiveness of their actions, their commitment to electoral politics has also weakened. We leave it to Chapter 7, however, to compare the impact of declining efficacy with the effect of other factors.

Summary

In light of the theory we expounded in Chapter 2, the findings we presented in Chapter 4, and the evidence that others have offered, this section reveals no surprises. Resources such as income, education, experience, and political efficacy sustain political activism. People draw upon their resources to offset the demands that arise from involvement in electoral politics.

---

[22] Our measure of external efficacy in presidential years is a scale built from two questions: "I don't think public officials care much what people like me think" and "People like me don't have any say about what the government does." Individual responses to these two questions correlate 0.45 between 1952 and 1988, and correlate 0.25 with the question measuring internal efficacy. Similar effects of external efficacy also emerge from our analysis of electoral participation in midterm elections. With data from the 1972–1974–1976 NES Panel Study, however, Finkel has shown that as much as a third of the relationship between external efficacy and turnout and as much as five-sixths of the relationship between efficacy and campaign participation may be owing to participation causing efficacy, rather than efficacy causing participation. The reciprocal effects of participation appear to be greatest for those with the fewest years of formal schooling. If these findings generalize, then the numbers we report overstate the impact that external efficacy has on electoral participation. Steven E. Finkel, "Reciprocal Effects of Participation and Political Efficacy: A Panel Analysis," *American Journal of Political Science* 29 (November 1985), pp. 891–913. Also see Jan Leighley, "Participation as a Stimulus of Political Conceptualization," *Journal of Politics* 53 (February 1991), pp. 198–211.

Evaluations of the Political System

Many observers blame the decline in citizen participation in electoral politics on the electorate's deep and growing alienation from the political system as a whole. In their view, declining participation casts a vote of no confidence in the political order. Turned off by government, Americans have tuned out of politics.[23]

Civic Responsibility

Citizens are much less likely to feel obligated to take part in electoral politics now than they were four decades ago—a trend that parallels the decline of popular involvement in elections. The electorate's sense of civic duty rose nearly 10 percentage points between 1952 and 1960, increasing together with public involvement. (See Figure 5-4.) Americans' sense of their duty to participate remained

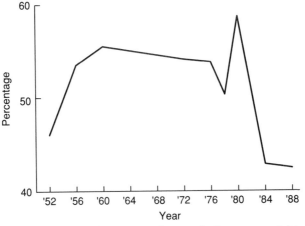

If a person does not care how an election comes out, he should not vote in it. (Disagree)

Figure 5-4   Civic Duty, 1952–1988.
Source: 1952–1988 National Election Studies.

[23] Walter Dean Burnham, "Shifting Patterns of Congressional Voting Participation in the United States," paper delivered at the annual meeting of the American Political Science Association, 1981.

fairly constant between 1960 and 1980, counter to the trend of voter turnout, but then dropped in the 1980s, along with voters' propensity to participate.

Although some observers take the sense of civic responsibility to be an important stimulus to participation,[24] many others have already expressed doubt that the declining sense of civic duty explains much, if any, of the decline in the public's political involvement.[25] Our analysis reinforces their skepticism. Strong feelings of civic duty make a small impact on the probability of voting in presidential elections—about 6 percent—but they have no discernable effect on the probability of attempting to persuade, of working in a campaign, or of contributing money.[26] Apparently, people do not participate in politics merely because they believe they have an obligation to the system.[27]

Confidence in Government

The case for the importance of evaluations of the system does not improve when we consider popular confidence in the government.

[24]Campbell et al., *The American Voter*, p. 106; Almond and Verba, *The Civic Culture*, pp. 176–77; Verba and Nie, *Participation in America*, pp. 133–36; Ashenfelter and Kelley, "Determinants of Participation," pp. 49–53.

[25]Richard A. Brody, "The Puzzle of Political Participation in America," pp. 287–324 in Anthony King, ed., *The New American Political System* (Washington, D.C.: American Enterprise Institute, 1978); Warren E. Miller, "Disinterest, Disaffection, and Participation in Presidential Elections," *Political Behavior* 2 (November 1980), pp. 7–32.

[26]This estimate is drawn from analyses that are not reported in Tables 5-1 and 5-2. Given that duty has an impact only on voter turnout, self-perception may be at work. The survey question asks people if they endorse the idea that they have an obligation to vote even if they do not care how elections turn out. People who participate may conclude from their behavior that they do in fact feel that obligation. If they do, even the 6 percent effect is overstated.

[27]The civic duty question was not asked in 1964 and 1968 National Election Studies, so the analysis reported here was conducted on data from the 1956, 1960, and 1972–1988 elections only. Parallel conclusions emerge from our analysis of the 1978 midterm election (the only year for which we have complete data on the variables in the equation). Strong feelings of civic duty boost turnout in midterm years by about 4 percent, but have no appreciable impact on other forms of electoral participation.

As before, the trend of public confidence parallels the downward trend of public involvement. Public trust in government and assessments of its responsiveness have both eroded spectacularly over the last four decades, as Figures 5-5 and 5-6 clearly show. In 1958, for example, 76 percent of the American public said they "trust[ed] the government in Washington to do what is right" most of the time or almost always. In 1980, only 26 percent did. The electorate's confidence that "the government is run for the benefit of all people," that the government does not "waste a lot of the money we pay in taxes," and that "hardly any [of the people running the government] are crooked" has suffered equally. Between 1958 and 1988, Americans' trust in their government fell by almost half.

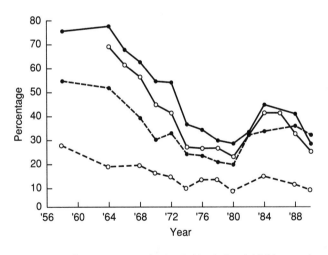

Figure 5-5 Trust in Government, 1958–1990.
Source: 1958–1990 National Election Studies.

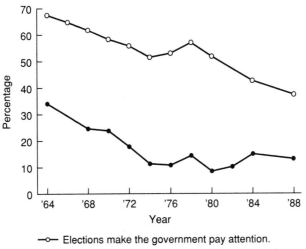

Figure 5-6 Government Responsiveness, 1964–1988.
Source: 1964–1988 National Election Studies.

The public's perception that the government is responsive dropped every bit as rapidly in the 1960s, 1970s, and 1980s. In 1964, two-thirds of the electorate believed that "elections make the government pay [a good deal of] attention to what the people think"; in 1988, just over a third did. In 1964, one out of three citizens believed that "over the years...the government pays [a good deal] of attention to what the people think when it decides what to do"; in 1988, fewer than one out of seven did.[28]

[28]A perception of government responsiveness and a sense of efficacy should not be confused. Responsiveness is an assessment of the government itself; efficacy is an individual's sense of his own personal political competence and his own ability to affect the political world around him. Confirmatory factor analysis establishes that internal efficacy, external efficacy, trust, and responsiveness are indeed four separate (though moderately correlated) dimensions. In presidential years, missing data forced us to confine our analysis to the 1964–1988 elections. In midterm years, analysis was confined to the 1974 and 1978 contests.

As before, many observers blame decaying confidence in government for the decline in electoral participation.[29] As before, however, the evidence argues against them. As our colleague Jack Citrin showed nearly two decades ago, trusting citizens are *not* more likely to vote, *not* more likely to engage in campaign activities, and *not* more likely to be interested in political campaigns or governmental affairs.[30] Our analysis confirms Citrin's conclusions. In both presidential and midterm years, once the other causes of electoral participation have been taken into account, neither feelings of trust in government nor beliefs about government responsiveness have any effect whatsoever on the likelihood that citizens will vote or will take part in any form of campaign politics.[31]

Summary

Despite the surface appeal of the idea that Americans have turned off and tuned out of politics, there is in fact no evidence that popular participation in elections constitutes a display of public confidence (or lack of it) in the political system.[32] The causes of the decline of electoral involvement most certainly lie elsewhere.

[29]Gans, "The Empty Ballot Box"; Robert Novak, on the "MacNeil/Lehrer Report," Public Broadcasting Service, November 7, 1978; Burnham, "Shifting Patterns"; Walter Dean Burnham, *The Current Crisis in American Politics* (New York: Oxford University Press, 1982), pp. 167–82.

[30]Part of the explanation for the lack of any relationship between trust and participation may lie with the survey questions themselves—they may not measure alienation from the political regime as much as "opposition to incumbent officeholders or largely ritualistic expressions of fashionable clichés." Jack Citrin, "Comment: The Political Relevance of Trust in Government," *American Political Science Review* 68 (September 1974), pp. 973–88, quoted at p. 984. Also see Raymond E. Wolfinger, David P. Glass, and Peverill Squire, "Predictors of Electoral Turnout: An International Comparison," *Policy Studies Review* 9 (Spring 1990), pp. 551–74.

[31]Our measure of trust in government is a four-item scale based on responses to the four questions displayed in Figure 5-5. The scale reliability is 0.72. Our measure of government responsiveness is a two-item scale based on responses to the two questions displayed in Figure 5-6. Responses to these two questions are correlated at 0.38.

[32]Cross-national data are also inconsistent with the disaffection hypothesis. Although Americans are 20 to 30 percent less likely to vote than Europeans, Americans are substantially more trusting of government and other political institutions than their European counterparts. Almond and Verba, *The Civic Culture*, pp. 176–77; David Glass, Peverill Squire, and Raymond E. Wolfinger, "Voter Turnout: An International

Evaluations of the Political
Parties and Their Candidates

The consequential evaluations, it turns out, have less to do with the legitimacy of the whole political system than with the attractiveness of the choices the system offers. The real business of American elections, after all, is to select the nation's leaders, and the choices themselves are important determinants of the benefits voters receive from their efforts. Some voters sometimes see major stakes in the decision: They stand to receive considerable gain and gratification from a victory. Other voters other times see little to accomplish in the election. They neither identify with the alternatives nor expect any policy advantages to accrue from the outcome of the election.

Over the last thirty years, the electorate's identification with the Democratic and Republican parties has weakened considerably. In each election year between 1952 and 1964, at least one-third of the voters considered themselves strong Democrats or strong Republicans. (See Figure 5-7.) From that point on, however, partisan attachments weakened, and by the end of the 1970s, fewer than one American in four identified strongly with a political party. Although partisan allegiances did rebound slightly during the 1980s, by the close of the decade fidelity to the two political parties was substantially weaker than it was during the 1950s.

In addition, citizens' evaluations of the party they prefer have also turned more negative over the last several decades. Since 1952, the NES has asked citizens to describe what they like and dislike about the two political parties. As shown in Figure 5-8, from 1952 to 1978 the margin of the good things people said about the party they liked best over the bad things they said about it declined steadily. Evaluations grew slightly more positive in the 1980s, but they remained well below the levels of approval that voters professed in the 1950s and 1960s.

Comparison," *Public Opinion* (December/January 1983), pp. 49–55; Seymour Martin Lipset and William Schneider, *The Confidence Gap* (New York: Free Press, 1983), p. 410.

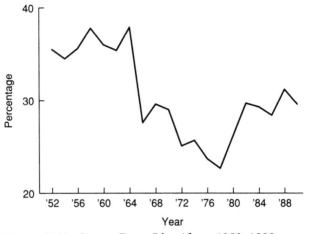

Figure 5-7   Strong Party Identifiers, 1952–1990.
Source: 1952–1990 National Election Studies.

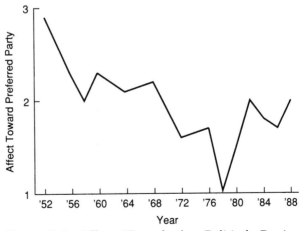

Figure 5-8   Affect Toward the Political Parties,
1952–1988.
Source: 1952–1988 National Election Studies.

Given these two trends of recent electoral history, it is no surprise at all that the electorate cares less and less about which party wins the election. Although nearly two out of three citizens professed to care a good deal whether the Democrats or the Republicans won the White House in 1952, only about half gave much of a damn in 1980. (See Figure 5-9.) Similarly, where two-thirds proclaimed an interest in the outcome of elections for the House of Representatives in 1970, barely half really cared much in 1990.

Finally, given these three aspects of recent electoral history, it is understandable that citizens' preferences between the presidential candidates have become much less intense. Since 1952, NES has also asked its respondents to describe what they like and what they dislike about the two presidential nominees. As reported in Figure 5-10, citizens felt much more strongly about their favorite candidates in 1964, 1968, and 1984 than nominees in any other pres-

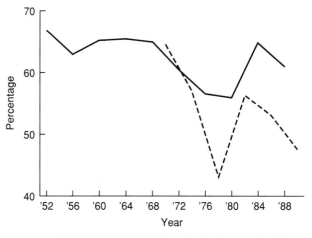

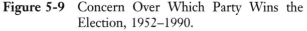

— Care a good deal which party wins the presidential election.

-- Care a good deal about the way the elections to the U.S. House of Representatives come out.

Figure 5-9 Concern Over Which Party Wins the Election, 1952–1990.

Source: 1952–1990 National Election Studies.

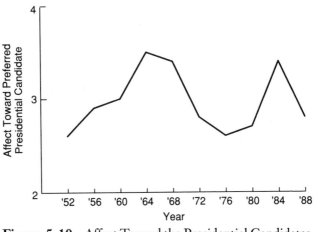

Figure 5-10   Affect Toward the Presidential Candidates, 1952–1988.
Source: 1952–1988 National Election Studies.

idential contest for which we have data. In 1964, 1968, and 1984, when Lyndon Johnson and Barry Goldwater, Hubert Humphrey and Richard Nixon, and Ronald Reagan and Walter Mondale offered choices and not echoes, citizens noticed the ideological differences and backed their favorites much more intensely. Even so, although the strength of the electorate's preferences waxes and wanes with the specific choices elections offer, voters' satisfaction with their favorites clearly rose until 1964 and declined thereafter.

In the 1980s, then, the electorate saw much less benefit from its choices than it did in the 1960s. Its weakening identification with the Democrats and the Republicans diminished the rewards of seeing the "right side" win. Its weakening preference for the candidates reflected the abatement of the benefits of having one leader in office rather than another. With greater skepticism about the value of helping one candidate to beat the other, there was less incentive for citizens to take part in elections.[33]

[33] Anthony Downs, *An Economic Theory of Democracy* (New York: Harper & Row, 1957); John Ferejohn and Morris Fiorina, "Closeness Counts Only in Horseshoes and Dancing," *American Political Science Review* 69 (September 1975), pp. 920–25.

Our analysis finds that the electorate's declining sense of a stake in election outcomes has contributed to its disengagement from electoral politics. Strength of party identification, evaluations of the political parties, concern over the outcomes of elections, and evaluations of the presidential candidates all affect the likelihood that citizens will vote or participate in campaign activities. As we report in Table 5-1, people who identify themselves as strong partisans are 10.6 percent more likely to vote than citizens who lean toward neither party. Strong partisans are 7.8 percent more likely to try to influence how others vote, 3.0 percent more likely to work for a campaign, and 5.1 percent more likely to contribute money to a party or candidate. People who evaluate one party more positively

---

There is a fair amount of evidence consistent with this line of reasoning. Strength of party allegiance is usually associated with the likelihood of participation in politics. See, for instance, Campbell et al., *The American Voter*; Verba and Nie, *Participation in America*, chap. 12; Milbrath and Goel, *Political Participation*, pp. 54–56; Steven E. Finkel and Karl-Dieter Opp, "Party Identification and Participation in Collective Action," *Journal of Politics* 53 (May 1991), pp. 339–71. Some scholars, in fact, have found a link between weakening allegiance to the political parties and declining turnout. Stephen D. Shaffer, "A Multivariate Explanation"; Carol A. Cassel and David B. Hill, "Explanations of Turnout Decline: A Multivariate Test," *American Politics Quarterly* 9 (April 1981), pp. 181–95; Burnham, *The Current Crisis*; Conway and Garber, "Stability and Change," p. 15. Some analysts claim that declining partisan allegiance is responsible for as much as one-quarter to one-third of the drop in turnout in presidential elections between 1960 and 1980 and even more of the decline in midterm years. Abramson and Aldrich, "The Decline of Participation," pp. 509–10. For a dissenting view, see Ashenfelter and Kelley, "Determinants of Participation." Still other analysts have blamed rising citizen disaffection from the political parties and their presidential nominees for the decline in turnout. Richard A. Brody and Benjamin I. Page, "Indifference, Alienation, and Rational Decisions," *Public Choice* 13 (Summer 1973), pp. 1–17; Milbrath and Goel, *Political Participation*, p. 140; Walter Dean Burnham, "The Appearance and Disappearance of the American Voter," pp. 35–73 in Richard Rose, ed., *Electoral Participation: A Comparative Analysis* (Beverly Hills: Sage, 1980), p. 66; Christian Goergen, "Explaining Turnout in 1988: About the Importance of Perceiving Differences between Parties and Candidates," paper presented at the annual meeting of the Midwest Political Science Association, 1991. Others have disputed this evidence. John Aldrich, "Some Problems in Testing Two Rational Models of Participation," *American Journal of Political Science* 20 (November 1976), pp. 713–33; Herbert F. Weisberg and Bernard Grofman, "Candidate Evaluations and Turnout," *American Politics Quarterly* 9 (April 1981), pp. 197–219.

than the other are 11.4 percent more likely to vote, 13.3 percent more likely to try to persuade others, 3.4 percent more likely to do campaign work, and 7.0 percent more likely to give money. Citizens who care about the outcome of the election are 6.4 percent more likely to vote, 10.7 percent more likely to persuade others, 1.7 percent more likely to donate their time, and 3.5 percent more likely to donate their money. Finally, people who strongly prefer one candidate to the other are 5.6 percent more likely to vote, 22.9 percent more likely to persuade others, 4.0 percent more likely to work for a party or candidate, and 3.3 percent more likely to make a campaign contribution.

In short, the better the options the more likely people will want to help make the choice. When citizens expect to get a benefit out of participation, whether it is policy or simple satisfaction, they are more inclined to devote their efforts to electoral politics.[34]

Social Involvement

Finally, the social matrix in which people live also structures the benefits and costs of political involvement in consequential ways. In casual interactions, families, friends, neighbors, associates, and co-workers underwrite the costs of information and manufacture the benefits of social approval and respect. Accordingly, people with dense webs of social contacts learn more about the candidates, the issues, and the opportunities to take part. They have greater exposure to social incentives—their obligations to others are more extensive, their opportunities to help others more numerous, and their actions

---

[34]These conclusions also hold for the 1974–1986 midterm elections, as reported in Table 5-2. Strength of party identification and concern over congressional election outcomes increased the likelihood that people voted, tried to persuade others, and contributed their time or money to one of the parties or candidates. Questions assessing the respondent's likes and dislikes of the parties and their candidates were not included in all of the NES midterm surveys and thus are not part of our analysis of participation in midterm years.

better scrutinized.[35] Thus, the better connected people are socially, the more likely they are to take part in electoral politics.[36]

In addition, citizens who are well established in relationships with co-workers, neighbors, and friends confront fewer barriers to political activism than people who are new to the community. New arrivals face the many demands of relocation—moving into new homes; transferring into new offices, factories, and schools; locating merchants and services—that distract from attention to politics.[37] They must reestablish themselves politically, most importantly by reregistering to vote.[38] Finally, they must wait for new channels of political information and encouragement to develop. They do not yet know anybody, and politicians, political parties, local interest groups, and activists do not yet know them.

We cannot directly measure the details of each person's social network, but we can use several simple indicators of the extent of each person's integration into her community. We know the length of her residence: People who live in one place for many years have more opportunity to develop broader networks of friends and associates.[39] We know whether she rents or owns her home: People

---

[35] See Gerald M. Pomper and Loretta Sernekos, "The 'Bake Sale' Theory of Voting Participation," paper presented at the annual meeting of the American Political Science Association, 1989, p. 13; Carole J. Uhlaner, "'Relational Goods' and Participation: Incorporating Sociability into a Theory of Rational Action," *Public Choice* 62 (September 1989), pp. 253–84.

[36] Wilber C. Rich and Abraham Wandersman, "Participation in Block Organizations," *Social Policy* 14 (Summer 1983), pp. 45–47; Carole J. Uhlaner, "Rational Turnout: The Neglected Role of Groups," *American Journal of Political Science* 33 (May 1987), pp. 390–422; Strate et al., "Life Span Civic Development and Voting Participation"; Jan E. Leighley, "Social Interaction and Contextual Influences on Political Participation," *American Politics Quarterly* 18 (October 1990), pp. 459–75; Stephen Knack, "Civic Norms, Social Sanctions, and Voter Turnout," *Rationality and Society* 4 (April 1992), pp. 133–56; Stephen Knack, "Social Connectedness and Voter Participation: Evidence from the 1991 NES Pilot Study," unpublished manuscript, Center for the Study of Public Choice, George Mason University, January 1992.

[37] Wolfinger and Rosenstone, *Who Votes?*, p. 53.

[38] There is good evidence that this one requirement significantly reduces voter turnout among the most mobile. Peverill Squire, Raymond E. Wolfinger, and David P. Glass, "Residential Mobility and Voter Turnout," *American Political Science Review* 81 (March 1987), pp. 45–65.

[39] Lane, *Political Life*, p. 267.

who own homes are less mobile than people who rent. We know the regularity with which she attends religious services: People who worship belong to churches and interact with other parishioners. Finally, we know whether she works in an office or a factory, works at home or is retired: People who work in factories and offices receive information and support in the workplace.

As Tables 5-1 and 5-2 show, people who are well integrated into their communities are substantially more likely to vote in national elections than those whose social networks are weaker. People who have lived in their communities for forty or more years are about 10.7 percent more likely to vote in presidential elections than those who have moved into the community within the year of the election.[40] Long-term residents are about 23.3 percent more likely than newcomers to cast ballots in midterm elections.[41] Homeowners are 7.5 percent more likely to vote in presidential years and 5.5 percent more likely to vote in midterm contests than renters. People who attend church every week are 15.1 percent more likely to vote in presidential elections and 10.2 percent more likely to vote in midterm years than people who never attend religious services.[42] Finally, people who work in factories and offices are 2.1 percent more likely to vote in presidential years than those who do not hold a job outside the home. In short, the greater the extent of social involvements, the greater the likelihood that people will cast votes in national elections.

Social integration has a much more modest impact on all other forms of participation in electoral politics. In presidential years,

---

[40]See Knack, "Civic Norms," and "Social Connectedness."

[41]These findings are consistent with those of Wolfinger and Rosenstone, *Who Votes?*, p. 54; Pomper and Sernekos, "The 'Bake Sale' Theory"; Verba and Nie, *Participation in America*, p. 145; Strate et al., "Life Span Civic Development and Voting Participation."

[42]These findings parallel those of Donald R. Matthews and James W. Prothro, *Negroes and the New Southern Politics* (New York: Harcourt, Brace and World, 1966), pp. 223–35; Katherine Tate and Ronald E. Brown, "The Black Church and Political Participation Revisited," paper presented at the annual meeting of the Midwest Political Science Association, 1991; and Ronald E. Brown and Monica Wolford, "Religious Resources and African American Political Action," paper presented at the annual meeting of the American Political Science Association, 1991.

length of residence in the community has no detectable impact on the likelihood that people will try to persuade others how to vote or that they will donate time or money to a political campaign. In midterm elections, long-time residents of the community are about 3.9 percent more likely to try to persuade others and about 2.6 percent more likely to work for a party or candidate. Church attendance, which had a huge effect on voter turnout, increases the probability of working for a party or candidate by only 1.0 percent; it has no impact at all on the willingness to engage in persuasion or to donate money to political campaigns. In presidential years, people employed outside the home are about 1.8 percent more likely to try to persuade others and 1.9 percent more likely to donate money to political campaigns, but no such effects emerge in midterm years.

The mixed results suggest that political leaders rely on more select social connections to mobilize volunteers and contributors to campaigns. Rather than working broadly and inefficiently through workplaces, churches, and communities, campaigns recruit volunteers and contributors from the ranks of prior activists.[43] Fundamentally, our point still stands, however: People receive information and rewards through their social networks, and the better placed they are within them, the more likely they are to take part in electoral politics.[44]

Conclusion

The main lessons of this chapter can be summarized easily. First, people who have ample resources are far more likely to participate in campaigns and elections than people who have few resources.

---

[43]The results might also suggest that our measures of social involvement are hopelessly weak, and that a more thorough mapping of social networks is needed to gauge the full effect of social influence. See Robert Huckfeldt and John Sprague, "Political Parties and Electoral Mobilization: Political Structure, Social Structure, and the Party Canvass," *American Political Science Review* 86 (March 1992), pp. 70–86.

[44]There is no measure of participation in groups and associations that appears with regularity in the National Election Studies. Thus, we are unfortunately unable to replicate this aspect of the analysis in Chapter 4 for the 1956 to 1988 elections.

Citizens with income, education, experience, and a sense of personal efficacy take greater part in electoral politics than people who lack them. They can better afford the costs of political involvement.

Second, people who see a great deal at stake in campaigns and elections are far more likely to participate than people who see little at stake. Citizens who identify strongly with the political parties, citizens who view their favorite party very positively, citizens who care deeply about the outcomes of elections, and citizens who prefer their favorite candidates strongly all take greater part in electoral politics than people who feel otherwise. They see greater benefits to be had from their involvement in electoral politics.

Finally, people who are well connected socially are far more likely to participate than people who are poorly connected. Citizens who are wealthy, educated, and older share social contacts with political leaders. Citizens who are part of dense webs of association of the workplace, church, and community receive more information and encounter more bountiful social benefits. They gain more social encouragement to participate in electoral politics.

To this point, though, we have discussed only the personal attributes of citizens and their connections to electoral activism. What we have related in this chapter is, in many ways, the familiar story. As we argued in Chapter 2 and demonstrated in Chapter 4, however, the familiar story is only half the story. Involvement in American politics is motivated not only by the personal but also by the political—by the activities of candidates, parties, interest groups, and activists. We present the political side of electoral participation next, in Chapter 6.

MOBILIZATION AND PARTICIPATION IN ELECTORAL POLITICS

The bottom line of this chapter is very simple. People participate in electoral politics because someone encourages or inspires them to take part. The very nature of elections motivates political leaders to mobilize public involvement: More votes than the opposition means victory. Accordingly, in any election campaign, candidates, political parties, campaign organizations, interest groups, and other activists do their best to muster participants. Candidates appear at factories, offices, and service clubs, parties canvass and staff phone banks, campaigns troll for contributors, and interest groups rally their troops. In any election campaign, moreover, the efforts of candidates, parties, campaigns, and interest groups are magnified by the subsequent social interactions of the people they reach. Families discuss campaigns, friends debate the options, and co-workers convey expectations. The essential feature of electoral politics, in short, is electoral mobilization.

In this chapter, we trace the means by which political leaders induce people to take part in elections. In the first part of the chapter, we measure the success of the efforts of political parties, election campaigns, and social movements to convince American citizens to vote, to persuade, to volunteer, and to give. In the second part of the chapter, we gauge the impact of institutionalized efforts to regulate and restrict citizen participation in elections—registration and election laws.

Mobilization, we conclude, is an essential part of the story of why people participate in elections. In fact, as we shall demonstrate in Chapter 7, the dynamic of mobilization in American politics is the key that unlocks the puzzle of electoral participation in America.

161

Mobilization by Political Parties

In a typical American election campaign, the Democratic and the Republican parties contact about one out of every four Americans to talk to them personally about the candidates and the election.[1] The efforts of parties to mobilize ebb and flow from election to election, as shown in Figure 6-1. In 1956, the political parties contacted about 17 percent of the electorate during the presidential election campaign, and over the next two decades the level of party mobilization grew steadily. Party mobilization reached its peak in 1972 when 29 percent of the electorate reported contact with a political party. Thereafter, mobilization dipped, with the parties reaching just 24 percent of the electorate during the 1988 presidential election campaign.

Party mobilization has also fallen of late in midterm election years. Party contact peaked in 1982, when Democrats and Republicans reached 31 percent of the electorate. In subsequent midterm elections, mobilization plummeted, and only 19 percent of American citizens reported contact with the political parties during the 1990 campaign.

The 1956–1980 National Election Studies (NES) data enable us to explore party mobilization quite broadly, first to understand its causes and then to appreciate its effects. Back in Chapter 2 we expounded on the idea that political leaders mobilize citizens strategically. Constrained by limited money, limited time, and finite other resources, they target their efforts and time their efforts carefully. Anxious to involve the greatest number of the right people with the least amount of expense, they mobilize people who are known to them, who are well placed in social networks, whose actions are effective, and who are likely to act. In addition, anxious that their actions have maximum effect, they time their efforts to coincide with salient issues, minimal distractions, imminent decisions, and

---

[1] Our measure of party mobilization relies on a question that has been asked on National Election Studies since 1956: "As you know, the political parties try to talk to as many people as they can to get them to vote for their candidates. Did anyone from one of the political parties call you up or come around and talk to you about the campaign?"

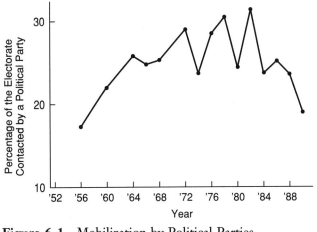

Figure 6-1 Mobilization by Political Parties, 1956–1990.

Source: 1956–1990 National Election Studies.

close political contests. In Chapter 4 we offered a great deal of evidence that politicians, interest groups, and activists in governmental politics make just these calculations.

The NES data allow us now to test these notions more directly. In Tables 6-1 and 6-2 we present summaries of our analysis of the causes of party mobilization for both presidential and midterm election years.

Targeting Mobilization

The goal of political parties is to win enough votes to elect their candidates to office. Mobilization efforts are designed to help make that happen, by inducing people to vote, persuade, contribute, and volunteer. Given their limited resources, however, parties must decide on whom they will target their efforts. Resources they devote to people who are unlikely to turn out or unlikely to support them are resources wasted.

Accordingly, parties give considerable thought to how they might best mobilize their supporters. First, they concentrate their efforts on the parts of the electorate that are most likely to support them. They, like political scientists, know that mobilization can increase

Table 6-1   Summary: Causes of Being Contacted by a Political
Party, 1956–1988 Presidential Election Years

Variable	Effect on Probability of Being Contacted
Resources	
Income	9.5
Education	18.6
Age	22.1
Attachment to Parties	
Strength of party identification	5.3
Social Involvement	
Years in community, logarithm*	6.9
Church attendance	3.6
Homeowners*	4.2
Union family	1.9
Mobilization by Campaigns	
Close presidential election	1.3
Gubernatorial election	2.1
Open House seat	3.9
Unopposed House seat	−4.7
Mobilization by Social Movements	
Civil rights movement actions	4.3
Other Demographic Variables	
Women socialized before 1920	−4.4
Southern state	−3.8
Southern blacks before 1964	−15.4

Note: Entries are the partial effects of independent variables on the probability of
mobilization (in percentages).
*Effect is estimated for the 1968–1988 presidential election years only.
Source: Appendix E.

Table 6-2   Summary: Causes of Being Contacted by a Political Party, 1974–1986 Midterm Election Years

Variable	Effect on the Probability of Being Contacted
Resources	
Education	22.0
Income	9.5
Age	12.1
Attachment to Parties	
Strength of party identification	7.2
Social Involvement	
Years in community, logarithm	9.1
Church attendance	6.3
Homeowners	7.2
Mobilization by Campaigns	
Toss-up gubernatorial election	1.7
Toss-up Senate election	7.5
Toss-up House election	5.5
Open House seat	5.3
Other Demographic Variables	
Southern state	−4.4

Note: Entries are the partial effect of independent variables on the probability of mobilization (in percentages).
Source: Appendix E.

participation, but that it rarely changes preferences.[2] Effective get-out-the-vote campaigns "concentrate on turnout of the vote among voters and in neighborhoods which are likely to support the party;

[2] Bernard R. Berelson, Paul F. Lazarsfeld, and William N. McPhee, *Voting* (Chicago: University of Chicago Press, 1954), p. 175; Gerald H. Kramer, "The Effects of Precinct-Level Canvassing on Voting Behavior," *Public Opinion Quarterly* 34 (Winter 1970), pp. 560–72; Doris A. Graber, *Mass Media and American Politics*, 3rd ed. (Washington, D.C.: Congressional Quarterly Press, 1989), chap. 6.

and [they] ... avoid contacting opposition voters."[3] Thus, campaigns devote their efforts to reinforcing partisans, trying to sway the undecideds, and making sure that friendly voters register and go to the polls. They consign few resources to efforts to convert opponents.[4] Our findings, reported in Tables 6-1 and 6-2, confirm this element of party strategy. Political parties are about 5.3 percent more likely to contact strong partisans in presidential election years, and about 7.2 percent more likely to contact the party faithful in midterm election years. Similarly, the parties are 1.9 percent more likely to contact the households of labor union members. The logic is clear. Partisans and unionists are easy to identify. The party faithful appear on lists of previous contacts, have voted in party primaries, and have often been party activists in the past; labor unions have long been affiliated with the Democratic Party. Partisans and unionists, likewise, are quite likely to participate, as we have already seen. And, of course, given the stability and power of partisan identification and the historic partisan allegiances of organized labor, the political parties know how they are likely to vote. The behavior of party acolytes holds few surprises, and political campaigns like nothing more than to minimize surprises.[5]

Second, political parties target people who are centrally located within social networks. The well connected, for one, are easier to reach. Homeowners, churchgoers, and long-time residents, for instance, are easier for parties to find than the footloose and fancy-free: They are more likely to have personal relationships with party activists, to belong to organizations that candidates visit, and to

---

[3] Kramer, "The Effects of Precinct-Level Canvassing," p. 572.
[4] David E. Price and Michael Lupfer, "Volunteers for Gore: The Impact of a Precinct-Level Canvass in Three Tennessee Cities," *Journal of Politics* 35 (May 1973), pp. 410–38; Robert Huckfeldt and John Sprague, "Political Parties and Electoral Mobilization: Political Structure, Social Structure, and the Party Canvass," *American Political Science Review* 86 (March 1992), pp. 70–86.
[5] Huckfeldt and Sprague, "Political Parties and Electoral Mobilization"; Angus Campbell, Philip E. Converse, Warren E. Miller, and Donald E. Stokes, *The American Voter* (New York: John Wiley and Sons, 1960), chap. 6. For a revealing look at the electoral relationships between the labor unions and political parties in three cities, see J. David Greenstone, *Labor in American Politics* (Chicago: University of Chicago Press, 1977).

appear on "in-house" lists of past activists, contributors, and contacts. The well connected are also better placed to pass mobilization along. Homeowners, churchgoers, and long-time residents simply know more other people. By contacting them, parties turn direct contact into ever widening circles of discussion and suggestion. The evidence also supports these claims. People who have lived in a community for most of their lives are 6.9 to 9.1 percent more likely to be contacted by a political party than people who are new to the community. Homeowners are 4.2 to 7.2 percent more likely to be mobilized than those who do not own their homes. Finally, people who attend religious services regularly are 3.6 to 6.3 percent more likely to be mobilized than people who are unchurched. Jesse Jackson's campaigns for the Democratic presidential nomination in 1984 and 1988, for example, worked through African-American churches to build an organization, recruit support, raise money, and register and encourage people to vote on election day. Pat Robertson pursued a parallel strategy through Protestant pentecostal congregations in his bid for the 1988 Republican nomination.[6]

Finally, political parties target the people who are most likely to respond by voting, persuading, volunteering, or contributing. In presidential years, Table 6-1 shows, political parties are 18.6 percent more likely to contact citizens with a college degree than those with only a grade school education. To give one example near to our hearts, friends of U.S. Representative David Price (D–N.C.) asked Price's fellow alumni from Yale's political science department to contribute to his 1988 reelection campaign. Likewise, in presiden-

---

[6]Aldon D. Morris, *The Origins of the Civil Rights Movement: Black Communities Organizing for Change* (New York: Free Press, 1984); Katherine Tate and Ronald E. Brown, "The Black Church and Political Participation Revisited," paper presented at the annual meeting of the Midwest Political Science Association, 1991; Sheila D. Collins, *The Rainbow Challenge* (New York: Monthly Review Press, 1986), p. 134; Ronald E. Brown and Monica Wolford, "Religious Resources and African American Political Action," paper presented at the annual meeting of the American Political Science Association, 1991; Clyde Wilcox, *God's Warriors: The Christian Right in Twentieth Century America* (Baltimore: Johns Hopkins University Press, 1992), chaps. 7–9; Allen D. Hertzke, "The Role of Churches in Political Mobilization: The Presidential Campaigns of Jesse Jackson and Pat Robertson," pp. 177–98 in Allan J. Cigler and Burdett A. Loomis, *Interest Group Politics*, 3rd ed. (Washington, D.C.: Congressional Quarterly Press, 1991).

tial years political parties are 9.5 percent more likely to contact the richest Americans than the poorest. In 1988, for example, the Bush for President Committee sponsored a series of luncheons for the Wall Street brokerage and investment community that, with very little effort, raised millions of dollars. Finally, in presidential years political parties are 22.1 percent more likely to contact the most experienced voters, those age sixty-five or older, than the least experienced voters, those eighteen years old. Candidate stops at retirement communities have become staples of presidential campaigns. In sum, political parties are more likely to contact the well educated, the wealthy, and the elderly, and the same pattern holds in midterm years (Table 6-2).

Equally, political parties bypass the people who cannot carry through on requests for electoral action. Before 1964, for instance, the states of the former Confederacy deprived African-Americans of their political rights through intimidation and legal proscription (as we will discuss in more detail later in this chapter). As our estimates show, before 1964 the political parties were 15.4 percent less likely to contact southern blacks than other Americans. The white supremacist parties of the southern states had no great interest in mobilizing black citizens, of course, but even if they had, it would have been wasted effort—blacks in Dixie were not allowed to take part anyway. In similar fashion, the political parties were about 4.4 percent less likely to mobilize women who reached voting age before 1920, the year in which women were first allowed to vote nationwide. Evidently, party strategists reasoned that presuffrage female voters were already socialized to the idea that politics was for men and were accordingly less likely to vote. The irony of the logic, however, was that it became self-fulfilling. As we found in Chapter 5, women were in fact no less likely to take part in electoral politics than any other citizens. The whole difference was that they were not encouraged by the political parties to take part.[7]

---

[7] It is quite possible that the parties learned the right lesson about presuffrage women voters in the 1920s but failed to update their information. All of the women affected in our earliest sample were in their sixties, seventies, and eighties in 1956, and so they had spent much more of their adult lives with the right to vote than without it. They were perhaps very differently socialized than the large cohort of women who were already in middle age at the time of the Nineteenth Amendment. Women's behavior, that is, changed after the parties' expectations were set.

The logic of party targeting, in sum, conforms to expectations. Political parties contact the people they expect to support them, who occupy central positions socially, and who are likely to respond by taking part.

Timing Mobilization

The scarcity of party resources not only requires parties to target their efforts strategically, it also demands that they time them strategically. The whole purpose of campaigns is to win elections. Consequently, the main criterion parties use to apportion resources is very simple: How much do we need to do to win? Political parties are most likely to mobilize when elections are closely contested—that is, when more voters, more persuaders, more workers, and more contributors stand a chance to make a real difference to who wins and who loses. Party effort is proportional to electoral necessity.

This simple rule captures the essence of party strategy. Consider elections headlined by presidential contests. Political parties contact about 1.3 percent more of the electorate in the midst of close presidential campaigns than in the course of landslide elections (Table 6-1). In the razor-close contest between John F. Kennedy and Richard M. Nixon in 1960, for example, party workers in Mayor Richard J. Daley's Chicago hustled voters (both the quick and the dead) to the polls right up until closing time. In the record-breaking victory of Lyndon B. Johnson over Barry Goldwater in 1964, in contrast, the Johnson campaign had to go to great lengths to guard against complacency.

Even in the absence of tight presidential races, political parties mobilize around other tough-fought campaigns. Parties are 3.9 percent more likely to mobilize citizens in districts with the most competitive races for the U.S. House of Representatives: seats for which no incumbent is running. On the other side, parties are 4.7 percent less likely to contact voters in districts with the least competitive races for the House: races in which candidates run unopposed. Finally, parties are 2.1 percent more likely to contact voters in states in which the most important statewide official, the governor, is up for election. In presidential years, then, political parties mobilize when elections are up for grabs, when greater public involvement stands the best chance of tipping the outcome. [8]

Parties rise equally to the occasion in midterm years. Forced to choose between races for the U.S. Senate, for the U.S. House, and for the governor's mansion, political parties focus their efforts on the toss-ups—the races that the pundits rate as too close to call. [9] In midterm elections between 1974 and 1986, parties were 1.7 percent more likely to mobilize voters in states with highly competitive races for governor. (See Table 6-2.) They were 7.5 percent more likely to contact people living in states with very close contests for senator. Finally, they were 5.5 percent more likely to mobilize people living in districts with highly contested races for House seats.[10]

Political parties, in short, time their efforts for maximum effect. They muster their forces to vote, to volunteer, and to contribute in the most intense campaigns, in elections where every little bit can make a difference. They bear down in the hard ones, and they coast through the easy and the hopeless ones.

The Impact of Party Mobilization

The political parties' efforts to mobilize have considerable effect. When parties make the effort, the people they contact are far more likely to participate in electoral politics than the people they pass over. As shown in Figure 6-2, people the Democrats and Republicans mobilize in the course of a presidential election campaign are

---

[8] On incumbency and electoral competitiveness, see Gary C. Jacobson, *The Politics of Congressional Elections,* 3rd ed. (New York: HarperCollins, 1992), chap. 3.

[9] Our pundits are the experts at *Congressional Quarterly,* who handicap every race for national and statewide office.

[10] Competitiveness is also the key to understanding the lethargic party mobilization in the southern states: As shown in Tables 6-1 and 6-2, political parties are about 4 percent less likely to contact southern voters in both presidential and midterm elections. Even to the present day, the South is the region with the weakest political parties and the least intense party competition. In many of the contests for which we do not have information—races for lieutenant governor, attorney general, secretary of state, and state legislatures—Democratic candidates still run unopposed in November.

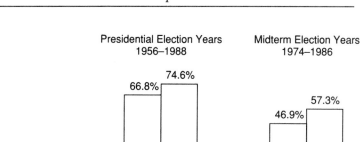

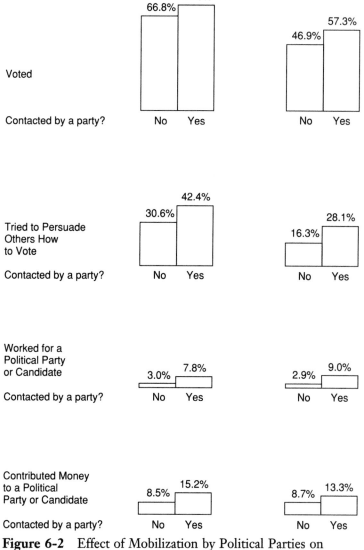

Figure 6-2   Effect of Mobilization by Political Parties on Participation in Electoral Politics, 1956–1988.

Source: Appendix D.

7.8 percent more likely to vote, 11.8 percent more likely to try to persuade others, 4.8 percent more likely to work for a party or candidate, and 6.7 percent more likely to make a financial contribution to a campaign.[11] Likewise, people the parties mobilize for midterm election campaigns are 10.4 percent more likely to turn out, 11.8 percent more likely to persuade, 6.1 percent more likely to volunteer, and 4.6 percent more likely to hand over cash.[12] These findings join a wealth of evidence that party mobilization increases turnout in local, state,[13] and national elections.[14]

[11] Our statistical model does not assume a simultaneous relationship between contact and participation. The real statistical problem, we believe, is not simultaneity but our unavoidable failure to include an unobserved variable—the parties' estimates of the likelihood that each person will participate if asked. In practice, we think the consequences for the consistency of our estimates are relatively small. We have already included in each equation most of the objective indicators that parties might rely on in forming their estimates, except for one: past involvement. Given the modest continuity in participation that we documented in Chapter 3, knowing who took part last time might not necessarily be a good guide to who might participate this time.

[12] At election time, political parties, candidates, and citizens' groups also mobilize people to register and vote. These efforts boost voter turnout, though not by much. The 1984, 1986, and 1988 National Election Studies asked respondents if during the campaign anyone had talked to them about registering or getting out to vote. A third of the electorate reported being contacted in each of these years, and citizens who were mobilized to register or vote were 3 percent more likely to cast a ballot in the 1984 and 1988 presidential elections and 5 percent more likely to do so in 1986. Mobilization to register and vote has a slightly greater effect on people who otherwise do not have the personal resources to overcome the hurdles of voter registration and get themselves to the polls on election day: the poor, those with few years of formal schooling, blacks, Puerto Ricans, and Mexican-Americans. See Bruce E. Cain and Ken McCue, "The Efficacy of Registration Drives," *Journal of Politics* 47 (November 1985), pp. 1221–30; Carole J. Uhlaner, "Rational Turnout: The Neglected Role of Groups," *American Journal of Political Science* 33 (May 1989), pp. 390–422.

[13] Gosnell's experiments found that citizens who received mailed appeals encouraging them to vote were about 9 percent more likely to turn out in the 1924 and 1925 Chicago aldermanic elections. Harold F. Gosnell, *Getting Out the Vote: An Experiment in the Stimulation of Voting* (Chicago: University of Chicago Press, 1927). Eldersveld's experiments (singly and with Dodge) demonstrated that personal contact increased turnout in the Ann Arbor, Michigan, municipal elections of 1953 and 1954. Samuel J. Eldersveld and Richard W. Dodge, "Personal Contact or Mail Propaganda? An Experiment in Voting and Attitude Change," pp. 532–42 in Daniel Katz, Dorwin Cartwright, Samuel Eldersveld, and Alfred M. Lee, eds., *Public Opinion and Propaganda* (New York: Dryden Press, 1954); Samuel J. Eldersveld, "Experimental Propaganda Techniques and Voting Behavior," *American Political Science Review*

Naturally enough, because so many people vote, party mobilization has its largest effect on the probability that people who are otherwise least likely to turn out—blacks, Puerto Ricans, Mexican-Americans, the poor, and the least educated—actually will turn out to vote.[15] Correspondingly, because so few people persuade, volunteer, and contribute, party mobilization has its largest effect on the probability that people who are otherwise most likely to participate

---

50 (March 1956), pp. 154–65. Blydenburgh's experiments found that telephone and personal contact boosted turnout rates in local legislative races in Monroe County, New York, in 1967. John C. Blydenburgh, "A Controlled Experiment to Measure the Effects of Personal Contact Campaigning," *Midwest Journal of Political Science* 15 (May 1971), pp. 365–81. Receipt of campaign literature increased turnout in state and local elections in Ohio in 1986. Gregory A. Caldeira, Aage R. Clausen, and Samuel C. Patterson, "Partisan Mobilization and Electoral Participation," *Electoral Studies* 9 (September 1990), pp. 191–204. Carton demonstrated, finally, that community leaders who engaged in voter contacting activities were able to increase voter turnout in a Detroit city income tax referendum. Paul Carton, *Mobilizing the Black Community: The Effects of Personal Contact Campaigning on Black Voters* (Washington, D.C.: Joint Center for Political Studies, 1984).

[14]Berelson and colleagues found that contact with a party increased turnout in the 1948 presidential election by about 8 percent. Berelson, Lazarsfeld, and McPhee, *Voting*, pp. 174–75. Kramer found that citizens contacted by one of the parties or candidates were about 30 percent more likely to vote in the 1952, 1956, 1960, and 1964 presidential elections. Kramer, "The Effects of Precinct-Level Canvassing." Huckfeldt and Sprague found that contact with a political party increases participation in electoral activities beyond voting. Huckfeldt and Sprague, "Political Parties and Electoral Mobilization." Contact with a party or candidate also stimulates voter turnout in presidential primaries and in congressional elections. See Barbara Norrander, "Turnout in the 1988 Presidential Primaries: Testing Alternative Models," paper presented at the annual meeting of the Midwest Political Science Association, 1989; Michael Lupfer and David E. Price, "On the Merits of Face-to-Face Campaigning," *Social Science Quarterly* 53 (December 1972), pp. 534–43; Price and Lupfer, "Volunteers for Gore."

[15]This conclusion is consistent with the findings that have emerged from a number of case studies. Lupfer and Price found a door-to-door canvass in a congressional campaign to be most effective in stimulating turnout in low-income and in black precincts. Lupfer and Price, "On the Merits of Face-to-Face Campaigning," p. 539; Price and Lupfer, "Volunteers for Gore," p. 434. Carton found that community leadership activity around the Detroit income tax campaign had greater effects among the poor. Carton, *Mobilizing the Black Community*. Also see Sidney Verba, Norman H. Nie, and Jae-on Kim, *Participation and Political Equality: A Seven-Nation Comparison* (New York: Cambridge University Press, 1978), chap. 5.

in other electoral activities—whites, the wealthy, and the well educated—actually will more extensively take part in elections.[16]

Contact with political parties promotes participation by several different routes. Contact with party workers, perhaps, reshapes people's perceptions and changes people's attitudes about the parties, the candidates, the election, and the efficacy of political action. By this line of reasoning, party appeals for support deepen citizens' affection for the parties and their candidates. They elevate voters' concern about the outcome of the election. They frame people's perceptions about the closeness of elections and the need for personal involvement. They enhance citizens' belief in their own political efficacy. Mobilization by political parties, in this view, works indirectly. It fosters perceptions and beliefs that promote political involvement.

As plausible as these arguments seem, none proves to have much force when put to a test.[17] Contact with political parties causes people to evaluate the parties and the candidates only 3 percent more positively. Mobilization by political parties moves people to become only 6 percent more liable to care about the outcome of the election. The efforts of political parties make people only 2 percent more likely to see the fall presidential election as a cliffhanger. Finally, contact with the parties lifts people's internal efficacy by only 5 percent and raises people's external efficacy by only 3 percent—statistically significant effects, to be sure, but not very big ones.

---

[16]This follows statistically from the assumptions that underlie probit analysis: Because of the shape of the cumulative normal density function, independent variables have the greatest effect on people who are on the cusp of participation and the least effect on people who are either certain to participate or certain not to participate. The statistical assumption, however, makes good substantive sense. Political parties clearly cannot convert people who have very little interest in taking part, no matter how hard they try, but they can prevail upon people who are already interested.

[17]In presidential election years we estimated the marginal effect of being contacted by a party on each of these perceptions, controlling for the demographic attributes of the respondent. We used ordinary least squares to estimate the equations for the perceived closeness of the election, feelings of external efficacy, and evaluations of the parties and their candidates; we used probit to estimate the equations for internal efficacy and concern over election outcomes.

Mobilization by political parties, in short, does not do much to change people's perceptions of the relative costs and benefits of participation in electoral politics. All told, barely a tenth of the total impact that party mobilization has on electoral participation stems from its effect on people's perceptions about the candidates, parties, and elections.[18] The rest results from two other processes.

First, party mobilization underwrites the costs of political participation. Party workers inform people about upcoming elections, tell them where and when they can register and vote, supply them with applications for absentee ballots, show them the locations of campaign headquarters, and remind them of imminent rallies and meetings. Campaigns drop by to pick up donations, telephone reminders on the day of the election, and drive the lazy, the harried, the immobile, and the infirm to the polls.

The 1986 reelection campaign of Republican representative Frank Wolf in northern Virginia illustrates these principles at work. The Wolf campaign began by merging the district's voter registration rolls with the state's Republican voter list to identify a pool of Republicans who were eligible to vote in the district. Campaign workers contacted over 25,000 of these households. If citizens said they supported Wolf, the campaign asked them to work for the campaign and offered to supply them with absentee ballots. In the weeks before the election, the campaign reestablished contact with every household that contained a Wolf supporter, and in the final six days of the campaign it sent postcards to remind them to vote. On election day, the campaign posted observers at the polling places and had them check off voters' names as they cast their ballots. Starting at two o'clock in the afternoon, staff and volunteers contacted the supporters who had not yet voted and urged them to get to the polls. Throughout the campaign, Wolf's team did everything it could to coax, assist, and bother people to turn out for Wolf.[19]

---

[18]This estimate represents the proportion of the total effect of party mobilization on participation that occurs indirectly through these attitudes. This estimate, if anything, may be overstated if these political perceptions are themselves causes of the likelihood of being mobilized.

[19]Thomas Herity and John D. Brady, "Saving Money with a PC, " *Campaigns and Elections* (March/April 1988), p. 53.

Second, mobilization occasions the creation of selective social incentives for political involvement. It taps networks of family, friends, neighbors, co-workers, and associates and exploits the complex relationships of social identity, expectation, and obligation. People participate not because parties ask them, but because people they know and respect ask them.

Electoral campaigns go to great lengths to engage social networks and to capitalize on the bonds of friendship. They detail volunteers to canvass their own neighborhoods and workplaces. They encourage supporters to sponsor "watch parties" and "coffee klatches," the political equivalents of Tupperware parties, for a little socializing and persuasion.[20] They call on their backers to contact old army buddies, business associates, and college classmates to solicit campaign funds.[21] The basic idea is simple: to give weight to requests for assistance by presenting them through people to whom it is difficult to say "no." [22]

Absent access to real friendship, moreover, campaigns mimic social intimacy. Direct mailers, for example, send many million solicitations to people whom candidates would not know from Adam, but they try their best to fabricate a sense of familiarity and closeness between the candidates and potential contributors. They craft appeals to make recipients feel as if they have received letters from friends in desperate need: "I need help from my friends," "Can I count on you again?" and "Would you do a special favor for me?" are common solicitation phrases.[23] "Wife letters," first used on a

---

[20] Supporters of Walter Mondale's bid for the Democratic presidential nomination raised $1.2 million through 6,000 "watch parties" in 1983. U.S. Senator Al Gore (D–Tenn.) used the same technique to generate over $50,000 in his 1984 Senate campaign. See Hal Malchow and Fran May, "Television Watch Parties: 1984's Fund Raising Innovation," *Campaigns and Elections* (Fall 1985), pp. 18–22.

[21] For a fascinating look at the variety of campaign styles, in which personal contacts loom large, see Richard F. Fenno, Jr., *Home Style: House Members in Their Districts* (Boston: Little, Brown and Co., 1978).

[22] One measure of the degree to which party mobilization taps into social networks is that it has its largest effect on the probability that people will attempt to influence the voting choices of others.

[23] Larry J. Sabato, *Campaign and Elections* (Glenview, Ill.: Scott, Foresman/Little, Brown, 1989), pp. 96–97.

mass scale by Richard Viguerie, the conservative godfather of direct mail, use the very same logic: Candidates' wives send "personal" letters to female constituents asking support. Through the miracle of the autopen, the missives appear to be hand-written. Their content typically centers on the candidate's family, even the family's pet; they sometimes enclose family snapshots.[24] As cynical as they sound, these "personal" contacts work. They, like true personal contacts, create a sense of identification and obligation, a bond of friendship.

Party mobilization is a powerful inducement to participation in electoral politics. By subsidizing information and by creating social connections, political campaigns lower the cost and increase the benefits of voting, persuading, volunteering, and contributing. As we shall demonstrate in Chapter 7, the parties' strategic decisions not to mobilize account for a substantial portion of the recent decline of citizen involvement in American elections.

Mobilization by Electoral Campaigns

In any electoral campaign, the political parties are not the only players who take the field. More and more, candidates for national, state, and local offices build their own campaign organizations apart from the Democratic and Republican parties. Interest groups, promoters, and people with axes to grind pursue their own agendas in elections, sometimes in tandem with the campaigns and sometimes independently. Finally, the print and broadcast media both cover and configure the election campaigns.

The activities of campaigns, interest groups, and the media, like the activities of political parties, promote electoral involvement. They, too, underwrite the costs of political participation, especially the costs of information. They, too, occasion the creation of social incentives for activism. Even at their most neutral, the media publicize news that informs people, personalities that engage people, causes that inspire people, appeals that galvanize people, and

---

[24]Larry J. Sabato, *The Rise of Political Consultants* (New York: Basic Books, 1981), p. 245.

controversies that entangle people in discussions with their families, friends, neighbors, and co-workers.

Campaigns and issue advocates, it stands to reason, operate by the same strategic logic as the political parties: They engage only as much of their scarce resources as necessary. They, like parties, expend more effort when more is at stake and when outcomes hang in the balance. Clearly, the media's attention follows, if for a slightly different reason: Close, conflictual, and important elections are simply more engrossing both to them and to their consumers.[25]

Presidential Campaigns and Midterm Campaigns

These strategic considerations go a long way toward accounting for the differences in voter participation between presidential and midterm election years. First, the presidential campaigns have resources at their disposal that are an order of magnitude larger than the resources of any other candidates. Political campaigns spend twice as much in the aggregate in presidential elections as in midterm elections, and the volume of campaign propaganda produced by presidential candidates all but drowns out everything else. Second, presidential elections engage activists as no other elections do. They offer interest groups the prospect of commitment from the most important actor in national government, and they present promoters of causes with the opportunity to gain a national platform for their convictions. Finally, presidential elections captivate the media as no other elections do. Press coverage is almost five times greater in presidential elections than in midterm elections.[26]

---

[25] In particular, the media are consumed with interest in the "horse-race" aspects of political campaigns, often to the exclusion of anything more substantive. See, for example, John Foley, Dennis A. Britton, and Eugene B. Everett, Jr., *Nominating a President: The Process and the Press* (New York: Praeger, 1980); Michael J. Robinson and Margaret A. Sheehan, *Over the Wire and on TV* (New York: Russell Sage Foundation, 1983).

[26] Thirty-nine percent of the stories that led off broadcasts of the CBS Evening News in the last eight weeks of the 1976, 1980, 1984, and 1988 presidential campaigns focused on the election; 20 percent of all the stories aired on the evening news reported on the election. In contrast, only 6 percent of the lead stories in the last eight weeks of the 1974, 1978, and 1982 midterm campaigns focused on the elections, and only 8 percent of all the stories aired reported on the contests.

Presidential contests, in short, are the quintessential "high stimulus" elections.[27] Unsurprisingly, then, voter turnout is some 15 percentage points higher in presidential years than in midterm years.

Competitive Presidential Campaigns

The same strategic rules suggest that campaigns, interest groups, and the media step up their exertions when the presidential campaign is a tight one and pace themselves when the outcome is a foregone conclusion, just as—we established earlier—political parties do. Likewise, the candidates' campaigns and supporters apportion their efforts to their needs: They contest every inch in campaigns that stand to be decided by tenths of percentage points, and they tacitly concede campaigns that look to be blowouts.[28] The media also cover competitive contests more intensely than runaways.[29] They stay attentive if the rivals are neck-and-neck down to the wire and grow bored if the dark horse pulls up lame in the back stretch.[30]

[27] Angus Campbell, "Surge and Decline: A Study of Electoral Change," *Public Opinion Quarterly* 24 (Fall 1960), pp. 397–418.

[28] Increasingly, the decision of whether to persevere or to withdraw is made not only by the campaigns. Contributors of electoral resources, especially money, carefully calculate candidates' viability, and they cut their losses when it appears they have backed losers. Once that happens, clearly, campaigns become strapped for resources for mobilization.

[29] Our analysis of the stories aired by the CBS Evening News in the eight weeks before the 1976 through 1988 presidential elections shows the following:

Year	Percentage Points Separating the Presidential Candidates in the Final Gallup Poll	Percentage of CBS Evening News Stories on the Campaign or Election
1976	1%	25%
1980	3	27
1984	18	11
1988	12	17

[30] Foley, Britton, and Everett, *Nominating a President;* Robinson and Sheehan, *Over the Wire and on TV.*

Table 6-3   Competitiveness of Presidential Campaigns,
1952–1988

Election	Candidates		Percentage Point Difference between Candidates in Final Gallup Poll
Year	Democratic	Republican	
1952	Stevenson	Eisenhower	2
1956	Stevenson	Eisenhower	19
1960	Kennedy	Nixon	2
1964	Johnson	Goldwater	28
1968	Humphrey	Nixon	1
1972	McGovern	Nixon	24
1976	Carter	Ford	1
1980	Carter	Reagan	3
1984	Mondale	Reagan	18
1988	Dukakis	Bush	12

Source: The Gallup Poll.

Presidential elections in the last half of the twentieth century
have offered a handful of cliff-hangers and an extraordinary number
of landslides. As shown in Table 6-3, the 1960 contest between John
Kennedy and Richard Nixon, and the 1976 contest between Gerald
Ford and Jimmy Carter, were dead heats going into election day.
At no time during the 1956 campaign, in contrast, was there much
doubt at all that Dwight D. Eisenhower would be reelected, and
the campaigns of Lyndon Johnson in 1964, Richard Nixon in 1972,
and Ronald Reagan in 1984 were blowouts of historic proportions.
When the votes were counted, Johnson won the largest percentage
of the popular vote ever recorded; Nixon won forty-nine of the
fifty states; and Reagan earned the largest popular vote ever
tallied.

As our analysis indicates, competitiveness at the top of the ticket
excites citizen participation across the board. The narrower the gap
between the two candidates in the final Gallup poll before the election, the greater the involvement in electoral politics. When elec-

tions are nail-biters, citizens are 3.0 percent more likely to vote, 7.8 percent more likely to attempt to persuade others, 1.0 percent more likely to work for a campaign, and 3.2 percent more likely to give a contribution to a campaign (see Table 5-1).[31]

Moreover, even with the existence of poll data, perceptions of the closeness of presidential elections vary from person to person: Some people think races are closer than surveys say, others think margins are wider. This may reflect ignorance, excitability, wishful thinking, accurate assessments of the leanings of friends and localities, or sober recollections of the inconstancy of public opinion

---

[31]There is ample evidence that electoral competition increases participation in a variety of settings. It affects voter turnout in gubernatorial elections and in elections to the U.S. House of Representatives. Samuel C. Patterson and Gregory A. Caldeira, "Getting Out the Vote: Participation in Gubernatorial Elections," *American Political Science Review* 77 (September 1983), pp. 675–89; Franklin D. Gilliam, "Influences on Voter Turnout for U.S. House Elections in Non-Presidential Years," *Legislative Studies Quarterly* 10 (August 1985), pp. 339–51; Gregory A. Caldeira, Samuel C. Patterson, and Gregory A. Markko, "The Mobilization of Voters in Congressional Elections," *Journal of Politics* 47 (May 1985), pp. 490–509. Close competition between the parties heightens interest in politics and increases turnout. Lester W. Milbrath and M. L. Goel, *Political Participation: How and Why Do People Get Involved in Politics?* (Chicago: Rand McNally, 1977), pp. 132–33; Harold W. Stanley, *Voter Mobilization and the Politics of Race* (New York: Praeger, 1987), p. 129; Gregory A. Caldeira and Samuel C. Patterson, "Contextual Influences on Participation in U.S. State Legislative Elections," *Legislative Studies Quarterly* 7 (August 1982), pp. 359–82; Gary W. Cox, "Closeness and Turnout: A Methodological Note," *Journal of Politics* 50 (August 1988), pp. 768–75; D. T. Denver and H. T. G. Hands, "Marginality and Turnout in British General Elections," *British Journal of Political Science* 4 (January 1974), pp. 17–35; Patterson and Caldeira, "Getting Out the Vote"; G. Bingham Powell, *Contemporary Democracies* (Cambridge: Harvard University Press, 1982), pp. 111–32. The decline in party competition at the turn of the century is part of the explanation for the decline of voter turnout in U.S. elections in the twentieth century. Paul Kleppner, *Who Voted? The Dynamics of Electoral Turnout, 1870–1980* (New York: Praeger, 1982); Michael E. McGerr, *The Decline of Popular Politics: The American North, 1865–1928* (New York: Oxford University Press, 1986). Finally, crossnational studies have demonstrated that electoral participation increases with party polarization. Markus M. L. Crepaz, "The Impact of Party Polarization and Postmaterialism on Voter Turnout," *European Journal of Political Research* 18 (March 1990), pp. 183–205.

polls. Regardless, individuals' perceptions of the competitiveness of elections also affect their involvement in campaigns. Citizens who think the presidential election is close are about 1.6 percent more likely to vote and about 1 percent more likely to take part in each of the other kinds of electoral activity (Table 5-1).[32] The effect is a small one, but as we will see in Chapter 7, changes in the perceived closeness of elections have in fact contributed to the pattern of electoral participation over the last four decades.

Presidential elections, in sum, mobilize greater citizen involvement in electoral politics, particularly when they are competitive. The activities of the campaigns, the media, and issue advocates inform people. The activities excite people, reinforce their social identities, and structure their interactions with family, neighbors, co-workers, and friends.

Although races for the White House are easily the most important and the most engaging campaigns, candidates for governor, senator, representative, and other offices wage their own campaigns alongside them, essentially independently even in presidential election years. Gubernatorial, senatorial, and congressional campaigns crowd the political landscape, each doing its best to rally citizens to take part. Like the presidential campaigns and their surrounding

---

[32] These findings clearly refute the "minimax regret" model that Ferejohn and Fiorina have advanced. John Ferejohn and Morris Fiorina, "Closeness Counts Only in Horseshoes and Dancing," *American Political Science Review* 69 (September 1975), pp. 920–25. Our findings are also at odds with the "expected utility" model, which argues that perceptions of the closeness of the election outcome should interact with the perceived benefits of voting: The closeness of the contest matters only when people think they will benefit from participating. Anthony Downs, *An Economic Theory of Democracy* (New York: Harper & Row, 1957), pp. 260–61; William H. Riker and Peter C. Ordeshook, *An Introduction to Positive Political Theory* (Englewood Cliffs, N.J.: Prentice-Hall, 1973), pp. 62–63. We found evidence of interactions between perceived benefits and perceptions of the closeness of the election outcome in none of the four electoral participation equations. Also see Angus Campbell, Philip E. Converse, Warren E. Miller, and Donald E. Stokes, *The American Voter* (New York: John Wiley and Sons, 1960), p. 99; Orley Ashenfelter and Stanley Kelley, Jr., "Determinants of Participation in Presidential Elections," *Journal of Law and Economics* 18 (December 1976), pp. 695–731; Milbrath and Goel, *Political Participation*, p. 137; and Howard L. Reiter, "Why Is Turnout Down?," *Public Opinion Quarterly* 43 (Fall 1979), pp. 297–311.

swarms of supporters, they and their backers engage in both direct and indirect mobilization: They provide information about the contestants and the issues, tell people where they should vote, furnish transportation to campaign events and the polls, advertise on television, on radio, and in newspapers, and ask citizens to contribute their time, money, and energy to campaign efforts.

Gubernatorial, senatorial, and congressional campaigns, obviously, affect smaller and more select groups of people and operate by different schedules than presidential campaigns. In the places and times they are operating, they mobilize public involvement in national elections.

Gubernatorial Campaigns

The proportion of the electorate exposed to a competitive race for governor has changed dramatically over time. To insulate gubernatorial elections from the effects of national politics, seventeen states rescheduled their gubernatorial elections out of presidential years between 1952 and 1988. States implemented most of the changes by lengthening gubernatorial terms from two to four years and, in doing so, dropping the election held in presidential election years. In the same period, the number of gubernatorial elections that were uncontested in November declined, especially in the South. The net effect of these changes, summarized in Figure 6-3 (see p. 184), is that over the last four decades fewer and fewer Americans were exposed to contested gubernatorial elections in presidential years. Nearly half the 1952 electorate saw contested gubernatorial elections; only 12 percent of the 1988 electorate did.

The presence or absence of contested gubernatorial campaigns significantly affects voter turnout. Citizens exposed to active gubernatorial campaigns in presidential election years are 5.0 percent more likely to vote,[33] even though gubernatorial elections do not

---

[33] These findings extend the work of Wolfinger and Rosenstone and Boyd that found that citizens exposed to gubernatorial elections were more likely to vote in the 1972 and 1980 elections. Raymond E. Wolfinger and Steven J. Rosenstone, *Who Votes?* (New Haven: Yale University Press, 1980); Richard W. Boyd, "Election Calendars and Voter Turnout," *American Politics Quarterly* 14 (January 1986), pp. 89–104.

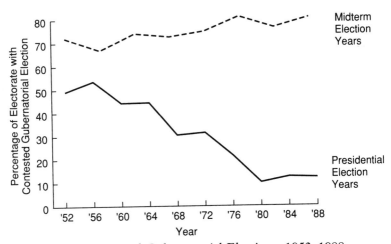

Figure 6-3   Contested Gubernatorial Elections, 1952–1988.
Source: Congressional Quarterly, *Guide to U.S. Elections,* 2nd ed. (Washington, D.C.: Congressional Quarterly, 1985); Richard Scammon, *America Votes* (Washington, D.C.: Government Affairs Institute, 1986, 1990).

have a significant effect on any of the other three forms of electoral participation (Table 5-1). Hence, as we will see in more detail in Chapter 7, the changes in the electoral calendar that removed gubernatorial elections from presidential years are one part of the explanation for decline in voter turnout since the 1960s. Competitions for crucial votes in contested races for governor spill over to mobilize voters in other campaigns.[34]

Senatorial and Congressional Campaigns

Likewise, competitions for votes in senatorial and congressional races boost citizen involvement in midterm election years. Just as closely fought campaigns for Congress induced parties to mobilize voters, the more competitive the race for Congress the more intense

[34]Richard W. Boyd, "Decline of U.S. Voter Turnout: Structural Explanations," *American Politics Quarterly* 9 (April 1981), pp. 133–59; Boyd, "Election Calendars."

the efforts of campaigns and their legions of followers to mobilize midterm voters.[35]

Motivated by real hopes of victory, campaigns pour extra resources into contests for open House seats: Open-seat contests attract the most experienced candidates, raise and spend the most money, capture the most media attention, and have the least certain outcomes.[36] The extra resources motivate citizens to take part; in midterm years, people who live in congressional districts in which incumbents are not contestants are 3.7 percent more likely to turn out to vote and 1.7 percent more likely to work for a party or candidate (Table 5-2). Motivated by real tastes of victory, campaigns devote additional resources to races so competitive that experts rate them toss-ups. Accordingly, citizens presented with these highly competitive races for the U.S. House are 6.0 percent more likely to vote and 2.5 percent more likely to contribute money to a party or candidate, and citizens presented with equally competitive races for the U.S. Senate are 3.7 percent more likely to give financial donations to electoral campaigns. Finally, careful not to waste their efforts, campaigns earmark fewer resources for uncontested House races. Their withdrawal reduces the likelihood of voting in midterm elections by 4.0 percent.[37]

Presidential Primary Campaigns

Presidential primary campaigns, like other electoral campaigns, create electoral organizations and draw media coverage that mobilize

---

[35] Some scholars have found that higher levels of campaign spending in congressional and gubernatorial elections stimulate higher voter turnout. Caldeira, Patterson, and Markko, "The Mobilization of Voters"; Patterson and Caldeira, "Getting Out the Vote"; P. A. Dawson and J. E. Zinser, "Political Finance and Participation in Congressional Elections," *Annals of the American Academy of Political and Social Science* 425 (May 1976), pp. 59–73; Gilliam, "Influences on Voter Turnout." More abundant resources allow campaigns more easily to mobilize voters, particularly through the media.

[36] Gary Jacobson, *The Politics of Congressional Elections*, 3rd ed. (New York: HarperCollins, 1992).

[37] Also see Caldeira, Patterson, and Markko, "The Mobilization of Voters"; and Gilliam, "Influences on Voter Turnout."

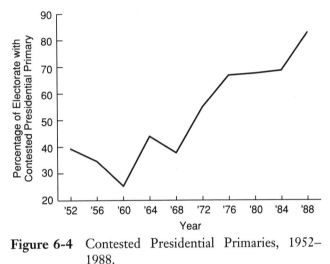

Figure 6-4　Contested Presidential Primaries, 1952–1988.

Source: Congressional Quarterly, *Guide to U.S. Elections,* 2nd ed. (Washington, D.C.: Congressional Quarterly, 1985); *Congressional Quarterly Weekly Report,* July 9, 1988, p. 1894; August 13, 1988, p. 2254.

citizens to take part. Nomination battles, in fact, are often as competitive and as interesting, and sometimes more competitive and more interesting, than general elections.

Since the 1960s, the proportion of Americans who have been asked to participate in contested presidential primaries has doubled (Figure 6-4); and with more opportunities to participate, more people have done so. Many observers believe, however, that the expansion of the presidential primary system has not increased but has suppressed citizen involvement in the November election.[38]

Our analysis bears out their belief. After taking the other causes of turnout into account, citizens who live in states with competitive presidential primaries are 3.7 percent less likely to vote in

---

[38]Nelson W. Polsby, *Consequences of Party Reform* (New York: Oxford University Press, 1983), p. 141; Boyd, "Decline of U.S. Voter Turnout"; Boyd, "Election Calendars"; Jeffrey E. Cohen, "Change in Election Calendars and Turnout Decline: A Test of Boyd's Hypothesis," *American Politics Quarterly* 10 (April 1982), pp. 246–54.

the November general election than citizens who were not offered chances to vote earlier, in the primaries (Table 5-1).

Presidential primaries, it seems, severely tax the resources of both citizens and the campaigns that mobilize them. Unlike contested gubernatorial and congressional elections, which are concurrent with the general election, presidential primaries occur five to nine months earlier. With limited time, attention, and other resources, citizens who participate in the primary have less left over for the general. Even more important, resources that candidates, parties, and interest groups use in primaries are no longer available for mobilization in the general election. The structural change in the nominating process, by increasing the demands on the public's and the politicians' resources, also contributed to the decline in voter turnout in presidential elections since the 1960s.[39]

The paradox, of course, is that additional opportunities to participate reduced the probability that people would vote on any given occasion and thereby lowered the aggregate turnout in particular elections. The proliferation of election dates after the turn of the century, offering separate elections for local, state, and national offices, as well as for nomination and election, may well be part of the reason for the long-term decline of turnout since the 1890s, as Richard Boyd suggests.[40] Similarly, the profusion of elected offices in the United States may be one reason that turnout is lower than in nearly every other democracy. As V. O. Key pointed out years ago, "The American voter is marched to the polls far more frequently than are his counterparts elsewhere. In a single year there may be, at different times, municipal primaries, municipal elections, presidential primaries, primaries to nominate candidates for state offices, the presidential election, and perhaps a special election or so."[41] No country approaches the United States in the frequency and variety

---

[39]Boyd also found that separate state primaries as well as state runoff primaries further reduced turnout in the 1980 election. Our findings add credence to the general proposition that Boyd has advanced concerning the decline in turnout. Boyd, "Decline of U.S. Voter Turnout"; Boyd, "Election Calendars."

[40]Boyd, "Decline of U.S. Voter Turnout"; Boyd, "Election Calendars."

[41]V. O. Key, Jr., *Politics, Parties, and Pressure Groups*, 5th ed. (New York: Thomas Y. Crowell, 1964), p. 579.

of elections, and few countries approach the United States in the infrequency of its voters' involvement.[42] Vigorously contested campaigns for president, governor, senator, and representative, in sum, promote public involvement in American national elections. Campaign organizations and interest groups give out information and provide services that lighten some of the burdens of taking part. They likewise evoke social identities and access social networks in ways that heighten some of the rewards of taking part. In reporting their activities, finally, the media convey their messages and provide the grist for social discussion.

In planning their actions, political campaigns are just as strategic as political parties, moving their resources into uses that promise the greatest payoff, the greatest chance of victory. Where consecutive campaigns in primary and general elections sap mobilization efforts, the simultaneous and independent actions of presidential, gubernatorial, senatorial, and congressional campaigns create a sort of mobilization synergy. The activities of any one bring out more participants for all.

Mobilization by Social Movements: The Impact of the Civil Rights Movement

Beyond political parties and campaign organizations, other groups such as interest groups, community organizations, and social movements also struggle to move people to take part in politics. They not only recruit people to join or embrace their cause, they mobilize them to take part in a variety of political activities, voting and electoral campaigns among them.

Without much doubt, the civil rights movement was the most important social movement in the United States in this century, and with its special focus on securing political rights for African-Americans, its impact on electoral politics was especially profound.

---

[42] Ivor Crewe, "Electoral Participation," pp. 216–63 in David Butler, Howard R. Penniman, and Austin Ranney, eds., *Democracy at the Polls* (Washington, D.C.: American Enterprise Institute, 1981), p. 232.

The term *civil rights movement* describes a broad coalition of political, social, and religious organizations that engaged in a wide range of activities with the general aim of securing political, economic, and social equality for black Americans.[43] Although long-established national organizations, such as the National Association for the Advancement of Colored People (NAACP) and the Congress of Racial Equality (CORE), were part of the civil rights movement, the heart of the movement was community and regional organizations of more recent vintage such as the Southern Christian Leadership Conference (SCLC), founded in 1957, the Student Nonviolent Coordinating Committee (SNCC), founded in 1960, and the Voter Education Project (V.E.P.), founded in 1962.

The civil rights movement created an array of political tactics designed to challenge segregationist authority, to mobilize the rank and file, and to galvanize public opinion. It brought suits against statutes that discriminated against blacks. It sponsored bus boycotts, sit-ins, and freedom rides to desegregate public transportation, public accommodations, and municipal facilities. It brought boycotts against white businesses that discriminated in employment against blacks. It led marches and rallies to dramatize the cause of integration and black equality. It demonstrated to protest police brutality and violence against civil rights workers and leaders. It led marches on Washington to rally for equality and opportunity. It applied pressure to members of Congress for passage of civil rights acts in 1957, 1964, and 1965, and for passage of subsequent renewals. It lobbied presidents for vigorous enforcement of civil rights legislation and more aggressive civil rights agendas. It conducted voter registration

---

[43]There are a number of fine accounts of the civil rights movement, among them: Aldon D. Morris, *The Origins of the Civil Rights Movement: Black Communities Organizing for Change* (New York: Free Press, 1984); Steven F. Lawson, *Running for Freedom: Civil Rights and Black Politics in America Since 1941* (Philadelphia: Temple University Press, 1991), chaps. 3–4; Doug McAdam, *Political Process and the Development of Black Insurgency, 1930–1970* (Chicago: University of Chicago Press, 1982); Pat Watters and Reese Cleghorn, *Climbing Jacob's Ladder: The Arrival of Negroes in Southern Politics* (New York: Harcourt, Brace and World, 1967); Steven F. Lawson, *Black Ballots: Voting Rights in the South, 1944-1969* (New York: Columbia University Press, 1976); David J. Garrow, *Protest at Selma: Martin Luther King, Jr. and the Voting Rights Act of 1965* (New Haven: Yale University Press, 1978).

drives to overcome discriminatory election laws and to reenfranchise African-American citizens. It recruited black candidates to run for public office. It mobilized black voters and campaign activists to influence party platforms and to elect blacks and sympathetic whites.

From small, isolated beginnings, civil rights movement activities grew steadily in number and extent during the late 1950s and 1960s (Figure 6-5).[44] In the early 1950s, the movement sponsored a few dozen actions a year, but by the end of the decade it initiated well over a hundred. As its efforts to break the political and economic domination of white Southerners grew more intense, its activity increased dramatically, to 440 actions annually by the first half of the 1960s. In the late 1960s, confronted by a powerful white backlash and riddled by internal factions, the civil rights movement's energy began to wane. By the 1970s, its heyday was clearly past, with fewer than 100 actions by the middle of the decade.

In its early years, the civil rights movement concentrated its efforts in the eleven former Confederate states of the South, initiating almost 80 percent of its actions in Dixie. Over time, however, the movement became increasingly national in scope and character. Between 1961 and 1965, 40 percent of its activities took place outside the South, and between 1966 and 1970, fully 70 percent of all civil rights movement events occurred outside of the region.[45]

As the civil rights movement matured and succeeded, its agenda evolved. Almost 90 percent of its actions in the 1950s had as their goal the attainment of legal equality, political power, and integration of accommodations, transportation, housing, education, facilities, and services. The same issues were the focus of two-thirds of the activities initiated between 1961 and 1965. After the passage

---

[44]Our measure of the civil rights movement activities is taken from the work of McAdam, *Political Process.* McAdam's measure is based on a meticulous coding of news stories about civil rights movement–initiated activities that appeared in the *New York Times Index* over a forty-year period. He describes the details of his coding procedures in his Appendix 1, where he also discusses some of the limitations of these data as well as their advantages over available alternatives. We were unable to uncover data sources that represent a more thorough tally of civil rights movement actions than McAdam's.

[45]McAdam, *Political Process*, Tables 7.2 and 8.3.

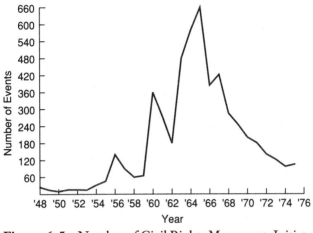

Figure 6-5   Number of Civil Rights Movement–Initiated Events, 1948–1976.
Source: Doug McAdam, *Political Process and the Development of Black Insurgency 1930–1970* (Chicago: University of Chicago Press, p. 121).

of the Civil Rights Act of 1964 and the Voting Rights Act (VRA) of 1965, however, the agenda expanded. Having finally won national endorsement of its claims to the full rights of citizenship for black Americans, the civil rights movement in the late 1960s devoted only a quarter of its efforts to the attainment of legal equality, political power, and integration of accommodations, facilities, and services. Instead, concern over white racism, police brutality, the general plight of black America, and dissension within the movement itself increasingly became its focus.[46]

[46]McAdam, *Political Process*, Tables 7.3 and 8.2. The institutional underpinnings of the civil rights movement also changed over time. During the early 1960s, more formal regional and national organizations began to supplement the indigenous local groups that were at the heart of the movement in the 1950s. Civil rights organizations greatly proliferated in number. Thus, although the NAACP, CORE, SNCC, and SCLC initiated nearly half of all civil rights movement actions in 1967, these organizations were responsible for less than 15 percent of all movement-initiated events three years later. McAdam, *Political Process*, pp. 182–86.

From its inception, then, one of the central goals of the civil rights movement was to secure full citizenship rights, particularly voting rights, for African-Americans, and its impact on the exercise of political rights—among both blacks and whites—was substantial.

The civil rights movement mobilized black citizens both indirectly and directly. Through its bold and confrontational but pacific tactics, it increased political awareness, political efficacy, racial identity, social expectations, and acceptance of personal risk among black Americans. Through its lawsuits, protests, marches, and sit-ins, it brought down the discriminatory Jim Crow election laws that had barred blacks from participation in southern political life for over two generations. Finally, through its voter registration drives, protests, and marches, it registered blacks to vote, organized blacks as voting blocs, and forced political candidates to mobilize black citizens and to compete for their support.[47]

The civil rights movement's efforts to empower black voters did not go unchallenged by segregationist white authority. The white reaction to the movement was notably violent, marked by assaults, assassinations, and bombings. Together with intimidation of black voters, segregationists worked to foster white racial identity, to shape social expectations, and to register Southern white voters to counterbalance blacks' gains.[48] As Doug McAdam shows, the actions of

[47] See Watters and Cleghorn, *Climbing Jacob's Ladder,* especially chap. 3; Lawson, *Black Ballots,* chaps. 9–10; *V.E.P. News* 2 (January 1968), p. 1. The black panther symbol, for example, originated as an icon to mark the names of sympathetic candidates to those Southern black voters who were illiterate.

[48] Earl Black, *Southern Governors and Civil Rights: Racial Segregation as a Campaign Issue in the Second Reconstruction* (Cambridge: Harvard University Press, 1976), p. 326; William C. Havard "The South: A Shifting Perspective," pp. 3–36 in William C. Havard, ed., *The Changing Politics of the South* (Baton Rouge: Louisiana State University Press, 1972), p. 22. Governor George Wallace, for example, led white voter registration drives in Alabama in 1965 and 1970. Harold W. Stanley, *Voter Mobilization and the Politics of Race: The South and Universal Suffrage, 1952–1984* (New York: Praeger, 1987), p. 51. Similar counter-mobilizations occurred in Mississippi. Lester Salamon "Mississippi Postmortem: The 1971 Elections," *New South* 27 (Winter 1972), p. 45. Between 1964 and 1971, 4.4 million Southern whites registered to vote compared to only 1.5 million Southern blacks. Garrow, *Protest at Selma,* p. 302, note 33.

white supremacists and state and local governments in opposition to integration and black political rights matched the actions of the civil rights movement to mobilize black voters step for step.[49] We find, accordingly, that the civil rights movement increased participation in elections among both black and white voters.[50] The greater the number of civil rights activities, the higher the voter turnout (Figure 6-6). Even relatively small numbers of activities significantly increased participation. Citizens who experienced an average of five civil rights activities in the seven years before the election were 3 percent more likely to vote, and citizens who experienced ten activities a year were 5 percent more likely to vote. At the height of the civil rights movement in the mid-1960s, Southerners were about 7 percent more likely to vote than they would otherwise have been.[51] Corroborating impressions of backlash and countermobilization among white Americans, the movement's effect on white turnout was about as large as its effect on black turnout.[52]

The civil rights movement also increased party mobilization, boosting voter turnout indirectly. Citizens living in the South at the height of the movement were about 4.3 percent more likely to be contacted by a political party than they otherwise would have been (see Table 6-1). In the wake of the movement and its segregationist

---

[49]McAdam, *Political Process*, pp. 142–45, 172–77.

[50]We use the data reported by McAdam in his Tables 7.2 and 8.3 to measure the level of civil rights movement activity that occurred in the region in which each NES respondent lived. Thus, our analysis takes into account changes in the level of civil rights actions over time as well as differences in the level of activity across regions. Unfortunately, McAdam was unable to provide us with state-level data which would obviously have made these estimates more precise. (For more details on our coding of civil rights actions, see our Appendix B.)

[51]For a discussion of the impact of civil rights organizations on black voter registration before the enactment of the VRA, see Donald R. Matthews and James W. Prothro, *Negroes and the New Southern Politics* (New York: Harcourt, Brace and World, 1966), pp. 164–66.

[52]If we estimate separate coefficients to test for differential impact of civil rights movement mobilization on blacks and whites, we find that the probit coefficient for blacks is only .005 greater than the coefficient for whites. The probability that the civil rights movement mobilized blacks more than whites is only .59.

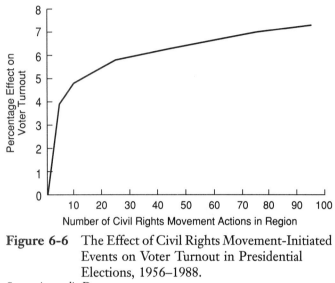

Figure 6-6   The Effect of Civil Rights Movement-Initiated
Events on Voter Turnout in Presidential
Elections, 1956–1988.
Source: Appendix D.

backlash, party strategists discovered hay to be made. As parties
saw more and more people poised to take action as racial tensions
mounted, they increased the intensity of their efforts to steer public
involvement.

The impact of racial confrontation on voter participation is not
peculiar either to the South or to the 1960s. In Chicago in 1983,
for example, fierce mobilization to support and oppose the mayoral
candidacy of U.S. Representative Harold Washington, an African-
American, boosted black turnout 17 percentage points and white
turnout 13 percentage points above the levels they had reached in
a less-heated mayoral contest four years before.[53] In Louisiana in
1991, churches, business organizations, civil rights groups, political
parties, and candidates banded together to oppose the gubernatorial candidacy of former Ku Klux Klan leader David Duke, and voter

[53] Paul Kleppner, *Chicago Divided: The Making of a Black Mayor* (Dekalb, Ill.: Northern
Illinois University Press, 1985), chap. 6.

participation soared.[54] All over the nation in 1984 and 1988 the Jesse Jackson campaign mobilized blacks to register and take part, and they did so in enormous numbers.[55]

Although the civil rights movement had its greatest impact on voter turnout, it stimulated other kinds of participation in elections as well, in interesting patterns. At the height of the movement, civil rights activities increased the probability that people would contribute money to a political party or candidate by 3 percent, and the effect on blacks was about the same as the effect on whites. When it came to work for a party or candidate, however, the activities of the civil rights movement increased the likelihood of participation among whites but had no effect at all among blacks. In the face of the African-American challenge, the political parties remained exclusionist, especially in the South. The hostility of the lily-white leadership of the Mississippi Democratic party, for example, forced black Mississippians to create their own alternative, the Mississippi Freedom Democratic party. The 1964 Democratic National Convention denied the new party the Mississippi credentials, but the 1968 Convention seated an integrated successor over the still-unrepentent, still-segregated, "official" Mississippi Democratic party delegation. In the North, the party organizations were not much more friendly. In 1972, the Democratic Convention purged the Illinois delegation led by Chicago machine mayor Richard J. Daley in favor of a reform delegation led by independent Chicago alderman William Singer and veteran civil rights activist Jesse Jackson.

---

[54]See Rhodes Cook, "In the Wake of Louisiana Defeat Duke Eyes National Bid," *Congressional Quarterly Weekly Report*, November 23, 1991, pp. 3475–79; Peter Applebome, "Fearing Duke, Voters in Louisiana Hand Democrat Fourth Term," *New York Times*, November 18, 1991, p. A1; Mike Williams, "Louisiana Blacks See Danger in Duke Victory," *Atlanta Journal and Constitution*, November 12, 1991, p. A3; Peter Applebome, "On Eve of Louisiana, Nothing Is Certain," *New York Times*, November 15, 1991, p. A21; Sallie Hughes, "On Election Day, Memories, Fears Weigh on Voters," *Miami Herald*, November 17, 1991, p. A31.

[55]Thomas E. Cavanagh and Lorn S. Foster, *Jesse Jackson's Campaign: The Primaries and the Caucuses* (Washington, D.C.: Joint Center for Political Studies, 1984); Katherine Tate, "Black Political Participation in the 1984 and 1988 Presidential Elections," *American Political Science Review* 85 (December 1991), pp. 1159–76.

The response of the white-dominated party organizations to the civil rights movement was to mobilize whites, not blacks.[56] In sum, the African-American movement for social, political, and economic rights mobilized both blacks and whites to vote and to contribute money to political parties and candidates, but mobilized only whites to work for political parties. On one hand, the movement's challenge to whites' domination of blacks heightened racial hostility and the social pressures among whites to oppose it, thus providing new incentives for whites to participate. On the other hand, the movement's efforts to foster collective action, to register voters, and to turn blacks out to vote reinforced racial identities, expectations, and sense of common purpose, thus supplying new motivations for blacks' political involvement. They overcame fears of white violence and dismantled legal barriers to blacks' exercise of political rights, diminishing old obstacles to black political activism. Political mobilization worked, in short, by assuming some of the costs of political participation—by subsidizing information, shouldering burdens—and by augmenting some of the benefits of political participation—by effecting the creation of social expectations and rewards.

The Legal Organization of Participation and Mobilization

Political participation and mobilization take place within a framework of electoral institutions that allocate participatory burdens and rewards. The requirements of local, state, and national election laws impose additional costs on participation, especially for people who lack the required resources. Likewise, the requirements of local,

[56]One mark of the resistance of the parties to the insurgents is the succession of delegate challenges at the Democratic Conventions between 1964 and 1972. In those years, civil rights and reform forces challenged the state party delegations of Mississippi, Alabama, Georgia, North Carolina, Texas, South Carolina, California, Illinois, and fourteen other states. The Republican Party, on the other hand, was spared the credentials battles only because of its clear disinterest in black voters after the Goldwater candidacy in 1964. See Congressional Quarterly, *Guide to U.S. Elections*, 2nd ed. (Washington, D.C.: Congressional Quarterly Press, 1985), pp. 115, 119–20, 123–24.

state, and national election laws place additional strains on mobilization. They force political leaders to come up with even more resources to offset the increased burdens on citizens; they make it unprofitable for political leaders to mobilize some constituencies at all.

The institutions of American elections, of course, are the deliberate creations of local, state, and national governments. Twice in American history, both times in the late nineteenth century, governments opted to impose more stringent regulations on voting, with the explicit intent to disfranchise entire classes of voters.[57] Southern states adopted measures to deprive black citizens of their voting rights, and almost all states implemented registration requirements, ostensibly to curb vote fraud practiced by urban, immigrant political machines. We will consider the effects first in the South and then nationwide.

Jim Crow Election Laws

In 1877, Reconstruction ended, and federal troops withdrew from the South. Soon after the federal departure, white supremacist "Redemption" governments in the former Confederate states created an assortment of election laws designed to strip blacks of their political rights: poll taxes, white primaries, voter registration, literacy tests, and grandfather clauses. By 1903, this patchwork of legal requirements effectively shut southern blacks (and many poor southern whites) out of the electoral process. The impact on voter participation was momentous. In 1888, 62.5 percent of adult male Southerners cast ballots in the presidential election; in 1904, only 28.6 percent did.[58]

---

[57]This account leaves aside the obvious effects of explicit disfranchisement: the exclusion of women before the Nineteenth Amendment, and the continued exclusion (in most states) of children, felons, and aliens.

[58]The figures come from J. Morgan Kousser, *The Shaping of Southern Politics: Suffrage Restriction and the Establishment of the One-Party South, 1880–1910* (New Haven: Yale University Press, 1974), Table 1.1. Other detailed accounts of schemes to keep southern blacks from voting can be found in V. O. Key, Jr., *Southern Politics in State and Nation* (New York: Vintage, 1949), chaps. 25–29; and C. Vann Woodward, *The Strange Career of Jim Crow*, 2nd ed. (New York: Oxford University Press, 1966).

One provision of the Jim Crow electoral laws, the poll tax, required that citizens pay an assessment in order to register to vote. In 1903, every Southern state except one imposed a poll tax, and in four states the tax was cumulative: To register, citizens in those states had to pay the current year's tax plus the taxes for all earlier and unpaid years of eligibility. By the mid-1950s, poll taxes remained a requirement in only five Southern states—Alabama, Arkansas, Mississippi, Texas, and Virginia. Even so, one out of every two blacks in the South (and one out of every four nationally) had to pay a tax to exercise the franchise. The Twenty-fourth Amendment to the Constitution, adopted in 1964, forbade the requirement of poll taxes in federal elections, and two years later the Supreme Court, ruling in a Virginia case, abolished the practice altogether.[59]

A second aspect of electoral Jim Crow, literacy tests, required voters to prove their ability to read and write to election judges before they were allowed to vote. Before 1890, no Southern state required verification of literacy as a prerequisite to voting, but six states adopted the requirements before 1910 and a seventh enacted it in 1921. By design, literacy tests left vast discretion to local registrars, to provide an opportunity for discrimination.[60] To bias the application of the tests even further, states included a variety of provisions to exempt illiterate whites. "Grandfather clauses" allowed otherwise unqualified persons to vote if they met certain qualifications, such as descent from a legal voter or service in the state's Confederate militia, that blacks could not possibly meet. Other provisions allowed illiterates to participate if they owned real property or if they could demonstrate "good moral character." In 1915, the Supreme Court struck down grandfather clauses, but it let literacy tests stand.[61]

Thus, in 1952, six out of ten Southern blacks (and four out of ten blacks nationally) lived in states that still imposed literacy tests that could be applied in biased fashion. Section 4 of the VRA of 1965 suspended those discriminatory literacy tests that remained in the

[59] *Harper v. Virginia State Board of Elections*, 383 U.S. 663 (1966).
[60] Key, *Southern Politics*, pp. 560–76.
[61] *Guinn v. United States*, 238 U.S. 347 (1915).

South, and the Voting Rights Act Amendments of 1970 abolished literacy tests nationwide.[62]

A third element of Southern exclusion, the white primary, straightforwardly prohibited blacks from voting in primary elections. In the Solid South, of course, the Democratic primary was where the real decisions were made about who would hold public office. It took nearly half a century, until 1944, for the U.S. Supreme Court to rule the white primary unconstitutional.[63] Southern states resisted the Court's ruling by trying to divorce the primary from governmental processes and by tightening up other ways (most notably literacy tests) of keeping blacks from voting.[64]

Finally, some Southern states and many Northern states adopted systems of periodic registration, which required people to reregister at intervals of as little as one year to retain their eligibility to vote. Not only did periodic registration significantly increase the costs of voting, it also provided more regular opportunities to purge "undesirables" from the rolls. Although only fourteen states had periodic registration in the 1950s, one out of four African-Americans came under the jurisdiction of the system. By 1972, periodic registration remained in only three states.

Three of the legal requirements the southern states adopted to obstruct black voting rights—literacy tests, poll taxes, and periodic registration—remained in force after World War II, and they were the major reason for the 11 percent voter participation rate of southern blacks in the 1952 presidential election. By our estimates, summarized in Table 5-1, literacy tests reduced the probability that blacks would vote by 16.0 percent, poll taxes reduced the probability by 10.2 percent, and periodic registration reduced the probability by 11.6 percent. Black citizens unfortunate enough to live in states

---

[62] Section 4 of the 1965 act suspended the use of literacy tests and other similar provisions (education or knowledge tests, character tests, and voucher requirements) in any state or political subdivision where any such test or device was in effect in November 1964 and where less than 50 percent of the voting-age residents were registered or where less than 50 percent voted in the November 1964 presidential elections. This formula covered the states of Alabama, Arkansas, Mississippi, Texas, Virginia, Alaska, three counties in Arizona, one in Hawaii, and one in Idaho.

[63] *Smith* v. *Allwright* 321 U.S. 649 (1944).

[64] Key, *Southern Politics*, pp. 626–32.

with all three provisions were 35 percent less likely to vote than their counterparts in states without them.[65] As their designers intended, and as our analysis confirms, the Jim Crow election laws had insignificant effects on whites. As we will demonstrate in more detail in Chapter 7, the major factor in the spectacular rise in black voter turnout, particularly in the South, was the abolition of these three discriminatory election laws.[66]

The impetus behind the abolition of exclusionary election laws was the VRA of 1965, even though its provisions suspended only the literacy test, and only in selected areas of the country. (The poll tax, as we have mentioned, was forbidden by constitutional amendment at about the same time.) The attack on election laws themselves, however, was only one provision of this landmark act. Other key provisions empowered the attorney general to send federal examiners into six Southern states and parts of a seventh to list applicants who wished to register to vote,[67] authorized federal election observers in the same jurisdictions, and required that any proposed changes in voting laws, procedures, or practices be "pre-cleared" with the Justice Department.

Voter turnout did in fact rise in the Southern jurisdictions covered by the VRA, and it did so beyond the 16.0 percent increase in black turnout that came from suspension of literacy tests. The increase in African-American turnout, however, was in general not the direct result of the activities of the federal government itself.

---

[65] Because of the nonlinearity underlying the probit model, the joint effect of several variables is not equal to the arithmetic sum of their individual effects.

[66] Rusk and Stucker demonstrate the enormous impact of these same provisions at the time of their adoption. Jerrold G. Rusk and John J. Stucker, "The Effect of the Southern System of Election Laws on Voting Participation," pp. 198–250 in Joel H. Silbey, Allan G. Bogue, and William H. Flanigan, eds., *The History of American Electoral Behavior* (Princeton: Princeton University Press, 1978). See also James E. Alt, "Race and Voter Registration in the South Before and After the Voting Rights Act," forthcoming in Chandler Davidson and Bernard Grofman, eds., *The Impact of the Voting Rights Act in the South* (Princeton: Princeton University Press, 1993).

[67] To be precise, federal examiners did not register voters. Rather, they reviewed applicants' qualifications for voting and placed the names of those qualified to vote on a list of eligible voters. State or local election officials were then obligated under the VRA to place the names of those persons listed by the federal examiners on the official voting lists.

Federal examiners, in fact, were few in number and were stationed in relatively few Southern jurisdictions. In the ten years following the VRA, the Justice Department dispatched federal examiners to only sixty counties and parishes in five Southern states, jurisdictions that contained only 9.3 percent of the South's blacks.[68] The first year's effort, the most intense under the act, was staffed by just 130 examiners.[69]

Consequently, the direct impact of the federal examiners on voter registration in the South was rather small. Examiners enrolled only 153,034 of the 774,861 African-Americans who registered in the first three years of the VRA—19.7 percent; in total, they enlisted only 160,417 of the 2,123,005 blacks who registered in the five Southern states into which examiners went—7.6 percent.[70] In the South as a whole, federal examiners signed up only 16 percent of the 932,298 blacks who registered to vote in the two years following the VRA.[71]

Our findings are entirely consistent with these aggregate numbers (Table 5-1). Blacks who lived in counties supervised by federal examiners were perhaps as much as 2 to 3 percent more likely to vote, but the estimate does not begin to approach statistical

[68] U.S. Commission on Civil Rights, *The Voting Rights Act: Unfulfilled Goals* (Washington, D.C.: U.S. Government Printing Office, September 1981), Table C-2.

[69] *Annual Report of the U.S. Civil Service Commission, 1966* (Washington, D.C.: U.S. Government Printing Office, 1966), p. 5. Complaints about inadequate numbers of examiners were commonplace. See Watters and Cleghorn, *Climbing Jacob's Ladder,* pp. 261–65; Lawson, *Black Ballots,* pp. 332–35; Steven F. Lawson, *In Pursuit of Power: Southern Blacks and Electoral Politics, 1965–1982* (New York: Columbia University Press, 1985), pp. 20–21; *The Shameful Blight: The Survival of Racial Discrimination in Voting in the South* (Washington, D.C.: The Washington Research Project, 1972), pp. 51–60; U.S. Commission on Civil Rights, *The Voting Rights Act: Ten Years After* (Washington, D.C.: U.S. Government Printing Office, January 1975), pp. 31–37; Garrow, *Protest at Selma,* pp. 182–89.

[70] *Report of the Attorney General of the United States, 1966* (Washington, D.C.: U.S. Government Printing Office, 1966), p. 111. Three-quarters of the blacks enrolled by federal examiners were registered in the first eleven months following enactment; 96 percent were enrolled during the first twenty-three months.

[71] These estimates exclude the state of Texas for which there are no registration data broken down by race before the VRA. Calculations are from data provided in United States Commission on Civil Rights, *Political Participation* (Washington, D.C.: U.S. Government Printing Office, May 1968), Appendix VII, Tables 1 and 2.

significance.[72] Even though the federal examiners deputized under the VRA had little direct effect on black voter participation in the South, they did have important indirect effects.[73] African-Americans who lived in jurisdictions into which federal examiners *could* be sent under the VRA were 26.4 percent more likely to vote in 1968 and 1972 than they would have been otherwise; whites in the same counties were 19.5 percent more likely to vote.[74]

On one hand, the *threat* that federal examiners might be sent into their communities persuaded many local election officials to allow blacks to register.[75] In Mississippi, Harold Stanley reports:

> Attorney General Joe Patterson called relaxation of Mississippi's voting requirements "a matter of self-preservation.... I don't like the relaxation of our laws any more than you do but when we see a cyclone coming we need to protect ourselves the best way possible." Patterson said if Mississippians reject the state laws, federal registrars "will swarm in here like grasshoppers on a spring morning and register one group of people on a wholesale basis"...registering Negroes "as quickly as possible while whites would still go to the Circuit Clerk's office to adhere to rigid voting requirements."[76]

[72]The probit coefficient is .131 with a standard error of .437. The low reliability of this estimate in part results from the small number of blacks in the sample who lived in examiner-supervised counties or parishes. Our estimates of the effect of federal registrars are considerably lower than Alt's estimates from aggregate, county-level data. See Alt, "Race and Voter Registration in the South."

[73]For a discussion of some of the broader political consequences and issues raised by the VRA, see Bernard Grofman and Chandler Davidson, eds., *Controversies in Minority Voting: The Voting Rights Act in Perspective* (Washington, D.C.: Brookings Institution, 1992).

[74]Although our best estimate is that the VRA had a slightly bigger effect on blacks than whites, statistically speaking there are only 70 chances in 100 that the two coefficients are different from one another.

[75]Watters and Cleghorn, *Climbing Jacob's Ladder,* p. 261; Stanley, *Voter Mobilization,* p. 95. Local compliance was probably also aided by the discovery that three in five of the new registrants were white.

[76]Jackson *Clarion-Ledger,* August 3, 1965, quoted in Stanley, *Voter Mobilization,* p. 95. The persuasive effect of the federal examiners was consistent with the Justice Department's hopes for the implementation of the VRA. As John Doar, head of the Civil Rights Division of the Justice Department, wrote, "Our objective [is] to obtain full compliance with the '65 Act...but to do this with a minimum amount of federal intrusion into the registration business of the states." "The prevailing viewpoint...is to convince our friends in these [covered] states that they should do the job themselves." John Doar, Memo to the Attorney General, August 1965, Civil

On the other hand, the possibility of intervention by federal examiners gave hope and legal protection to the efforts of CORE, SNCC, the NAACP, and the Voter Education Project (V.E.P.) to register black voters. V.E.P. funded over 100 registration programs in 1966 and 1967 and sponsored 60 voter registration drives in 1967 alone.[77] By one estimate, V.E.P.–affiliated programs registered about 100,000 blacks in 1966, or about a third of the African-Americans registered in that year.[78] As Attorney General Nicholas Katzenbach observed, "Counties which have seen extensive Negro registration, whether by local officials or by federal examiners, are counties in which registration campaigns have been conducted. In counties without such campaigns, even the presence of examiners has been of limited gain."[79]

The impact of the VRA on voter participation in the South, then, stemmed less from the direct intervention of federal agents than from the mobilizing efforts of the civil rights movement and its segregationist opponents and from the "voluntary" compliance of local election officials who feared federal involvement in their own communities if they did not allow blacks to register.[80]

Rights Division Office Files, Department of Justice, quoted in Lawson, *In Pursuit of Power*, p. 18; and John Doar, testimony before the Special Equal Rights Committee, October 5, 1965, Box 91, Democratic National Committee Files, Lyndon Baines Johnson Library, quoted in Lawson, *In Pursuit of Power*, p. 19.

[77] *V.E.P. News* 2 (January 1968), p. 1. For an account of the V.E.P. activities, see Watters and Cleghorn, *Climbing Jacob's Ladder*.

[78] V.E.P., "What Happened in the South, 1966" (Atlanta: Voter Education Project, December 14, 1966), p. 8. Studies of V.E.P.'s activities documented that registration drives boosted voter registration of blacks by an average of 9 percent in counties without federal examiners and 4 percent in counties where federal examiners were also at work. Southern Regional Council, *The Effects of Federal Examiners and Organized Registration Campaigns on Negro Voter Registration* (Atlanta: Southern Regional Council, July 1966), quoted in United States Commission on Civil Rights, *Political Participation*, p. 155.

[79] Quoted in Garrow, *Protest at Selma*, p. 186.

[80] Under the Nixon administration, enforcement of the VRA languished. Between July 1968 and June 1974, the Justice Department enrolled only 10,859 registrants and dispatched federal examiners to only one additional county. Attorney General John Mitchell lobbied Congress to drop the preclearance provision of the 1965 VRA when it came up for renewal in 1970. When Mitchell failed to prevail upon Congress, he ordered the Civil Rights Division to relax its enforcement of the preclearance process.

(continued)

Even beyond the legal structures erected to prevent blacks from exercising their political rights, however, stood a system of intimidation, physical violence, and economic reprisal that proved very difficult to dislodge. Even in the face of federal examiners and election observers, the coercion continued,[81] and even today, decades after the passage of the VRA, discrimination, harassment, and intimidation continue to make it difficult for blacks and other minorities to register and to vote.[82]

Indeed, even after taking into account all the ways that blacks, Puerto Ricans, and Mexican-Americans differ from other citizens, African-Americans remain 4.4 percent less likely to vote in presidential elections, and Puerto Ricans and Mexican-Americans remain 5.7 percent less likely to vote in presidential elections, as Table 5-1 shows. Members of all three minority communities remain about 9 percent less likely to vote in midterm elections, as Table 5-2 shows. The residual racial and ethnic difference in electoral participation turns up only for voter turnout: African- and Latino-Americans are no less likely than whites to try to influence others, to work for

---

(continued)
The 1968 data are reported in the *V.E.P. News* 2 (October 1968), p. 2. The 1974 data are reported in United States Commission on Civil Rights, *The Voting Rights Act: Ten Years After,* Appendix 3. See also Howard Ball, Dale Krane, and Thomas P. Lauth, *Compromised Compliance: Implementation of the 1965 Voting Rights Act* (Westport, Conn.: Greenwood Press, 1982), pp. 67–71; *The Shameful Blight,* p. 58; Charles V. Hamilton, *The Bench and the Ballot: Southern Federal Judges and Black Voters* (New York: Oxford University Press, 1973), pp. 241–45; Lawson, *In Pursuit of Power,* pp. 125, 164–69; Lawson, *Running for Freedom,* pp. 137–38.

[81]Matthews and Prothro, *Negroes and the New Southern Politics;* U.S. Commission on Civil Rights, *The Voting Rights Act: The First Months* (Washington, D.C.: U.S. Government Printing Office, 1965), pp. 2, 35; Watters and Cleghorn, *Climbing Jacob's Ladder,* chap. 5; Lester M. Salamon and Stephen Van Evera, "Fear, Apathy, and Discrimination: A Test of Three Explanations of Political Participation," *American Political Science Review* 67 (December 1973), pp. 1288–1306; Lawson, *In Pursuit of Power,* p. 127; Armand Derfner, "Racial Discrimination and the Right to Vote," *Vanderbilt Law Review* 26 (April 1973), pp. 523–84.

[82]U.S. Commission on Civil Rights, *The Voting Rights Act,* chaps. 3–4; Kenneth H. Thompson, *The Voting Rights Act and Black Electoral Participation* (Washington, D.C.: Joint Center for Political Studies, 1982), pp. 19–20; Frank Parker, *Black Votes Count: Political Empowerment in Mississippi After 1965* (Chapel Hill: University of North Carolina Press, 1990); Ball, Krane, and Lauth, *Compromised Compliance.*

political parties, or to donate money to campaigns. These results suggest that discrimination is not only a historical problem, that biased administration of voter registration laws, inconvenient placement of polling places, inadequate numbers of polling booths, and outright intimidation continue to hinder access to the ballot box. Only where there are institutional opportunities to discriminate do racial and ethnic differences in participation persist. De facto barriers to political involvement will not fall until de jure requirements fall.

Voter Registration Laws

In 1800, Massachusetts became the first state to require its citizens to register before the election in order to be able to vote. Before the Civil War, few states, most in New England, followed the Bay State's lead. In the decades after the Civil War, however, most states adopted voter registration requirements. Between 1876 and 1912, in fact, almost half of the Northern states wrote voter registration clauses into their constitutions, and many more adopted them as statutes.[83]

The enactment of voter registration requirements in the North was a political response to massive waves of immigration in the late nineteenth and early twentieth centuries. Unscrupulous and corrupt urban political machines, middle-class, native-stock reformers argued, employed poor, uneducated, and unsophisticated Irish, Italians, Bohemians, Greeks, Poles, and Jews to perpetrate election fraud. Voter registration, the reformers believed, would put an end to stolen elections by making it more difficult for immigrants, blacks, Indians, Chinese, and Mexicans to vote, either legally or illegally.[84]

---

[83] Joseph P. Harris, *Registration of Voters in the United States* (Washington, D.C.: Brookings Institution, 1929), chap. 3; Kevin P. Phillips and Paul H. Blackman, *Electoral Reform and Voter Participation* (Washington, D.C.: American Enterprise Institute, 1975), p. 8.

[84] In fact, the first states to adopt voter registration laws after the Civil War were mostly the urban industrial states of the Northeast and Midwest, and many of the registration statutes that they wrote applied only to residents of cities over a certain population. See Harris, *Registration of Voters in the United States*, chap. 3. The exact nature of the "problem" differed from place to place—in the North it was European immigrants; in the West it was Chinese and Japanese; in the Southwest it was Mexicans; in the South it was blacks—but the political coalitions that advanced registration were remarkably similar: middle class, white, native stock, often the era's "progressives." Richard Hofstadter, *The Age of Reform* (New York: Random House,

(continued)

With the adoption of registration laws, voter turnout in the North dropped 17 percent between 1896 and 1916.[85] These same voter registration laws persist to the present day and, as we will show, they continue to suppress voter participation, particularly among those who lack the resources to work their way through the maze of bureaucratic requirements.[86] As Rosenstone and Wolfinger put it, "Registration is often more difficult than vot-

---

(continued)
1955), pp. 175–81; William J. Crotty, *Political Reform and the American Experiment* (New York: Thomas Y. Crowell Co., 1977), chap. 1; William H. Riker, *Democracy in the United States* (New York: Macmillan, 1953); Frances Fox Piven and Richard A. Cloward, *Why Americans Don't Vote* (New York: Pantheon Books, 1988.

[85] The data are from Walter Dean Burnham, "The Turnout Problem," pp. 97–133 in A. James Reichley, ed., *Elections American Style* (Washington, D.C.: Brookings Institution, 1987), p. 113. There is a fair amount of controversy over how much of this 17 percent decline in turnout should be attributed to changes in registration laws or to the political parties and their electoral campaigns, and how much is simply an artifact of census undercounts of the eligible electorate in the nineteenth century. For a sampling of the debate see: Walter Dean Burnham, "The Changing Shape of the American Political Universe," *American Political Science Review* 59 (March 1965), pp. 7–28; Philip E. Converse, "Change in the American Electorate," pp. 263–337 in Angus Campbell and Philip E. Converse, eds., *The Human Meaning of Social Change* (New York: Russell Sage, 1972); Walter Dean Burnham, "Theory and Voting Research: Some Reflections on Converse's 'Change in the American Electorate,'" *American Political Science Review* 68 (September 1974), pp. 1002–23; Jerrold G. Rusk, "Comment: The American Electoral Universe: Speculation and Evidence," *American Political Science Review* 68 (September 1974), pp. 1028–49; Kleppner, *Who Voted?*; McGerr, *The Decline of Popular Politics*; John B. Sharpless and Ray M. Shortridge, "Biased Underenumeration in Census Manuscripts," *Journal of Urban History* 1 (August 1975), pp. 409–39; Peter R. Knights, "Potholes in the Road of Improvement? Estimating Census Underenumeration by Longitudinal Tracing: U.S. Census, 1850–1880," *Social Science History* 15 (Winter 1991), pp. 517–26; John W. Adams and Alice Bee Kasakoff, "Estimates of Census Underenumeration Based on Genealogies," *Social Science History* 15 (Winter 1991), pp. 527–43; Donald A. DeBats, "Hide and Seek: The Historian and Nineteenth-Century Social Accounting," *Social Science History* 15 (Winter 1991), pp. 545–63; Kenneth Winkle, "The U.S. Census as a Source in Political History," *Social Science History* 15 (Winter 1991), pp. 565–77; Richard H. Steckel, "The Quality of Census Data for Historical Inquiry: A Research Agenda," *Social Science History* 15 (Winter 1991), pp. 579–99.

[86] Stanley Kelley, Jr., Richard E. Ayres, and William G. Bowen, "Registration and Voting: Putting First Things First," *American Political Science Review* 61 (June 1967), pp. 359–79; Steven J. Rosenstone and Raymond E. Wolfinger, "The Effect of Registration Laws on Voter Turnout," *American Political Science Review* 72 (March 1978), pp. 22–45.

ing. It may require a longer journey, at a less convenient hour, to complete a more complicated procedure—and at a time when interest in the campaigns is far from its peak."[87] The more difficult it is to register to vote, the lower the probability that people will register, and if they do not register, they cannot vote.

The rules that govern registration vary widely across the fifty states. Some states require that citizens register at least fifty days before the election, but others allow citizens to register on election day itself, and North Dakota does not ask citizens to register at all. Some states allow election officials to deputize citizens to set up tables in shopping centers, factories, offices, and government centers, or to go house-to-house to register people to vote, but other states do not allow outreach. Some states permit registration by postcard, and others enroll voters when they get drivers' licenses. Some states staff registration offices only a few hours several days a week, but others register voters every day, including Saturdays. Some states remove people who have failed to vote from registration rolls, but others do not purge at all.

Each of these provisions puts a small impediment on the ease with which people can register, but the provision that stands out consistently as having the greatest impact on registration and turnout is the closing date, the last day states allow people to register before an election.[88] Very early closing dates have all but disappeared over the last four decades. In the 1950s, states required 40 percent of the electorate to register more than thirty days before the election. The 1970 Voting Rights Act Amendments, however, mandated closing dates for presidential elections no more than thirty days in advance, and the Supreme Court declared in 1972 that thirty days was "an ample period of time" for other elections, even though a year later it permitted Arizona and Georgia to retain fifty-day closing dates.[89] As a result of these national requirements, in 1988 only 5 percent of the electorate had to register more than a month before election day. Even so, over 90 percent of American citizens must still

[87]Rosenstone and Wolfinger, "The Effect of Registration Laws," p. 22.
[88]Kelley et al., "Registration and Voting"; Rosenstone and Wolfinger, "The Effect of Registration Laws."
[89]*Dunn v. Blumstein*, 405 U.S. 330 (1972); *Marston v. Lewis*, 410 U.S. 679 (1973); and *Burns v. Forston*, 410 U.S. 686 (1973).

register two or more weeks before the election, and that proportion has not shrunk since the 1950s. Only 3 percent of the electorate lives in states that either allow election-day registration or require no registration at all.

The longer before an election people must act to ensure their eligibility to vote, the more likely they will fail to do so. Compared to citizens who live in states that allow registration right up to election day, citizens who live in states with thirty-day closing dates are 3.0 percent less likely to vote, and citizens who live in states with sixty-day closing dates are 5.6 percent less likely to vote. (See Table 5-1.) Early closing dates, by requiring people to register long before campaigns have reached their climax and mobilization efforts have entered high gear, depress voter participation in American elections.

Early closing dates have their greatest impact on the people who are least likely to vote anyway: Given that they lack the resources to overcome the costs of turning out, it is surely no surprise that they also lack the resources to offset the additional burdens of registration. Sixty-day closing dates reduce the turnout of the poorest Americans by 6 percent but depress the turnout of the wealthiest Americans by only 3 percent. They diminish the turnout of the grade-school educated by 6 percent but lessen the turnout of the college educated by only 4 percent. Early closing dates, finally, inhibit African-Americans, Mexican-Americans, and Puerto Ricans slightly more than other citizens.[90]

Over the last few decades other registration requirements have also been liberalized, but there is little evidence that they had any effect on voter turnout. In the 1950s, most states required one year of residency before registering. The 1970 Voting Rights Act Amendments imposed a maximum thirty-day residency requirement for presidential elections and permitted new residents to vote at their previous residences either in person or by absentee ballot. In 1972, the Supreme Court struck down Tennessee's one-year requirement, thereby restricting residency requirements for other than presidential elections as well. Despite public concerns that

---

[90]As before, the unequal effects are a consequence of the statistical assumptions that underlie the probit model. Nevertheless, they make substantive sense in that little can be done to change the prospects of people who are almost certain to turn out, but much can be done to change the prospects of people who may or may not turn out.

onerous residency requirements kept Americans from the polls,[91] neither our analysis nor earlier scholarly analyses of registration in 1960 and turnout in 1972 finds evidence that residency requirements depressed turnout.[92] We suspect that few citizens knew about residency requirements and even fewer paid any attention to them. Thus, the relaxation of residency requirements in the early 1970s did little to effect voter participation. Reformers turned all their attention to a provision that made little difference and ignored the one that suppressed turnout the most: the closing date.

Summary

The basic message of this section is abundantly clear: The legal restrictions on the exercise of the franchise adopted in the early part of the century and maintained to the present day place significant burdens on American citizens and lower the probability that they will participate in political life. Although neutral on their face, the conditions on the use of political rights burden the least advantaged much more than the most advantaged. In fact, restrictive election laws afflict minorities, the poor, and the uneducated twice over: They make it doubly difficult for the disadvantaged to participate in politics, and they make it doubly doubtful that political leaders will devote the resources to efforts to mobilize them.

On the whole, however, the recent record is one of improvement. Primarily because of the pressures generated by the civil rights movement, the United States has moved recently toward liberalization of its requirements for exercise of the franchise. By our estimates, the easing of the burdens on American voters should have increased participation in electoral politics—particularly voter turnout. In fact, as we will show in Chapter 7, it did—but other factors overwhelmed it.

Conclusion

Mobilization, in all its forms, causes people to take part in electoral politics. Citizens who are contacted by political parties, exposed to

---

[91] *Report of the President's Commission on Registration and Voting Participation* (Washington, D.C.: U.S. Government Printing Office, November 1963), p. 13.
[92] Kelley et al., "Registration and Voting"; Rosenstone and Wolfinger, "The Effect of Registration Laws."

intensely fought election campaigns, or inspired by the actions of social movements are more likely to vote, to persuade, to campaign, and to give. Mobilization, we have seen, does not much affect people's perceptions about the parties, the candidates, the election, or their place in the political system. Instead, mobilization works, first, because it subsidizes the cost of electoral participation: Candidates, parties, interest groups, and social movements provide information, transportation, absentee ballots, voter registration forms, and the like. Mobilization works, second, because it occasions social contacts that provide additional benefits for electoral participation: Working through social networks, candidates, parties, interest groups, and social movements exploit friendships and social obligations.

Political mobilizers target and time their efforts strategically. They concentrate their energies on people who seem likely to participate if asked: people who themselves have resources or strong partisan allegiances. They economize by contacting people who are easy enough to identify and who seem likely to contact others in turn: people who are centrally placed in social networks. Finally, they save their scarce resources for contests whose outcomes their efforts might affect: for close, competitive elections.

The willingness of citizens to participate and the ability of leaders to mobilize, we have also shown, depend crucially on the canons that govern elections. For purposes that were all too often deliberately exclusionary, states wrote electoral laws that put significant burdens on both leaders and citizens, especially the most disadvantaged. The Jim Crow election laws of the South and the voter registration laws of the North directly increased the costs of voting and of mobilization. Onerous election laws make people, especially underprivileged people, much less likely to exercise their rights as citizens.

Between this chapter and Chapter 5, we have developed a complete, perhaps exhausting explanation of the causes of participation in electoral politics, an explanation that assesses both the personal and the political side of decisions to take part. The one remaining task, to which we now turn, is to weigh the two sets of explanations against each other, to see how the personal and political causes of citizen action have each contributed to the decline of electoral participation over the last thirty years.

SOLVING THE PUZZLE
OF PARTICIPATION IN
ELECTORAL POLITICS

Americans participate in electoral politics for a mixture of personal and political reasons. An abundance of political resources allows some citizens to bear the costs of involvement, and a lack of resources prevents others. Powerful interests and identities motivate some citizens to seek the benefits of participation, and weaker interests and identities fail to stir others. Finally, candidates, parties, campaigns, interest groups, and social movements mobilize some citizens and neglect others, step up their efforts at some times and scale them back at others. Their labors, when they occur, promote political participation, offsetting the costs and augmenting the social benefits of citizens' political activism.

In this brief chapter, we compare the contributions of the personal and the political to the solution of one of the puzzles with which we began this book: the puzzle of declining participation in American elections.[1] In the 1960s, we noted in Chapter 3, about 62 percent of eligible Americans turned out to vote in presidential elections, but in the 1980s, barely half did. In the 1960s, 10.4 percent of the electorate contributed money to a party or candidate, but in the 1980s, just 8.2 percent did. In the 1960s, 5.5 percent of adult Americans worked for a party or candidate, but in the 1980s, only 3.7 percent did. Put differently, the ranks of participants in electoral

---

[1]Richard A. Brody, "The Puzzle of Political Participation in America," pp. 287–324 in Anthony King, ed., *The New American Political System* (Washington, D.C.: American Enterprise Institute, 1978).

politics have dwindled by between a sixth and a quarter over the last three decades. Why is that? Why has participation in American elections declined during the last thirty years?

In Chapters 5 and 6 we showed some of the proposed solutions to the puzzle to be right, some to be wrong, and all to be importantly incomplete.[2] The decline of turnout, we have shown, occurred despite the stimulating effect of increased education and the liberating effect of reduced legal barriers (as Richard Brody in fact noted in his original framing of the puzzle). The causes of the decline, as recent analysts have asserted and as we have shown, include political efficacy, partisan identification, and satisfaction with the choices offered, all of which themselves have recently declined. The causes of the decline do not include, as several other analysts have suggested, disavowals of responsibility, distrust toward government, or generalized alienation from the political system: As we have shown, these attitudes had no effect on the probability that citizens took part. Finally, the causes of the decline include elements that almost every other analysis has overlooked: the intensity of efforts by candidates, parties, campaigns, interest groups, and social movements to mobilize people to take part. As we have shown, party contacts, electoral competition, and active social movements muster ordinary citizens into electoral politics.

We have yet to assess, however, the relative *magnitudes* of the effects of resources, interests, and strategic mobilization on participation in electoral politics. In this chapter we do just that. Drawing on the theory of participation we outlined in Chapter 2, and working from the empirical results we presented in Chapters 5 and 6, we decompose the trends of electoral participation into their underlying causes. We calculate how much of the decline in citizen participation can be attributed to changing resources, how much

[2]For a sampling of some of the other solutions proposed for Brody's puzzle, see Stephen D. Shaffer, "A Multivariate Explanation of Decreasing Turnout in Presidential Elections, 1960–1976," *American Journal of Political Science* 25 (February 1981), pp. 68–95; Paul R. Abramson and John H. Aldrich, "The Decline of Participation in America," *American Political Science Review* 76 (September 1982), pp. 502–21; Carol A. Cassel and Robert C. Luskin, "Simple Explanations of Turnout Decline," *American Political Science Review* 82 (December 1988), pp. 1321–30; Ruy A. Teixeira, *Why Americans Don't Vote: Turnout Decline in the United States, 1960–1984* (Westport, Conn.: Greenwood Press, 1987).

can be blamed on changing evaluations of the parties and their candidates, how much can be laid to changing degrees of involvement in communities, and how much results from changing patterns of electoral mobilization.

To aid in the assessment, we "transformed" the citizens of the 1960s into the citizens of the 1980s. One variable at a time, we gave each of the respondents to the 1960, 1964, and 1968 National Election Studies the characteristics of their counterparts in the 1980s: their more advanced educations, more fragile sense of political efficacy, more diffident attachments to political parties, more skeptical assessments of the candidates, more tenuous integration into communities, less frequent exposure to the mobilization efforts of parties, campaigns and social movements, and greater freedom from the burdens of discriminatory voter registration and election laws.[3] For each variable, then, we computed how much more or less likely members of the 1960s electorate would have been to participate in elections had they been like the members of the 1980s electorate.

The results, to foreshadow, are dramatic. In every case the changing pattern of mobilization by parties, campaigns, and social movements accounts for at least half of the decline in electoral participation since the 1960s. Explanations of political involvement that have focused exclusively on the personal attributes of individual citizens—their demographic characteristics and political beliefs—have missed at least half the story.

[3] We use the probit equations reported in Appendix D to estimate the magnitude of the effect each of the political and social changes that occurred between the 1960s and 1980s had on the decline in electoral participation. In the first step, we used the equations to generate the predicted probabilities of participation for each respondent to the 1960, 1964, and 1968 National Election Studies. We then altered the scoring of the independent variable of interest to reflect the change in that variable between the 1960s and the 1980s. (For example, to estimate the impact of rising levels of education, we raised each respondent's level of education to reflect the increased level of formal education that prevailed in the 1980s.) Finally, we calculated the probability of participation under this simulated condition. The difference between the actual probability of taking part in the 1960s and the simulated probability of taking part under the conditions of the 1980s, averaged across the respondents, yielded an estimate of the marginal effect on participation of that particular change. We repeated this procedure for each variable to calculate its contribution to the decline in electoral participation since the 1960s.

The Decline of Voter Turnout Since the 1960s

The most interesting, most important, and most conjectured puzzle of recent American electoral history is the 11-percentage-point decline in reported voter turnout since the 1960s.

As we already noted, the decline in voter turnout is all the more problematic, of course, because it runs counter to two important demographic and structural changes that should have fostered voter participation but did not.

First, the educational attainment of the American public has increased markedly during the last thirty years. In 1960, only four out of ten American adults had earned a high school diploma, and only one out of thirteen had taken a college degree. In 1988, in contrast, three out of four adults had completed high school, and one out of five had finished college. The knowledge and skills that facilitate political involvement have never been more broadly distributed.

Second, the legislated barriers to voter participation have diminished significantly during the last thirty years. Constitutional amendments, federal statutes, and federal court decisions have abolished the poll tax and literacy tests and all but ended periodic voter registration. In addition, court rulings and state laws have made it easier for people to register to vote closer to election day. The legal obstacles to citizen involvement in elections have not been lower in this century.

As our simulation indicates, voter turnout would indeed have increased had education and legal requirements been the only elements of the electoral landscape to have changed over the last three decades (see Table 7-1). Had the stimulative effects of better education and the emancipating effects of liberalized election laws not occurred, the decline of voter turnout would have been even more severe—nearly 16 percentage points. Instead, more widespread access to education raised voter turnout 2.8 percentage points above what it would have been had Americans been no better educated than they were in the 1960s. Removal of impediments to the exercise of the franchise advanced voter turnout by 1.8 percentage points. Other changes, however, more than canceled the gains.

Where better education augmented the electorate's resources, other developments reduced them. Between the 1960s and the

Table 7-1 Decomposition of the Decline in Voter Turnout in Presidential Election Years Between the 1960s and 1980s

The Change	Effect on Percentage Change in Turnout Between 1960s and 1980s	Percentage of Decline in Turnout Explained
An easing of voter registration laws	+ 1.8	
Increased formal education	+ 2.8	
A younger electorate	− 2.7	17
Weakened social involvement	− 1.4	9
Declining feelings of efficacy	− 1.4	9
Weakened attachment to and evaluations of the political parties and their candidates	− 1.7	11
A decline in mobilization	− 8.7	54
		100
Net change in voter turnout:	−11.3	

Source: Appendix D.

1980s, the voting-age population grew substantially younger. When the Twenty-sixth Amendment lowered the voting age to eighteen in 1972, the size of the voter group least likely to participate increased by 40 percent overnight, accounting for the substantial drop in voter participation in that one year. Throughout the 1960s and 1970s, moreover, the enormous postwar "baby boom" generation moved into the electorate—in Raymond Wolfinger's vivid analogy, "like a pig through a boa constrictor." Where only 27 percent of the 1960 electorate was under the age of thirty-five, 40 percent of the 1984 electorate belonged to the youngest age group. This simple demographic change reduced aggregate rates of voter turnout. As our estimates indicate, the younger and less experienced electorate accounted for about a sixth of the decline in voter participation, 2.7

percentage points, between the 1960s and the 1980s. All by itself, in fact, the electorate's youthful inexperience erased nearly all of the positive effects of its more extensive education. The electorate of the 1980s was not only less able to draw upon the resources of experience, it also faced the electoral arena with a diminished sense of the efficacy of its actions. Between the 1960s and the 1980s, more and more citizens came to believe that politics and government were so complicated that ordinary people could not understand them; internal efficacy fell. Likewise, more and more citizens came to doubt that public officials cared about the views of the people and came to wonder whether they had any say in what the government did; external efficacy fell. Declining efficacy accounted for about a tenth of the total decline in voter participation, or 1.4 percentage points. It was not, however, by any means a primary or even a substantial cause of declining voter turnout, as some have argued.[4]

On the benefit side of the ledger, voter participation declined because people saw fewer benefits from involvement. First, Americans were far less satisfied with the choices the 1980s offered them—Jimmy Carter, Ronald Reagan, Walter Mondale, George Bush, Michael Dukakis—than with the choices the 1960s offered them—John Kennedy, Richard Nixon, Lyndon Johnson, Barry Goldwater, Hubert Humphrey, George Wallace. They cared far less about who actually won the White House. They had many fewer good things to say even about their favorite political parties and candidates. In addition, Americans had much weaker partisan loyalties in the 1980s than they had in the 1960s. The percentage of strong partisans in the electorate fell from 35 percent in the 1960s to only 29 percent in the 1980s. Weakening identification with the Democrats and the Republicans undermined the rewards of helping the "right side" to win. Taken together, the electorate's diminished sense that anything was at stake in elections and its weakening ties to political parties

[4]Curtis B. Gans, on the "MacNeil/Lehrer Report," Public Broadcasting Service, November 7, 1978; Curtis B. Gans, "The Empty Ballot Box: Reflections on Nonvoters in America," *Public Opinion* (September/October 1978), pp. 54–57; Shaffer, "A Multivariate Explanation of Decreasing Turnout"; Abramson and Aldrich, "The Decline of Electoral Participation."

accounted for about a tenth of the decline in voter turnout—1.7 percentage points.[5]

Finally, Americans were much less integrated into the social life of their communities in the 1980s than they had been in the 1960s. Fewer people lived near where they were born, and fewer people attended religious services regularly. Their shallower social attachments also accounted for about a tenth of the drop in voter participation since the 1960s, about 1.4 percent. Fewer people had ties of long standing to the friends and associates who expect them to participate and reward them when they do.

Between the 1960s and the 1980s, in sum, Americans withdrew from voting because they had fewer resources to devote to politics and less to gain from taking part. Although they had more of the knowledge and skills that derive from education, they had less of the knowledge and fewer of the skills that arise from experience and less of the self-confidence that comes from a sense of personal efficacy. They were less closely involved in social life, less closely identified with political parties, and less deeply invested in the outcomes of elections. Altogether, our estimates indicate, the electorate's depreciated resources and diminished involvements, identifications, and stakes account for 7.2 percent of the 15.9 percent "real" decline in reported voter turnout since the 1960s.

To consider the conclusion differently, however, the usual suspects in research on voter participation fall well short of explaining the most important puzzles of recent American politics. The personal attributes of Americans—their resources, involvement in communities, identifications with political parties, and opinions of the candidates—leave over half of the decline in voter turnout still missing and unaccounted for, but we know now just exactly where to find the remainder. Half of the decline of voter turnout since the 1960s occurred because electoral mobilization declined.

First, partisan mobilization declined. Political parties and campaign organizations increased their efforts to contact people in the 1960s, never failing to mobilize less than a quarter of the American electorate directly. As campaigns abandoned the labor-intensive

---

[5] Abramson and Aldrich, "The Decline of Electoral Participation," pp. 509–10.

canvassing methods of the 1960s for the money-intensive media strategies of the 1980s, they contacted fewer and fewer Americans.

Second, electoral competition declined. Kennedy defeated Nixon in 1960 and Nixon defeated Humphrey in 1968 by less than 1 percent of the votes cast; Reagan beat Carter in 1980 and Bush beat Dukakis in 1988 by margins of 9 and 8 percentage points, respectively. The average margin of victory for incumbents in House races increased from 63 percent in the 1960s to 67 percent in the 1980s. Between 1968 and 1980, seventeen states moved gubernatorial elections and their campaign activities out of presidential election years and into midterm years. Fewer competitive campaigns for the White House, the Congress, and the governor's mansion meant fewer occasions for voter mobilization.

Third, demands on campaign resources intensified. The number of contested presidential primaries nearly doubled between 1968 and 1980. By increasing the number of separate occasions on which voters were called to the polls, the proliferation of presidential primaries spread the resources of both citizens and campaigns thinner and thinner.

Finally, social movement activity declined. The civil rights protests, marches, boycotts, and voter registration drives of the 1960s tapered off in the 1980s. The movement's ebb removed a powerful stimulus to participation for both blacks and whites.

The decline of electoral mobilization from the 1960s to the 1980s, our simulation indicates, produced 8.7 percent of the 15.9 "real" decline in voter turnout over the same three decades. Had candidates, parties, campaigns, interest groups, and social movements been as active in mobilizing voters in the 1980s as they were in the 1960s, even leaving the legal structure and the condition of individual voters unchanged, reported voter participation would have fallen only 2.6 percent, rather than the 11.3 percent that it did.

The resolution of the puzzle of voter turnout, then, is clear. The attributes of individual citizens alone are not sufficient to account for declining public involvement in American elections. People vote because they have the resources to bear the costs and because they have the interests and identities to appreciate the benefits. But people also turn out to vote substantially because somebody helps them or asks them to participate. The actions of parties, campaigns, and social movements mobilize public involvement in American elections. The "blame" for declining voter turnout, accordingly, rests as much on political leaders as on citizens themselves.

The Rise and Decline of Black Voter Turnout

The puzzles of citizen participation in American elections do not begin and end with the decline of national voter turnout. As we observed back in Chapter 3, the postwar trends of voter participation among African-Americans differed significantly from the trends of the rest of the population. In the 1952 and 1956 presidential elections, barely one-third of the black population reported voting. Over the next decade and a half, however, African-American turnout expanded, and in the 1968 and 1972 elections, nearly two-thirds of the black population participated in the selection of the president. From there, black turnout declined, in parallel with the decline in voter participation nationally.

With the theory we proposed in Chapter 2 and the analysis we offered in Chapters 5 and 6, we can also account for the rise and decline of African-American voter turnout. As before, we decompose the changes in black turnout from one era to another by transforming the black electorate from one decade into the black electorate in another decade, characteristic by characteristic. We analyze the increase of black voter turnout in the 1950s and 1960s and the decrease of black voter turnout in the 1970s and 1980s separately. Table 7-2 summarizes the source of the rise in black turnout between the 1950s and the late 1960s.

Unsurprisingly, the relaxation of discriminatory voter registration laws made the largest single contribution, by far, to the rise in black turnout in the 1950s and 1960s. The prohibition of the poll tax and literacy tests, the move to permanent (instead of periodic) systems of registration, the shortening of the closing date, and the implementation of the Voting Rights Act (VRA) of 1965 opened doors to black voters. Taken together, the elimination of legal barriers that had been used to shut blacks out of the political

Table 7-2   Decomposition of the Increase in Black Voter Turnout in Presidential Election Years Between the 1950s and 1968–1972

The Change	Effect on Percentage Change in Turnout Between 1950s and 1968–1972	Percentage of Rise in Black Turnout Explained
Weakened social involvement	− 1.3	
An increase in personal resources	+18.6	24
Increasing feelings of efficacy	+11.3	1
Strengthened attachment to and evaluations of the political parties and their candidates	+ 4.8	13
An increase in mobilization	+ 6.6	18
An easing of voter registration laws	+15.8	44
		100
Net change in black voter turnout:	+34.8	

Source: Appendix D.

process increased African-American turnout by 15.8 percentage points, accounting for almost half the gains of the 1950s and 1960s.[6]

There was more to encourage black voters to participate, however, than simply permitting them to vote. Throughout the 1950s and 1960s the civil rights movement grew and spread, reaching its peak around the campaign for voting rights during the Johnson ad-

[6]This estimate is remarkably parallel to estimates of the negative impact of the initial adoption of poll taxes and literacy tests on voter turnout in the South. See Jerrold Rusk, "Comment: The American Electoral Universe: Speculation and Evidence," *American Political Science Review* 41 (September 1974), pp. 1028–49.

ministration. Throughout the 1950s and 1960s, moreover, the political parties paid increasing attention to newly enfranchised African-American voters—Southern blacks were 15 percent more likely to be contacted by political parties after 1964 than before. More intensive civil rights movement activities and more extensive contacts with political parties mobilized black voters, increasing black turnout by 6.6 percentage points.

In addition to the political innovations, black turnout increased because of changes in the political outlooks and personal characteristics of black Americans. On the benefits side, as the national Democratic party became the champion of civil rights, the differences between the parties widened and blacks perceived more benefits from political participation. In the 1964 presidential election, President Lyndon B. Johnson, the sponsor of the 1964 Civil Rights Act, confronted Senator Barry Goldwater, who had voted against it. In the 1968 presidential election, Vice President Hubert H. Humphrey, a veteran crusader for civil rights and the author of the first civil rights plank to appear in a party platform since Reconstruction, battled former Vice President Richard M. Nixon and segregationist Alabama governor George C. Wallace, both of whom pursued deliberate "Southern strategies" of appeals to Southern whites. In response, African-Americans developed stronger partisan loyalties to the Democratic party and reached more positive evaluations of Democratic presidential nominees. Their growing attachment to the Democrats increased their turnout by 4.8 percentage points.

On the resource side, African-Americans' fortunes increased. The experiences of the civil rights era fostered greater political efficacy, which contributed 0.3 percentage points to the increase in black turnout. More important, the policy achievements of the civil rights movement, especially the 1964 Civil Rights Act and the programs of the Great Society, significantly increased opportunities for African-Americans and gave them access to better educations and jobs. In the space of fifteen years, the proportion of black Americans who had completed high school rose 20 percentage points to 61 percent. In the space of fifteen years, the proportion of black Americans who earned incomes that placed them in the lowest third of American families declined 15 percentage points to 56 percent. Better educations, better incomes, and a slight aging of the black population extended the money, skills, and experience of the black community and increased black voter turnout by 8.6 percentage points, accounting for about a quarter of the gains between the 1950s and the 1960s.

Although increasing mobility and declining church attendance loosened blacks' connections to their communities and slightly depressed black turnout, on the whole the rise in black turnout was dramatic: an increase of almost 35 percentage points in the course of only fifteen years. The largest part of the increase stemmed from the demolition of the legal barriers that excluded black Americans from voting, of course, but deeper attachments to political parties, more abundant resources, and increasing encouragement and mobilization by political parties and social movements all played important parts.

These same forces that were so instrumental in raising black turnout to its peak in the 1968 and 1972 presidential elections also produced the decline in participation in the two decades after. As shown in Table 7-3, the years of schooling of black Americans continued to grow throughout the 1970s and 1980s and raised African-American turnout by 2.6 percentage points. Likewise, the legal obstacles to voter participation continued to drop throughout the 1970s and 1980s and lifted African-American turnout by 2.6 percentage points. As with all Americans, the decline in voter turnout among African-Americans would have been far worse had not education continued to rise and barriers continued to fall.

All in all, though, personal and political causes of black voter turnout moved in directions that depressed political involvement. By the end of the 1980s, African-Americans as a group had fewer political resources. During the 1970s and 1980s, the black population grew considerably younger and less experienced, cutting voting rates by 3.2 percent, more than offsetting the gains from better education. By the end of the 1980s, African-Americans were less well integrated into supportive communities. Mobility increased, home ownership fell, and church attendance waned, reducing turnout rates by 0.8 percentage points. By the end of the 1980s, finally, African-Americans as a group perceived fewer benefits from participation. As the Democratic party's commitment to social welfare programs

Table 7-3   Decomposition of the Decrease in Black Voter Turnout in Presidential Election Years Between 1968–1972 and the 1980s

The Change	Effect on Percentage Change in Turnout Between 1968–1972 and 1980s	Percentage of Decline in Black Turnout Explained
An easing of voter registration laws	+ 2.6	
Increased formal education	+ 2.6	
A younger electorate	− 3.2	18
Weakened social involvement	− .8	4
Declining feelings of efficacy	0.0	0
Weakened attachment to and evaluations of the political parties and their candidates	− 2.6	14
A decline in mobilization	− 6.2	34
A decline of voter registration efforts around the Voting Rights Act	− 5.2	29
		99
Net change in black voter turnout:	−12.8	

Source: Appendix D.

faded, blacks' identification with the party slipped. As the Democratic party's nominees turned more centrist, most distinctly in the case of the only winner, Jimmy Carter, blacks' enthusiasm for the ticket flagged. Rising disaffection from the Democratic party and its candidates reduced African-American voter turnout by 2.6 percentage points.

By far the most important drag on African-American voter turnout, however, was the atrophy of instruments of mobilization.

In the 1970s and 1980s, efforts to register black voters slowed considerably, as the inspiration of the 1965 VRA faded into history. In the 1970s and 1980s, the civil rights movement slowed, as white resistance and internal disputes sapped its energy. In the 1970s and 1980s, political parties lagged in their efforts to contact black voters, as they did in their efforts to contact all Americans. In the 1970s and 1980s, gubernatorial campaigns disappeared, as states moved gubernatorial elections out of presidential years. In the 1970s and 1980s, finally, contested presidential primaries—which twice featured an African-American, Jesse Jackson—diverted campaigns' and voters' efforts into the primaries and out of the November elections. As political parties, campaigns, and social movements subsidized fewer costs and created fewer benefits, black voter turnout declined by 11.4 percentage points. Curtailed mobilization accounts for nearly two-thirds of the drop in African-American voter participation since 1968.

The forces that brought African-Americans into electoral politics, in sum, were the same forces that brought other Americans into electoral politics, although in different proportions. Abundant resources, attractive benefits, and active mobilization sustained black voter turnout, but mobilization mattered most of all. The historic deprivation of the African-American community makes the mobilizing activities of outside forces like political parties and indigenous forces like the civil rights movement all the more important.

The Decline of Work for Parties and Contributions to Campaigns

The puzzles of citizen participation in American elections extend beyond the decline of voter turnout to a more general decline of involvement in campaign activities of all sorts. From the 1960s to the 1980s, the percentage of Americans who volunteered to work for political parties or candidates dropped 1.9 percentage points, and the percentage of Americans who contributed money to a campaign fell 2.6 points. By this point in the chapter, the reasons for the decline are so familiar that we will try to avoid belaboring them.

Involvement in electoral politics declined, first of all, because resources diminished. As shown in Tables 7-4 and 7-5, the electorate's increasing youth and inexperience and its declining sense of efficacy reduced campaign work and contributions by small amounts, with gains in education offsetting the losses in both cases.

Involvement in campaigns declined, second of all, because interests and identities weakened. Looser attachments to the political parties and less-favorable evaluations of their candidates accounted for about one-fifth of the decline in both campaign work and contributions across the 1970s and the 1980s.

Involvement in electoral politics declined, most of all, because the efforts of parties, campaigns, and social movements abated. Less-

Table 7-4   Decomposition of the Decline in Working for a Political Party or Candidate in Presidential Election Years Between the 1960s and 1980s

The Change	Effect on Percentage Change in Working for a Party or Candidate Between 1960s and 1980s	Percentage of Decline in Working for a Party or Candidate Explained
Increased formal education	+ .4	
A younger electorate	− .2	9
Weakened social involvement	− .1	4
Declining feelings of efficacy	− .3	13
Weakened attachment to and evaluations of the political parties and their candidates	− .5	22
A decline in mobilization	−1.2	52
		100
Net change in working for a political party or candidate:	−1.9	

Source: Appendix D.

Table 7-5 Decomposition of the Decline in Contributing Money to a Political Party or Candidate in Presidential Election Years Between the 1960s and 1980s

The Change	Effect on Percentage Change in Contributing Money Between 1960s and 1980s	Percentage of Decline in Contributing Money Explained
Increased formal education	+1.4	
A younger electorate	− .2	5
Weakened social involvement	.0	0
Declining feelings of efficacy	− .5	13
Weakened attachment to and evaluations of the political parties and their candidates	− .8	20
A decline in mobilization	−2.5	62
		100
Net change in contributing money to a political party or candidate:	−2.6	

Source: Appendix D.

vigorous attempts to involve people in politics reduced volunteer activity in campaigns by 1.2 percentage points. Less vigorous attempts to involve people in politics reduced financial contributions to campaigns by 2.5 percentage points. The failure of political leaders and institutions to solicit, support, and encourage political participation accounted for over half the decline in work for political parties and almost two-thirds of the decline in contributions to political campaigns.

Conclusion

Thus, for all three kinds of citizen involvement in elections, not only for voting but also for campaign work and contributions, changes in the personal characteristics and political outlooks of the individuals in the electorate explain at best only half of the three-decade decline in political participation. Political parties, campaign organizations, and social movements presented voters with fewer chances to take part in elections, fewer opportunities to share the burdens of political involvement, and fewer occasions to gain the rewards and satisfactions of political activity. Citizens did not fail the political system; if anything, the political system failed them.

Our theory of political participation not only explains *who* participates in electoral politics, it also explains *when* people participate in electoral politics.

Part of the solution to the puzzle of electoral participation lies in the ways in which the American people have changed: changes in their resources, social ties, and evaluations of the political parties and candidates. An equally large part of the solution to the puzzle lies in the changes that have taken place in the political world that people confront: changes in the actions of political parties, the nature of political campaigns, and the actions of social movements. The level of electoral participation in the United States waxes and wanes in response to political mobilization. People participate in electoral politics in all of its forms when they are mobilized to do so. When political mobilization falls, so does the propensity of people to take part.

CONCLUSION: THE SCOPE AND
BIAS OF POLITICAL PARTICIPATION

Political participation is the product of strategic interactions of citizens and leaders. Few people spontaneously take an active part in public affairs. Rather, they participate when politicians, political parties, interest groups, and activists persuade them to get involved. Working through social networks of family, friends, neighbors, co-workers, and associates, leaders supply information and occasion the creation of social rewards. Their strategic choices, their determinations of who to mobilize and when to mobilize, shape the contours of public participation in American politics. They give political meaning to political participation.

As we have shown throughout this book, the political logic of political participation captures the essence of public involvement in American politics. It explains who participates in politics and who does not, why people engage in some kinds of political activity but not in others, and why more people participate at some moments than at others. It also explains political action in both elections and government, in both local politics and national politics.

Over and over we have shown that resources, interests, and social positions distinguish people who participate in politics from people who do not. People who have better educations, better incomes, more experience, and greater senses of political competence are better able to meet the costs of political involvement. People who have more direct interests, stronger preferences, and more distinct identities are better positioned to see the benefits of political involvement. People who occupy social positions that expose them to information and to social incentives bear less burdensome costs and

228

receive more substantial benefits from their involvement in public affairs.

But this is only half of the story. Again and again we have shown that the strategic opportunities that political contests present to politicians, parties, interest groups, and activists distinguish times when large numbers of people participate in politics from times when fewer do. Participation in governmental politics rises when salient issues reach the public agenda and falls when they leave it. It rises when governments approach crucial decisions and falls afterward. Participation in electoral politics rises when political parties contact, when competitive election campaigns stimulate, when social movements inspire, and falls when they do not. Political leaders focus their mobilization efforts on the moments when public involvement matters the most to the outcome. Participation in American politics rises and falls with the incentives the system presents to its leaders.

The political logic of political participation, in sum, accounts for heretofore puzzling aspects of public involvement in American politics. It tells why citizens dropped out of electoral politics despite gains in education, and why they moved into governmental politics despite deterioration of political efficacy. It tells why public involvement in elections peaked in the 1960s, and why public involvement in national government surged in the early 1980s. It tells why African-Americans turned out in increasing numbers in the 1960s and in decreasing numbers in the 1970s. It tells why citizens participated in governmental activities in greater numbers in the summer and in lesser numbers in the winter. The political logic of political participation, in short, solves the puzzles with which we began this book. It tells the rest of the story of participation in America.

Our analysis in this book, of course, has (of necessity) concerned itself with only seven kinds of political action, only one period, and only one country. Our argument, however, generalizes to other activities, to other times and other places.

The logic of mobilization helps to account for differences between the United States and Europe in the political involvements of their citizenry. On the one hand, American citizens turn out to vote at rates 20 to 30 percentage points below their counterparts in Europe.[1] On the other hand, Americans take part in government—in particular by contacting public officials—at rates substantially above Europeans'.[2] The reasons are fairly straightforward. Voter turnout in the United States trails that in Europe because the United States has some of the world's most onerous voter registration requirements and one of the world's weakest party systems. Where institutional arrangements discourage citizens from taking part and political parties fail to mobilize citizens to act, participation in elections is low.[3] Yet citizen participation in American government leads that in European governments because the United States has one of the world's most decentralized political systems and some of the world's most numerous, most active, and most powerful interest groups. Where politicians, associations, and activists mobilize citizens to pressure, participation in government is high.[4]

---

[1] Although barely 50 percent of Americans cast a ballot in presidential elections, between 80 and 90 percent of the electorates in Austria, Belgium, Germany, and Portugal regularly vote in national elections. Seventy to 80 percent of the electorates in Ireland, France, the United Kingdom, and Japan take part.

[2] Sidney Verba, Norman H. Nie, and Jae-on Kim, *Participation and Political Equality* (New York: Cambridge University Press, 1978), pp. 58–59; Samuel H. Barnes, Max Kaase et al., *Political Action: Mass Participation in Five Western Democracies* (Beverly Hills: Sage, 1979), pp. 541–42.

[3] Verba, Nie, and Kim, *Participation and Political Equality*, chap. 6; G. Bingham Powell, Jr., "American Voter Turnout in Comparative Perspective," *American Political Science Review* 80 (March 1986), pp. 17–43; Robert W. Jackman, "Political Institutions and Voter Turnout in the Industrial Democracies," *American Political Science Review* 81 (June 1987), pp. 405–23; David P. Glass, Peverill Squire, and Raymond E. Wolfinger, "Voter Turnout: An International Comparison," *Public Opinion* (December/January 1984), pp. 49–55; Raymond E. Wolfinger, David P. Glass, and Peverill Squire, "Predictors of Electoral Turnout: An International Comparison," *Policy Studies Review* 9 (Spring 1990), pp. 551–74.

[4] Our argument meshes as well with recent theories of involvement in social movements, interest groups, and community action. Mobilization of citizen activism by governments, politicians, entrepreneurs, and patrons plays a prominent role in recent scholarship. On social movements, see Charles Tilly, *From Mobilization to Revolution* (Reading, Mass.: Addison-Wesley, 1978); Doug McAdam, *Political Process and the Development of Black Insurgency, 1930–1970* (Chicago: University of Chicago Press, 1982); Luther P. Gerlach and Virginia H. Hine, *People, Power, Change: Movements of Social Transformation* (New York: Bobbs-Merrill, 1970); Anthony Obershall, *Social Conflict and Social Movements* (Englewood Cliffs, N.J.: Prentice-Hall, 1973). On interest groups, see Mancur Olson, Jr., *The Logic of Collective Action* (Cambridge: Harvard University Press, 1965), chap. 6; Robert H. Salisbury, "An Exchange Theory

Likewise, the logic of mobilization helps to account for differences between the nineteenth and twentieth centuries in the political involvements of American citizens. In the United States, voter turnout during the last half of the nineteenth century averaged 78 percent, a full 21 percentage points above voter turnout during the last half of the twentieth century. Part of the reason for the difference, we know from Chapter 6, is the twentieth century's more restrictive election laws, which made it difficult for poor whites and nearly impossible for Southern blacks to vote. Part of the reason, too, is the twentieth century's better enumeration methods, which drastically reduced the Census Bureau's population undercounts.[5] Part of the reason for the difference, though, is surely the contrast between the political parties of the nineteenth and twentieth centuries, their styles of campaigning, and their strategies of voter mobilization. As electoral historians report, the social, religious, and economic conflicts of the nineteenth century were intensely politicized and tied inextricably to political parties: Elections not only pitted Republicans against Democrats, they aligned Protestants against Catholics, nativists against immigrants, industrialists against agrarians, and northerners against southerners. Nineteenth-century parties mounted elaborate spectacles of campaign pageantry, parades, mass demonstrations, and rallies. They sustained newspapers noted for no-holds-barred partisanship. They created campaign clubs and marching companies to advertise their tickets. They "built cadres of party workers to encourage men to go to the polls." The intense partisan mobilization of the nineteenth century did more than entertain. It heightened people's interest in politics. It informed people and helped them to understand the logical connection between the issues of the day and the casting of their ballots. It reinforced ethnic, religious, class, and regional

---

of Interest Groups," *Midwest Journal of Political Science* 13 (March 1969), pp. 1–32; Jack L. Walker, Jr., *Mobilizing Interest Groups in America: Patrons, Professions and Social Movements* (Ann Arbor: University of Michigan Press, 1991). On community action, see Robert H. Salisbury, *Citizen Participation in the Public Schools* (Lexington, Mass.: Lexington Books, 1980); Steven J. Rosenstone, "Separate and Unequal: Report of the 1989 Detroit Area Study," unpublished manuscript, University of Michigan, 1989; Paul Freedman, "Mobilization and Participation," unpublished manuscript, University of Michigan, 1992.

[5]See Chapter 6, note 85.

identities and provided solidary and purposive benefits to those who stood with their neighbors. It got people to vote.[6] In sum, differences between the United States and Europe, between the nineteenth century and the twentieth century reflect differences in the activities of political leaders and institutions. Leaders either supply or deny incentives for people to take part in their politics.

Political leaders clearly do not mobilize public involvement just for its own sake. Instead, they mobilize participation in pursuit of their own advantage: to win elections, pass bills, amend rulings, and influence policies. Accordingly, when these leaders face new political, economic, and social incentives, their willingness to mobilize citizen involvement in elections and in government changes to exploit the new opportunities and accommodate the new constraints.

This is nowhere more aptly demonstrated than in the recent history of the United States. Over the last forty years, American politics, economy, and society have undergone significant and interrelated changes. The population has changed. Citizens have become more affluent, educated, and mobile. Their partisan, ethnic, religious, and community identifications have weakened. Equally, the political system has changed. Party organizations fueled by patronage have almost disappeared. Labor unions have atrophied. Television has nationalized American culture and public discourse. Government has assumed greater and more varied responsibilities. The end result of all these changes, Benjamin Ginsberg and Martin Shefter have argued, is the "declining importance of elections in America" and the rising importance of "politics by other means."[7]

Political, economic, and social changes have dramatically altered the mix of incentives for political mobilization. Electoral campaigns have seen once dependable blocs of committed, partisan voters shrink. They have lost loyal cadres of union and patronage workers. They have witnessed the efficiencies of television and direct mail in reaching a mobile, disconnected citizenry. In response, political campaigns have evolved from labor-intensive to capital-intensive

[6]Michael E. McGerr, *The Decline of Popular Politics: The American North, 1865–1928* (New York: Oxford University Press, 1986), chap. 2, quoted at p. 12; Paul Kleppner, *Who Voted? The Dynamics of Electoral Turnout, 1870–1980* (New York: Praeger, 1982).
[7]Benjamin Ginsberg and Martin Shefter, *Politics by Other Means: The Declining Importance of Elections in America* (New York: Basic Books, 1990).

organizations. Face-to-face canvassing in neighborhoods has given way to polls and focus groups as means of assessing the public's opinions and reactions to issues. Door-to-door electioneering in wards and precincts has given way to direct mail and television spots. Grass-roots organization has given way to professional staff. Campaigns in the 1990s need to expend more of their energies soliciting the support of an uncommitted electorate.[8]

At the same time, interest groups have discovered better opportunities for mobilization. Affluence and education have created a citizenry newly attentive to causes such as environmentalism and racial justice. Great wealth, federal tax laws, and new government responsibilities have fostered a new class of individual, institutional, and governmental patrons for collective action. New political problems and new governmental obligations have extended the reach of public decision making and endowed government with greater means for responding to public demands. In response, a larger and broader array of interest groups has surfaced to link citizens to city halls, statehouses, and Capitol Hill. More interests and more groups have the motivation and the capacity to mobilize public involvement.[9]

Through the strategic choices of candidates, parties, interest groups, and activists, political, economic, and social change has tipped the balance of political participation in America. Face-to-face contact with political parties and campaign organizations is a thing

---

[8]Nelson W. Polsby and Aaron Wildavsky, *Presidential Elections: Contemporary Strategies of American Electoral Politics,* 8th ed. (New York: Free Press, 1991); Elizabeth Kolbert, "Campaign Ads Replace Campaigning in California," *New York Times,* May 22, 1992, p. A2; Dan Baltz, "Candidates, Public Depend Less on News Media for the Message," *Washington Post,* May 19, 1992, p. A2; James M. Perry, "Call It New Media, Teledemocracy or Whatever; It's Changing the Way the Political System Works," *Wall Street Journal,* June 24, 1992, p. A20; Sidney Blumenthal, *The Permanent Campaign: Inside the World of Elite Political Operatives* (Boston: Beacon Press, 1980); Larry J. Sabato, *The Rise of Political Consultants: New Ways of Winning Elections* (New York: Basic Books, 1981); Benjamin Ginsberg, "A Post Election Era?" *PS: Political Science and Politics,* March 1989, p. 19; W. Lance Bennett, *The Governing Crisis: Media, Money, and Marketing in American Elections* (New York: St. Martin's Press, 1992).

[9]Walker, *Mobilizing Interest Groups in America;* R. Kenneth Godwin, "Money, Technology, and Political Interests: The Direct Marketing of Politics," pp. 308–25 in Mark P. Petracca, ed., *The Politics of Interests: Interest Group Politics Transformed* (Boulder: Westview Press, 1992).

of the past. Candidates now speak directly to the electorate through new campaign technologies, bypassing political and social institutions. At the same time, more and more interest groups muster public pressures on local, state, and national governments. As we noted at the very beginning of this book, fewer citizens participate in elections and more participate in government now than did a generation ago. This, we believe, is the reason. The political, economic, and social changes of the last few decades wounded campaign organizations and gave them incentives to persuade rather than to mobilize, while the same changes promoted interest groups and encouraged them to mobilize.

The political uses of citizen participation help to make sense of the puzzles of political participation in modern American politics. The withdrawal of citizens from electoral politics is not wholly of their own choosing, is neither the product of satisfaction nor despair. The influx of citizens into governmental politics is likewise not wholly of their own choosing, is neither the product of enthusiasm nor cynicism. Both, rather, are the product of the strategic choices of political leaders from among the opportunities with which they are presented, and within the constraints under which they must operate.

Once we take political participation out of the realm of the attitudinal and place it in the sphere of the political, once we find its causes not only in individuals but also in the political system, the meaning of citizen participation in a democracy changes dramatically. By itself, citizen involvement implies neither legitimacy nor vigilance, neither contentment nor estrangement, neither virtue nor indifference. Instead, political participation tells us more about a political system than about its citizens. It indicates a society in which people have the resources to bear the costs of participation. It indicates a society in which people have enough interests at stake in political decisions to seek the benefits of participation. Most important, it indicates a society in which the leaders have incentives to involve the people in the ongoing tasks of governance.

Mobilization, Participation, and Political Equality

If political participation has political sources, it must have political effects. After all, political leaders would not go to the trouble to mobilize citizen involvement unless it brought them some meaningful benefit.

Both as scholars and as citizens, however, we must ultimately confront the political effects of political participation beyond the small, the singular, and the episodic. What difference does it make to the functioning of a democracy that public involvement is higher at some times than at others? What difference does it make that many people take part in some kinds of politics while few people take part in others?

The extent of public involvement matters, clearly, because participants are not impartial. As E. E. Schattschneider observed three decades ago:

> The outcome of every conflict is determined by the *extent* to which the audience becomes involved in it. That is, the outcome of all conflict is determined by the *scope* of its contagion. The number of people involved in any conflict determines what happens; every change in the number of participants, every increase or reduction in the number of participants affects the result.... Every change in the scope of conflict has a bias. By definition, the intervening bystanders are not neutral.[10]

As Tables 8-1 and 8-2 show, there is a systematic relationship between the scope of political conflict—the extent of citizen participation—and the bias in the composition of participants, just as Schattschneider averred. Each table displays both "representation ratios" and "indexes of equality." The ratios indicate the degree to which different groups in the population are underrepresented (ratios less than 1.0) or overrepresented (ratios greater than 1.0) among political activists. The indexes show the degree of equality across population groups: The higher the value, the greater the equality.[11] Two things are immediately obvious.

First, the pool of political activists is enormously unrepresentative of the population, no matter how many people are involved. In

[10]E. E. Schattschneider, *The Semi-Sovereign People: A Realist's View of Democracy in America* (New York: Holt, Rinehart and Winston, 1960), pp. 2, 4–5 (emphasis in original).

[11]The representation ratios are the ratio of the percentage of participants from that population group to the percentage of citizens from that population group. The equality index is the ratio of two representation ratios: those of the least advantaged and the most advantaged population groups. Appendix F details the derivation, the properties, and the justification for these measures.

Table 8-1   Inequality in Participation in Governmental Politics, 1976–1988

Activity	Total Percentage Participating	Representation Ratio Years of Education			Index of Equality
		0–8	9–15	16+	
Signed petition	34.8	.34	.87	1.44	.24
Attended local meeting	18.0	.31	.78	1.46	.21
Wrote Congress	14.6	.38	.72	1.56	.24
Attended rally	9.1	.29	.57	1.58	.18
Wrote letter to newspaper	5.0	.26	.70	1.68	.15
Made a speech	4.6	.28	.50	1.89	.06
Wrote an article	2.4	.08	.50	1.96	.04

Source: Roper Surveys, 1976, Nos. 76-1, 76-2, 76-6, 76-7; 1980, Nos. 80-1, 80-2, 80-6, 80-7; 1984, Nos. 84-1, 84-2, 84-6, 84-7; 1988, Nos. 88-1, 88-2, 88-6, 88-7.

governmental politics (Table 8-1), the college-educated are vastly overrepresented, while the grammar school–educated are substantially underrepresented. For example, of the people who write to Congress, those who attended college comprise only 35 percent of the population but account for 56 percent of those who write letters: Their share of the participants is 1.56 times larger than their share of the population. Those with the least education comprise 10 percent of the population but only 4 percent of those who write to Congress: Their share of the participants is only .38 times their share of the population. The index of equality is just .24.

In electoral politics, likewise, the fragment of the population that is most abundantly endowed with education and income is dramatically overrepresented, and the segment of the electorate that is most impoverished is strikingly underrepresented (Table 8-2). In the most conspicuous case, the wealthiest 5 percent of the population constitute 17 percent of the financial contributors to campaigns (their

Table 8-2   Inequality in Participation in Electoral Politics, 1952–1988

Activity	Total Percentage Participating	Representation Ratios Years of Education					Index of Equality
		0–8	9–11	12	13–15	16+	
Voted	66.1	.85	.83	1.00	1.12	1.26	.67
Influenced others	26.7	.61	.75	.94	1.33	1.61	.38
Contributed money	8.9	.33	.51	.87	1.37	2.41	.15
Attended meetings	7.8	.48	.50	.85	1.43	2.14	.24
Worked on campaign	4.6	.48	.50	.87	1.33	2.25	.23

Activity	Total Percentage Participating	Representation Ratios Family Income (percentile)					Index of Equality
		0–16	17–33	34–67	68–95	96–100	
Voted	66.1	.76	.90	1.00	1.16	1.27	.60
Influenced others	26.7	.63	.79	.98	1.25	1.54	.41
Contributed money	8.9	.25	.51	.80	1.54	3.25	.08
Attended meetings	7.8	.49	.73	.93	1.31	2.27	.22
Worked on campaign	4.6	.48	.74	.85	1.37	2.42	.20

Note: Analysis is based on data from presidential and midterm years combined.
Source: 1952–1988 American National Election Studies.

representation ratio is 3.25), but the poorest 16 percent constitute only 4 percent (their representation ratio is only .25).[12] The index of equality—at .08—indicates an extraordinary degree of class bias in participation.

In sum, no matter which form citizen participation takes, the pattern of class inequality is unbroken. Inequalities are not dispersed, they are cumulative.[13]

Second, the greater the number of participants in political activity, the greater the equality in political participation. As Figures 8-1 and 8-2 show, the correspondence between the extent of public involvement and the representativeness of the clique of participants is strong and direct. The bias toward the advantaged in such common activities as voting, signing petitions, and attending meetings is serious, but it is substantially less than the bias toward the advantaged in such select activities as making speeches, working for candidates, and contributing money to campaigns.

Given participation's dependence on political resources, demonstrated amply throughout this book, the relationship between the scope of conflict and the degree of bias is not surprising. People participate in politics because they possess resources sufficient to overcome the demands that involvement places upon them. The most popular activities—signing petitions, persuading others, attending meetings—are invariably the least expensive. The least common activities—writing articles for the newspaper, making speeches, contributing money to campaigns—are invariably the most demanding. The resource demands of political participation skew the activist community toward the most advantaged.

Unequal distributions of political resources are not, however, the sole reason for the class inequalities among the politically involved. The class biases in political involvement derive as well from class biases in political mobilization. As our colleague Jack Walker put

[12] Although the income categories available on the Roper surveys are too crude to permit us to make reliable estimates of the degree of income inequality in participation in governmental politics, in every kind of governmental participation the poor are underrepresented relative to the rich.

[13] Robert A. Dahl, *Who Governs? Democracy and Power in an American City* (New Haven: Yale University Press, 1961), chap. 19.

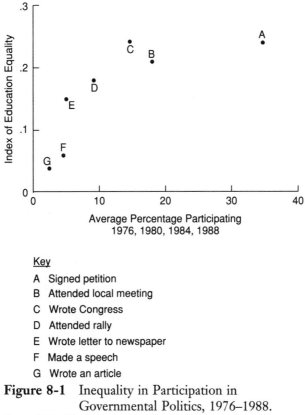

Key

A   Signed petition
B   Attended local meeting
C   Wrote Congress
D   Attended rally
E   Wrote letter to newspaper
F   Made a speech
G   Wrote an article

Figure 8-1   Inequality in Participation in
Governmental Politics, 1976–1988.
Source: Table 8-1.

it, "Our system of political mobilization does not do a good job of covering those at the bottom of the social order."[14] From the argument we propounded in Chapter 2, the reasons are more than clear. First, political mobilizers target people who are both convenient and predictable, people with whom they share social connections.

[14]Jack L. Walker, Jr., "Three Modes of Political Mobilization," paper presented at the annual meeting of the American Political Science Association, 1984, p. 33.

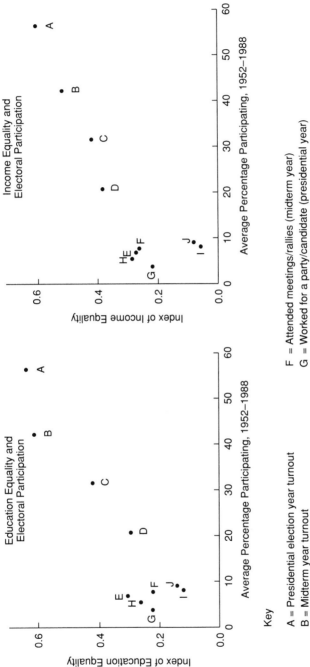

Figure 8-2 Inequality in Participation in Electoral Politics, 1952–1988.

Source: 1952–1988 National Election Studies, except for turnout. See Appendix B.

Politicians, activists, and the leaders of interest groups contact people who, like they, come from the upper echelons of American society. Second, political mobilizers target people who are identifiable and accessible, who are members of voluntary associations. The associational universe is heavily weighted in favor of the advantaged.[15] Finally, political mobilizers target people who are likely to respond and to be effective. They target the educated, the wealthy, and the powerful.[16] Thus, the pressures that political leaders face to use their own resources most efficiently build a class bias into their efforts to mobilize. In the American participatory system, class differences in mobilization typically aggravate rather than mitigate the effects of class differences in political resources. Once again, inequalities are cumulative, not dispersed.

History teaches, however, that it does not always have to be that way. Given the right set of incentives, political mobilizers expand their efforts, extend public involvement, and ameliorate inequality. As Figures 8-3 and 8-4 demonstrate, participatory equality rises and falls as public involvement in single activities surges and subsides. When many citizens write letters to Congress, they are more representative of the population than when fewer people write (Figure 8-3). Likewise, when many citizens turn out to vote, they are more representative of the electorate than when fewer people vote (Figure 8-4). Class equality in participation was greatest in the high-turnout elections of the 1960s and least in the low-turnout elections of the 1980s. As turnout declined between 1960 and 1988, class inequalities multiplied.[17] As Schattschneider might put it, increasing the scope of conflict decreases class bias.

[15] Schattschneider, *The Semi-Sovereign People*, chap. 2; Kay Schlozman, "What Accent the Heavenly Chorus? Political Equality and the American Pressure System," *Journal of Politics* 46 (November 1984), pp. 1006–32.

[16] Political parties, we found in Chapter 6, are much more likely to contact the wealthy and the well educated. In addition, parties are more likely to reach the advantaged through their more active involvements in social networks and associations.

[17] Walter Dean Burnham, "The Appearance and Disappearance of the American Voter," pp. 112–39 in Richard Rose, ed., *Electoral Participation: A Comparative Analysis* (Beverly Hills: Sage, 1980); Thomas E. Cavanagh, "Changes in American Voter Turnout, 1964–1976," *Political Science Quarterly* 96 (Spring 1981), pp. 33–65; Walter Dean Burnham, "The Turnout Problem," pp. 97–133 in A. James Reichley, ed., *Elections American Style* (Washington, D.C.: Brookings Institution, 1987); Walter Dean Burnham, "The Class Gap," *New Republic*, May 9, 1988, p. 30.

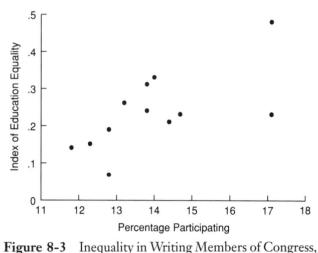

Figure 8-3   Inequality in Writing Members of Congress, 1980–1988.

Source: Roper Surveys, 1980, Nos. 80-1, 80-2, 80-6, 80-7; 1984, Nos. 84-1, 84-2, 84-6, 84-7; 1988, Nos. 88-1, 88-2, 88-6, 88-7.

The correspondence between the scope of public involvement and the degree of class equality *over time* cannot be a consequence of varying demands on resources. Resource endowments and the costs of political participation just do not change that rapidly (particularly in the case of governmental participation, where the fluctuations in citizen involvement are as large from month to month as they are from year to year). Rather, it is the result of mobilization. As we argued in Chapter 2 and have shown throughout, when the stakes are high and the outcomes are uncertain, politicians, political parties, interest groups, and activists devote greater efforts to mobilization. When political leaders offset the costs of political involvement—when they provide information, subsidize participation, occasion the provision of social rewards—they make it possible for people who have few resources of their own to participate. When leaders mobilize extensively, that is, they muster even the disadvantaged into politics.

The capacity of political mobilization to promote participatory equality is no mere supposition. The more intense exertions of political parties and labor unions to include citizens in the electoral process are an important reason why voters are more representative

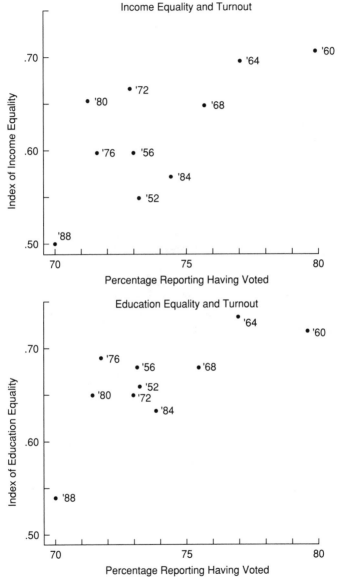

Figure 8-4   Inequality in Voter Turnout, 1952–1988.
Source: 1952–1988 National Election Studies.

of electorates in Europe that they are in the United States.[18] Similarly, the more passionate efforts of political parties to get people to the polls are an important reason why class equality in American voter turnout was greater a century ago than it is today.[19]

The most dramatic example of how political mobilization can undo the class biases of political participation, however, comes from the era of the civil rights movement in America. During the 1950s, when the political parties mobilized whites more than blacks and registration laws systematically excluded blacks (particularly in the South), the racial disparities in citizen participation were immense (see Table 8-3). During the 1960s and into the 1970s, in contrast, when the civil rights movement conquered Jim Crow, the federal government enforced voting rights, the political parties reached out to blacks, and the racial inequalities in political participation narrowed. During the 1980s, finally, political mobilization declined, and progress toward equal representation in the political community stalled.

Political mobilization, then, extends political participation, and more extensive public involvement promotes political equality. When political leaders undertake to mobilize, when they activate more than the easiest and the closest at hand, more people take

Table 8-3   Racial Inequality in Political Participation, 1952–1988

| | Index of Racial Equality in Participation | | |
| | 1952 | 1964 | 1980 |
Activity	to 1960	to 1976	to 1988
Voted	.51	.88	.88
Influenced others	.71	.97	.81
Worked on a campaign	.29	.78	.76
Contributed money	.37	.58	.39
Attended meetings or rallies	.74	.73	1.23

Source: 1952–1988 National Election Studies.

[18] Verba, Nie, and Kim, *Participation and Political Equality.*
[19] Kleppner, *Who Voted?*, chap. 3.

part, and when more people take part, the characteristics of the political class more faithfully mirror the characteristics of the whole polity. When political leaders expand the scope of conflict, in short, they counteract the system's usual bias toward the prosperous, the privileged, and the fortunate.

It is just possible, however, that political equality is of no consequence. It is just possible that it makes no real difference whether many citizens or only a few actually exercise their rights to participate in their own governance. It is just possible that the political system safeguards people's interests whether they participate or not.

But it hardly seems likely. In fact, Americans need not look very far back into their history for incontrovertible evidence that who participates matters. "The first step in applying the formula" of white supremacy in the postbellum American South, historian C. Vann Woodward has noted, "was the total disfranchisement of the Negro."[20] By 1905, the institutional bulwark of Jim Crow election laws effectively shut Southern blacks out of the political process, and within years they were segregated in nearly every aspect of Southern social and economic life, in theaters, boarding houses, toilets, water fountains, waiting rooms, ticket windows, sports, factories, unions, churches, voluntary associations, and housing. All-white mayors and councils, all-white governors and legislatures ransacked African-Americans' education and trampled African-Americans' constitutional rights.[21] Inequalities in participation led to inequalities in influence, which led to inequalities in policy outputs, which led to inequalities in resources, which led once more to inequalities in participation and the beginning of another vicious circle. Jim Crow was

[20] C. Vann Woodward, *The Strange Career of Jim Crow*, 2nd rev. ed. (New York: Oxford University Press, 1966), p. 83.
[21] Woodward, *The Strange Career of Jim Crow*; Gerald M. Pomper, *Elections in America: Control and Influence in Democratic Politics* (New York: Dodd, Mead and Company, 1970). Northern politicians were duplicitous and for much the same reason. The Fourteenth Amendment to the U.S. Constitution stipulated that "when the right to vote in any election...is denied to any of the male inhabitants of such State...the basis of representation therein shall be reduced in proportion which the number of such male citizens shall bear to the whole number of male citizens twenty-one years of age in such State." Electoral Jim Crow should have cost the South seats in Congress and votes in the Electoral College, but the federal government declined to enforce the Constitution. Because black citizens could not vote, nobody looked out for their interests.

self-perpetuating because the disadvantaged did not—indeed, could not—participate.

After World War II, the first step in the recovery of black Americans' economic and social rights was the restoration of their political rights. Even after the enactment of the landmark 1964 Civil Rights Act, the civil rights movement insisted on the necessity of a voting rights act to safeguard its gains, and it forced the hand of the President of the United States to get it. The results were dramatic. In the South and across the nation, violence against blacks declined, the quality of public services delivered to blacks increased, and the number of black public officials grew.[22] After the Voting Rights Act, fewer politicians could risk the consequences of ignoring black citizens. As the racial disparities in political participation narrowed, the incentives facing political leaders changed fundamentally. To be sure, massive racial inequalities in political participation persist to this day. African-Americans still possess fewer resources and still face tremendous obstacles to full incorporation in the American political system. Nevertheless, it is difficult to imagine that the gains blacks have made since the 1950s could have occurred had not racial inequalities in political participation lessened.

Granted, African-American political participation is an extreme case. Southern blacks were barred from political society, if not by legal sanction then by violence, intimidation, and harassment. The

---

[22]Harold W. Stanley, *Voter Mobilization and the Politics of Race* (New York: Praeger, 1987); Richard Bensel and Elizabeth Sanders, "The Impact of the Voting Rights Act on Southern Welfare Systems," in Benjamin Ginsberg and Allan Stone, eds., *Do Elections Matter?* (New York: M. E. Sharpe, 1986), pp. 52–70; William R. Keech, *The Impact of Negro Voting: The Role of the Vote in the Quest for Equality* (Chicago: Rand McNally, 1968). Black civil disturbances in American cities in the 1960s also had important consequences: These upheavals moved racial issues to the top of the American political agenda; they prompted members of Congress to lobby antipoverty agencies to direct more money to riot-torn communities; they stimulated a flurry of new policies and programs designed to address the grievances of urban blacks. James W. Button, *Black Violence: Political Impact of the 1960s Riots* (Princeton: Princeton University Press, 1978); David C. Colby, "A Test of the Relative Efficacy of Political Tactics," *American Journal of Political Science* 26 (November 1982), pp. 741–53; Albert K. Karnig and Susan Welch, *Black Representation and Urban Policy* (Chicago: University of Chicago Press, 1980); Peter Eisinger, "Black Employment in Municipal Jobs: The Impact of Black Political Power," *American Political Science Review* 76 (June 1982), pp. 380–92.

poor, the uneducated, and the unfortunate might not be able to afford to participate, they might not be mobilized to participate, but at least they are not forcibly excluded.

However true that is, though, the simple fact is that democratic government provides few incentives for leaders to attend to the needs of people who neither affect the achievement of their policy goals nor influence the perpetuation of their tenure in office.[23] Politicians can serve either the active or the inactive. The active contribute directly to their goals: They pressure, they contribute, they vote. The inactive offer only potential, the *possibility* that they might someday rise up against rulers who neglect them. Only the rare politician would pass up the blandishments of the active to champion the cause of those who never take part.[24]

Even the rare politician has limits. Suppose democratic leaders strive conscientiously to represent all citizens, the active and inactive alike. They still need to discover what the citizens want. As for the active, the leaders' task is easy: Participants speak for themselves and thereby shape the information that officials draw upon as they make their choices. The idle go unheard: They do not speak up, define the agenda, frame the issues, or affect the choices leaders make. Even with the best intentions, it is difficult to judge the interests of people who do not disclose them.[25]

---

[23] See, for example, V. O. Key, Jr., *Southern Politics in State and Nation* (New York: Vintage, 1949), pp. 507–8, 527.

[24] For some thought-provoking indications that class inequalities in turnout have real welfare consequences, see Kim Quaile Hill and Jan E. Leighley, "The Policy Consequences of Class Bias in State Electorates," *American Journal of Political Science* 36 (May 1992), pp. 351–65.

[25] Recognizing the overwhelming task of sifting through all the information that comes to leaders' attention, one might even pronounce the task impossible. See, for example, Raymond A. Bauer, Ithiel de Sola Pool, and Lewis Anthony Dexter, *American Business and Public Policy: The Politics of Foreign Trade*, 2nd ed. (Chicago: Aldine-Atherton, 1972); Lewis Anthony Dexter, "What Do Congressmen Hear: The Mail," *Public Opinion Quarterly* 20 (Winter 1956), pp. 16–27; John W. Kingdon, *Congressmen's Voting Decisions*, 2nd ed. (New York: Harper & Row, 1981); Philip E. Converse and Roy Pierce, *Political Representation in France* (Cambridge: Harvard University Press, 1986); Richard F. Fenno, Jr., *Home Style: House Members in Their Districts* (Boston: Little, Brown, 1978); John Mark Hansen, *Gaining Access: Congress and the Farm Lobby, 1919–1981* (Chicago: University of Chicago Press, 1991), pp. 227–30.

The extent of citizen involvement in American politics matters, then, because people defend and express their interests through participation. "If a group is inactive, whether by free choice, violence, intimidation, or law," Robert A. Dahl observed, "the normal American system does not necessarily provide it with a checkpoint anywhere in the process."[26]

The thirty-year decline of citizen involvement in elections and the more recent decline of citizen involvement in government has yielded a politically engaged class that is not only growing smaller and smaller but also less and less representative of the American polity. In fact, the economic inequalities in political participation that prevail in the United States today are as large as the racial disparities in political participation that prevailed in the 1950s. America's leaders today face few incentives to attend to the needs of the disadvantaged.

---

[26]Robert A. Dahl, *A Preface to Democratic Theory* (Chicago: University of Chicago Press, 1956), p. 138.

APPENDIX A

PARTICIPATION IN GOVERNMENTAL POLITICS: DATA SOURCES AND CODING

Aggregate Time-Series Analysis, 1973–1990

Percentage of voting-age population that wrote a letter to Congress. Source: *Roper Reports* Nos. 73–9 to 91–1, September 1973 to December 1990. *Question Wording:* "Now here is a list of things some people do about government and politics. Have you happened to have done any of these things in the past year? Written your congressman or senator." Coding: Percentage of valid responses.

Percentage of voting-age population that attended a local meeting on a town or school affair. Source: *Roper Reports* Nos. 73–9 to 91–1, September 1973 to December 1990. *Question Wording:* "Now here is a list of things some people do about government and politics. Have you happened to have done any of these things in the past year? Attended a public meeting on town or school affairs." Coding: Percentage of valid responses.

Percentage of voting-age population that signed a petition. Source: *Roper Reports* Nos. 73–9 to 91–1, September 1973 to December 1990. *Question Wording:* "Now here is a list of things some people do about government and politics. Have you

249

happened to have done any of these things in the past year? Signed a petition." Coding: Percentage of valid responses.

Percentage of voting-age population that was an officer of a club or organization. Source: *Roper Reports* Nos. 73–9 to 91–1, September 1973 to December 1990. *Question Wording:* "Now here is a list of things some people do about government and politics. Have you happened to have done any of these things in the past year? Served as an officer of a club or organization." Coding: Percentage of valid responses.

Percentage of voting-age population that served on a committee for a local organization. Source: *Roper Reports* Nos. 73–9 to 91–1, September 1973 to December 1990. *Question Wording:* "Now here is a list of things some people do about government and politics. Have you happened to have done any of these things in the past year? Served on a committee for some local organization." Coding: Percentage of valid responses.

Percentage of voting-age population that worked for a political party. Source: *Roper Reports* Nos. 73–9 to 91–1, September 1973 to December 1990. *Question Wording:* "Now here is a list of things some people do about government and politics. Have you happened to have done any of these things in the past year? Worked for a political party." Coding: Percentage of valid responses.

Freshman representatives and senators. Source: Norman J. Ornstein, Thomas E. Mann, and Michael J. Malbin, *Vital Statistics on Congress, 1989–1990* (Washington, D.C.: Congressional Quarterly Press, 1990), pp. 17–18, 19. Coding: Sum of percentage of House members serving first term and percentage of senators first elected within previous election cycle. Data are yearly.

Congressional activism. Source: "Resume of Congressional Activity," *Congressional Record Daily Digest,* 1973 to 1990. Coding: Natural logarithm of total number of bills introduced into both the House and Senate during the entire year. Data are yearly.

Presidential calls for letters. Source: *Public Papers of the Presidents,* 1973–1989; *Weekly Compilation of Presidential Documents,* 1990. Coding: 1 if prime-time televised speech within week of Roper Survey asked viewers to write to Congress, 0 otherwise. Data are weekly.

School-aged children per 1,000 voting-age population. Source: U.S. Department of Education, National Center for Education Statistics, *Digest of Educational Statistics*, 1990; U.S. Bureau of the Census, *Current Population Reports*, Series P-25, No. 732, Sept. 1978, No. 948, April 1984, No. 1059, April 1990. Coding: Number of children enrolled in public-elementary and secondary schools per thousand voting-age population. Data are yearly.

Change in real, per capita property tax collections. Source: U.S. Department of Commerce, *Survey of Current Business*, "Selected NIPA Tables," Tables 3.3 and 7.1, 1983–1991, and U.S. Department of Commerce, *The National Income and Product Accounts of the United States, 1929–82: Statistical Tables*, 1986, Tables 3.3 and 7.1; U.S. Census Bureau, *Current Population Reports*, Series P-25, No. 1045, January 1990, pp. 86–87. Coding: Difference between state and local property tax collected in current quarter and in quarter prior, deflated to 1990 dollars, normalized to population. Data are quarterly.

Watergate. Coding: 1 for period through September 1974, 0 otherwise.

Unemployment rate. Source: U.S. Department of Commerce, Bureau of Economic Analysis, *Business Statistics, 1961–1988*, pp. 44, 249; U.S. Department of Commerce, *Survey of Current Business*, 1989–1991. Data are monthly.

Presidential budget proposal as a percentage of current year. Source: *Congressional Quarterly Almanac*, 1973, pp. 982–83, 1974, pp. 938–39, 1975, pp. 910–11, 1976, pp. 690–91, 1977, pp. 206–07, 1978, pp. 52–53, 1979, pp. 186–87, 1980, pp. 136–37, 1981, pp. 254–55, 1982, pp. 180–81, 1983, pp. 430–31, 1984, pp. 136–37, 1985, pp. 430–31, 1986, pp. 538–39, 1987, pp. 580–81, 1988, pp. 190–91, 1989, pp. 76–77, 1990, pp. 120–21; U.S. Department of Commerce, *Survey of Current Business*, "Selected NIPA Tables," Table 7.1. Coding: Presidential budget proposal, deflated by current year inflation rate, as a percentage of current year's budget. Data are yearly.

Holiday in month. Coding: Number of national holidays—New Year's Day, Easter, Memorial Day, Independence Day, Labor Day,

Thanksgiving Day, and Christmas—within four weeks previous to a Roper survey. Data are weekly.

Days Congress in session. Source: *Congressional Directory*, 101st Congress, 1989, pp. 526–28; Commerce Clearing House, *Congressional Index*, 1989–1990, 1990, pp. 51–52. Coding: Number of days within the four weeks previous to a Roper survey that Congress was in session. Data are weekly.

Bills on floor. Source: *Congressional Record Daily Digest*, "Resume of Congressional Activity," 1973 to 1990. Coding: Natural logarithm of difference between number of bills reported from committee (both House and Senate) up to current month and number of bills passed (both House and Senate) up to month prior. Data are monthly.

Percentage of voting-age population with local budgets due. Source: Educational Research Service, "List of School Systems Responding to 1981–82 ERS Local School Budget Survey to Date," mimeo., December 1981; U.S. Department of Education, National Center for Education Statistics, *Digest of Educational Statistics*, 1990; U.S. Bureau of the Census, *Current Population Reports*, Series P-25, No. 732, Sept. 1978, No. 948, April 1984, No. 1059, April 1990. Coding: For each month, sum of voting-age populations of states and localities with school fiscal years beginning the next month. Data are monthly.

Percentage of voting-age population within two months of ballot access closing date. Source: U.S. Senate, Committee on Rules and Administration, "Election Law Guidebook, 1976," Sen. Doc. 94-216, 94th Cong., 2d sess., 1976, pt. 2; U.S. House of Representatives, Committee on House Administration, "Important Statutory and Regulatory Information and Accompanying Forms Relating to the Election of Candidates to the House of Representatives," 94th. Cong., 2d sess., 1976, pt. 4; U.S. Senate, Committee on Rules and Administration, "Senate Election Law Guidebook, 1980," Sen. Doc. 96-45, 96th Cong., 2d sess., 1980, pt. 3; U. S. Senate Committee on Rules and Administration, "Senate Election Law Guidebook, 1984," Sen. Doc. 98-23, 98th Cong., 2d sess., 1984, pt. 3; U.S. Senate, Committee on Rules and Administration, "Senate Election Law Guidebook, 1986," Sen. Doc.

99-28, 99th Cong., 2d sess., 1986, pt. 3; U.S. House of Representatives, Committee on House Administration, "U.S. House of Representatives Election Law Guidebook, 1988," Hse. Doc. 100-208, 100th Cong., 1st sess., 1988, pt. 2; U.S. Senate, Committee on Rules and Administration, "Senate Election Law Guidebook, 1990," Sen. Doc. 101-26, 101st Cong., 2d sess., 1990, part 3; U.S. Bureau of the Census, *Current Population Reports*, Series P-25, No. 732, Sept. 1978, No. 948, April 1984, No. 1059, April 1990. Coding: Sum of voting-age populations of states within two months before deadline for submission of ballot access petitions. For 1974 and 1978, closing dates coded from 1976 source, for 1982 from 1980 source. Data are monthly.

Individual Cross-Sectional Analysis, 1976

Unless otherwise noted, the source of these data is the American National Election Study, 1976, conducted by the Center for Political Studies at the University of Michigan and made available through the Inter-university Consortium for Political and Social Research.

Wrote to Congress. *Question Wording:* "Besides voting, people sometimes take part in several other types of political activities that are related to national politics and the government in Washington. Please look at this list of activities and tell me if you have done any of them in the last two or three years. Spoken to or written your congressman or some other national leader." Coding: 1 if yes; 0 if no.

Attended a meeting. *Question Wording:* "Now, how about activities in your local community? Please look at the next page and tell me if you have been involved in any of these local activities in the last two or three years? Attended meetings of city council or school board." Coding: 1 if yes; 0 if no.

Signed a petition. *Question Wording:* "Besides voting, people sometimes take part in several other types of political activities that are related to national politics and the government in Washington. Please look at this list of activities and tell me if you have done any of them in the last two or three years. Signed a petition either for or against action by the national government." "Now, how about activities in your local community? Please look at the next page and tell me if you have been involved in any of these local activities in the last two or three years? Signed a petition for or against action by the local government?" Coding: 1 if yes to either question; 0 if no to both.

Education. *Question Wording:* Summary item from series of questions: "What is the highest grade of school or year of college you completed? Did you get a high school diploma or pass a high school equivalency degree? Have you had any other schooling? What kind? Do you have a college degree? What degree is that?" Coding: Recoded to a zero-one interval, with 0 lowest and 1 highest.

Age. *Question Wording:* Summary item from question: "What is your date of birth?" Coding: actual.

Women. *Question Wording:* Observed by interviewer. Coding: 1 if female, 0 if male.

Blacks. *Question Wording:* Observed by interviewer. Coding: 1 if African-American, 0 otherwise.

Mexican-Americans and Puerto Ricans. *Question Wording:* "In addition to being an American, what do you consider your main ethnic or nationality group?" Coding: 1 if Mexican-American or Puerto Rican, 0 otherwise.

External efficacy. *Question Wording:* "Now I'm going to read some of the things people tell us when we interview them. Just tell me whether you agree or disagree with them. People like me don't have any say about what the government does. I don't think public officials care much what people like me think." Coding: For each item, coded 1 if disagree, 0 if agree, then summed and rescaled to a zero-one interval.

External efficacy (local). *Question Wording:* "I'm going to read some of the kinds of things people tell us about their local town or community government when we interview and ask you whether you agree or disagree with them. People like me don't have any say about what the local government does." Coding: 1 if disagree, 0 if agree.

Internal efficacy (local). *Question Wording:* "I'm going to read some of the kinds of things people tell us about their local town or community government when we interview and ask you whether you agree or disagree with them. Sometimes local politics and government seem so complicated that a person like me can't really understand what's going on." Coding: 1 if disagree, 0 if agree.

Unemployed. *Question Wording:* "We'd like to know if you are working now, or are you unemployed, retired, or what?" Coding: 1 if unemployed, 0 otherwise.

Working. *Question Wording:* "We'd like to know if you are working now, or are you unemployed, retired, or what?" Coding: 1 if working, 0 otherwise.

Income. *Question Wording:* "Please look at this page and tell me the letter of the income group that includes all members of your family in 1975 before taxes. This figure should include dividends, interest, salaries, wages, pensions, and all other income." Coding: Recoded to a zero-one interval, with 0 lowest and 1 highest.

Joined with others to work on a national problem. *Question Wording:* "Besides voting, people sometimes take part in several other types of political activities that are related to national politics and the government in Washington. Please look at this list of activities and tell me if you have done any of them in the last two or three years. Worked with others or joined an organization trying to do something about some national problem." Coding: 1 if yes; 0 if no.

Joined with others to work on a local problem. *Question Wording:* "Now, how about activities in your local community? Please look at the next page and tell me if you have been involved in any of these local activities in the last two or three years? Worked with others or joined an organization in your community to do something about some community problem." Coding: 1 if yes; 0 if no.

Contacted by party. *Question Wording:* "As you know, the political parties try to talk to as many people as they can, to get them to vote for their candidate. Did anyone from one of the political parties call you up or come around and talk to you about the campaign this year?" Coding: 1 if yes; 0 if no.

First-term senator. Source: *Congressional Directory*, 94th Congress, 2d session, 1976. Coding: 1 if senator first elected in 1974 or appointed or elected since, 0 otherwise.

First-term representative. Source: *Congressional Directory*, 94th Congress, 2d session, 1976. Coding: 1 if representative first elected in 1974 or in special election since, 0 otherwise.

School-aged children. *Question Wording:* "Do you have any children? How many? What are their ages?" Coding: 1 if any children ages 5 to 18 years, 0 otherwise.

PARTICIPATION IN ELECTORAL POLITICS: DATA SOURCES AND CODING

Individual-Level Survey Data

All individual-level data are taken from the American National Election Studies Cumulative Data File, 1952–1988, 5th release, and the American National Election Study, 1990 Post Election Survey.

Voter turnout. *Question wording:* "In talking to people about the election we find that a lot of people weren't able to vote because they weren't registered or they were sick or they just didn't have time. How about you, did you vote in the elections this November?" Coding: 1 if yes, 0 if no.

Try to persuade others how to vote. *Question wording:* "We would like to find out about some of the things people do to help a party or candidate win an election. During the campaign, did you talk to any people and try to show them why they should vote for one of the parties or candidates?" Coding: 1 if yes, 0 if no.

Attend political meetings or rallies. *Question wording:* "Did you go to any political meetings, rallies, dinners, speeches, or things like that in support of a particular candidate?" Coding: 1 if yes, 0 if no.

Work for a political party or candidate. *Question wording:* "Did you do any (other) work for one of the parties or candidates during the campaign?" Coding: 1 if yes, 0 if no.

Contribute money to a political party or candidate. *Question wording:* "During an election year people are often asked to make a contribution to support campaigns. Did you give any money to an individual candidate running for public office?" "Did you give money to a political party during this election year?" Coding: 1 if yes to either question, 0 if no to both questions.

Income. *Question wording:* "Please look at this page and tell me the letter of the income group that includes the combined income of all members of your family living here in [year] before taxes. This figure should include salaries, wages, pensions, dividends, interest, and all other income." Coding: 0 if 0–16th percentile, .25 if 17th–33d percentile, .50 if 34th–67th percentile, .75 if 68th–95th percentile, 1 if 96th–100th percentile.

Education. *Question wording:* "What is the highest grade of school or year of college you have completed?" "Did you get a high school diploma or pass a high school equivalency test?" "What is the highest degree that you have earned?" Coding: 0 if 8 grades or less, .25 if 9–12 grades with no diploma or equivalency, .50 if 12 grades, diploma, or equivalency, .75 if some college, 1 if college degree.

Unemployed. *Question wording:* "We'd like to know if you are working now, temporarily laid off, or are unemployed, retired, permanently disabled, a homemaker, a student, or what?" Coding: 1 if unemployed, 0 otherwise.

Age. *Question wording:* "What is the month, day and year of your birth?" Coding: age in years.

External efficacy. *Question wording:* "Now I'd like to read some of the kinds of things people tell us when we interview them. Please tell me whether you agree or disagree with these statements." "I don't think public officials care much what people like me think." "People like me don't have any say about what the government does." Coding: for each item, coded 0 if agree, 1 if disagree, then summed and rescaled to the zero–one interval.

Internal efficacy. *Question wording:* "Sometimes politics and government seem so complicated that a person like me can't really understand what's going on." Coding: 0 if agree, 1 if disagree.

Strength of party identification. *Question wording:* "Generally speaking, do you usually think of yourself as a Republican, a Democrat, an Independent, or what?" (If Republican or Democrat) "Would you call yourself a strong (Republican/Democrat) or not very strong (Republican/Democrat)?" (If independent, other, or no preference) "Do you think of yourself as closer to the Republican or Democratic party?" Coding: 0 if independent or apolitical, .33 if independent leaning toward a party, .67 if a weak partisan, 1 if a strong partisan.

Affect for a party. *Question wording:* "Is there anything in particular you like about the Republican party?" "Is there anything in particular you dislike about the Republican party?" "Is there anything in particular you like about the Democratic party?" "Is there anything in particular you dislike about the Democratic party?" Coding: the absolute value of difference between two sums, coded to the zero–one interval: the sum of Democratic party "likes" and Republican party "dislikes" minus the sum of Democratic party "dislikes" and Republican party "likes."

Care which party wins the presidential election. *Question wording:* "Generally, speaking, would you say that you personally care a good deal which party wins the presidential election this fall, or don't you care very much which party wins?" Coding: 0 if don't care very much, 1 if care a good deal.

Care which party wins congressional elections. *Question wording:* "Generally speaking, would you say that you personally cared a good deal about the way the elections to the U.S. House of Representatives came out?" Coding: 0 if don't care very much, 1 if care a great deal.

Affect for presidential candidate. *Question wording:* "Is there anything in particular you like about [the Republican candidate]?" "Is there anything in particular you dislike about [the Republican candidate]?" "Is there anything in particular you like about [the Democratic candidate]?" "Is there anything in particular you dislike about [the Democratic candidate]?" Coding: the absolute value of difference between two sums, coded to the zero–one interval: the sum of Democratic candidate "likes" and Republican candidate "dislikes" minus the sum of Democratic candidate "dislikes" and Republican candidate "likes."

Trust government to do the right thing. *Question wording:* "People have different ideas about the government in Washington. These ideas don't refer to Democrats or Republicans in particular, but just to the government in general. We want to see how you feel about these ideas." "How much of the time do you think you can trust the government in Washington to do what is right—just about always, most of the time, or only some of the time?" Coding: 0 if none or some of the time, .5 if most of the time, 1 if just about always.

Government run by a few big interests. *Question wording:* "Would you say the government is pretty much run by a few big interests looking out for themselves or that it is run for the benefit of all the people?" Coding: 0 if few big interests, 1 if benefit of all.

Government wastes money. *Question wording:* "Do you think that people in the government waste a lot of money we pay in taxes, waste some of it, or don't waste very much of it?" Coding: 0 if a lot, .5 if some, 1 if not very much.

Government officials are crooked. *Question wording:* "Do you feel that almost all of the people running the government are crooked, not very many are, or do you think hardly any of them are crooked?" Coding: 0 if quite a few, .5 if not many, 1 if hardly any.

Trust in government scale. Coding: Sum of the four previous questions divided by four.

Government pays attention to what people think. *Question wording:* "Over the years, how much attention do you feel the government pays to what the people think when it decides what to do—a good deal, some or not much?" Coding: 0 if not much, .5 if some, 1 if a good deal.

Elections make the government pay attention. *Question wording:* "And how much do you feel that having elections makes the government pay attention to what the people think, a good deal, some or not much?" Coding: 0 if not much, .5 if some, 1 if a good deal.

Government responsiveness scale. Coding: Sum of the responses to the previous two questions, divided by two.

Citizen duty. *Question wording:* "If a person doesn't care how an election comes out then that person shouldn't vote in it." Coding: 0 if agree, 1 if disagree.

Years in community. *Question wording:* "How long have you lived here in your present (city/town)?" Coding: actual number of years.

Church attendance. 1952–1968: *Question wording:* "Would you say you go to church regularly, often, seldom, or never?" Coding: 0 if never, .33 if seldom, .67 if often, 1 if regularly. 1970–1988: *Question wording:* "Would you say you go to (church/synagogue) every week, almost every week, once or twice a month, a few times a year, or never?" Coding: 0 if never, .33 if a few times a year, .67 if once or twice a month, 1 if every week or almost every week.

Homeowners. *Question wording:* "(Do you / Does your family) own your own home, pay rent or what?" Coding: 0 if not owned, 1 if owned.

Currently working. *Question wording:* "We'd like to know if you are working now, temporarily laid off, or are unemployed, retired, permanently disabled, a homemaker, a student, or what?" Coding: 1 if employed, 0 otherwise.

Contacted by a political party. *Question wording:* "The political parties try to talk to as many people as they can to get them to vote for their candidates. Did anyone from one of the political parties call you up or come around and talk to you about the campaign? Which party was that?" Coding: 0 if not contacted, 1 if contacted.

Perceived closeness of election. *Question wording:* "Do you think the presidential race will be close or will one candidate win by quite a bit?" Coding: 0 if will win by quite a bit, .5 if don't know or depends, 1 if close race.

Blacks. Observed by interviewer. Coding: 1 if black, 0 otherwise.

Mexican-Americans and Puerto Ricans. *Question wording:* "In addition to being an American what do you consider your main ethnic group or nationality group?" "Are you of Spanish or Hispanic origin or descent?" (If yes) "Please look at the booklet and tell me which category best describes your Hispanic origin." Coding: 1 if Mexican-American or Puerto Rican, 0 otherwise.

Live in Southern state. Observed by interviewer. Coding: 1 if lives in Alabama, Arkansas, Florida, Georgia, Louisiana, Mississippi,

North Carolina, South Carolina, Tennessee, Texas, or Virginia, 0 otherwise.

Live in border state. Observed by interviewer. Coding: 1 if lives in Missouri, Kentucky, Maryland, Oklahoma, or West Virginia, 0 otherwise.

Women. Observed by interviewer. Coding: 0 if man, 1 if woman.

Southern blacks prior to 1964. Coding: 1 if black living in the South between 1952 and 1962, 0 otherwise.

Women socialized prior to 1920. Coding: 1 if a woman born before 1911, 0 otherwise.

Aggregate Data

Aggregate Voter Turnout. Source: "Projection of the Population of Voting Age for States: November 1990," *Current Population Reports*, Series P-25, No. 1059, April 1990, Table 5; Congressional Quarterly, *Guide to U.S. Elections*, 2nd ed. (Washington, D.C.: Congressional Quarterly, 1985); Richard Scammon, *America Votes* (Washington, D.C.: Government Affairs Institute, 1986, 1990). Coding: In presidential years = [(votes cast for president)/(voting age population)]×100; in midterm years = [(votes cast for the highest vote getting race in each state)/(voting age population)]×100.

Close presidential election. Source: *The Gallup Poll Monthly*, various issues. Coding: Absolute value of the difference between the Democratic and Republican presidential candidates in the last Gallup poll conducted before the election.

Contested gubernatorial election. Source: Congressional Quarterly, *Guide to U.S. Elections*, 2nd ed. (Washington, D.C.: Congressional Quarterly, 1985); Richard Scammon, *America Votes* (Washington, D.C.: Government Affairs Institute, 1986, 1990). Coding: 1 if both a Democratic and Republican candidate are running in the gubernatorial election in the state, 0 otherwise.

Contested presidential primary election. Source: Congressional Quarterly, *Guide to U.S. Elections*, 2nd ed. (Washington, D.C.: Congressional Quarterly, 1985); *Congressional Quarterly Weekly Re-*

port, July 9, 1988, p. 1894; August 13, 1988, p. 2254. Coding: 1 if a contested presidential primary in the state, 0 otherwise.

Civil rights movement actions. Source: Doug McAdam, *Political Process and the Development of Black Insurgency, 1930–1970* (Chicago: University of Chicago Press, 1982), Tables 7.2 and 8.3. Coding: logarithm of the number of civil rights movement actions in the region over the previous eight years. The details of McAdam's coding procedures are described in his Appendix 1.

Literacy tests × **blacks.** Source: Bertram M. Bernard, *Election Laws of the Forty-eight States* (New York: Oceana Publications, 1950); Constance E. Smith, *Voting and Election Laws* (New York: Oceana Publications, 1960); Elizabeth Yadlosky, "Voting Laws of the 50 States and the District of Columbia," U.S. Library of Congress, Legislative Reference Service, May 18, 1964. Coding: 1 if a black living in a state with a literacy test with opportunities for discrimination (Alabama, Georgia, Mississippi, North Carolina, South Carolina), 0 otherwise.

Poll tax × **blacks.** Source: Bertram M. Bernard, *Election Laws of the Forty-eight States* (New York: Oceana Publications, 1950); Constance E. Smith, *Voting and Election Laws* (New York: Oceana Publications, 1960); Elizabeth Yadlosky, "Voting Laws of the 50 States and the District of Columbia," U.S. Library of Congress, Legislative Reference Service, May 18, 1964. Coding: 1 if black living in a state with a poll tax, 0 otherwise.

Periodic registration × **blacks.** Source: Bertram M. Bernard, *Election Laws of the Forty-eight States* (New York: Oceana Publications, 1950); Constance E. Smith, *Voting and Election Laws* (New York: Oceana Publications, 1960); Elizabeth Yadlosky, "Voting Laws of the 50 States and the District of Columbia," U.S. Library of Congress, Legislative Reference Service, May 18, 1964; Steven J. Rosenstone and Raymond E. Wolfinger, "The Effect of Registration Laws on Voter Turnout," *American Political Science Review* 72 (March 1978), pp. 22–45; League of Women Voters Education Fund, "Easy Does It: Registration and Absentee Voting Procedures by State" (Washington, D. C.: The League of Women Voters Education Fund, 1976, 1980, 1984, 1988); *The Book of States,* various years. Coding: 1 if a black living in a state with periodic voter registration, 0 otherwise.

1965 Voting Rights Act × blacks. Source: United States Commission on Civil Rights, *The Voting Rights Act: Ten Years After*, report, January 1975. Coding: 1 if a black living in a state in 1968 or 1972 covered by the 1965 Voting Rights Act, 0 otherwise.

1965 Voting Rights Act × whites. Source: United States Commission on Civil Rights, *The Voting Rights Act: Ten Years After*, report, January 1975. Coding: 1 if a white living in a state in 1968 or 1972 covered by the 1965 Voting Rights Act, 0 otherwise.

Voter registration closing date. Source: Bertram M. Bernard, *Election Laws of the Forty-eight States* (New York: Oceana Publications, 1950); Constance E. Smith, *Voting and Election Laws* (New York: Oceana Publications, 1960); Elizabeth Yadlosky, "Voting Laws of the 50 States and the District of Columbia," U.S. Library of Congress, Legislative Reference Service, May 18, 1964; Steven J. Rosenstone and Raymond E. Wolfinger, "The Effect of Registration Laws on Voter Turnout," *American Political Science Review* 72 (March 1978), pp. 22–45; League of Women Voters Education Fund, "Easy Does It: Registration and Absentee Voting Procedures by State" (Washington, D.C.: The League of Women Voters Education Fund, 1976, 1980, 1984, 1988); *The Book of States*, various years. Coding: Number of days prior to general election that one can last register to vote.

Counties where federal examiners were dispatched under the Voting Rights Act of 1965. Source: United States Commission on Civil Rights, *The Voting Rights Act: Ten Years After*, report, January 1975, Appendix 3. Coding: 1 in 1968 or 1972 if a county where federal examiners were sent, 0 otherwise.

Unopposed House seat. Source: Congressional Quarterly, *Guide to U.S. Elections*, 2nd ed. (Washington, D.C.: Congressional Quarterly, 1985); Richard Scammon, *America Votes* (Washington, D.C.: Government Affairs Institute, 1986, 1990). Coding: 1 if an election for the U.S. House of Representatives where either a Democratic or Republican candidate does not run in the general election, 0 otherwise.

Open House seat. Source: 1956–1972, Gary Jacobson, personal communication, May 28, 1991; 1974–1988, American National Election Studies Cumulative Data File, 1952–1988, 5th release. Coding: 1 if no incumbent is running for the U.S. House of Representatives, 0 otherwise.

Toss-up House election. Source: *Congressional Quarterly Weekly Report*, November 2, 1956; October 31, 1958; November 4, 1960; November 2, 1962; October 23, 1964; November 4, 1966; October 25, 1968; October 28, 1970; October 7, 1972; November 2, 1974; October 30, 1976; November 4, 1978; November 1, 1980; October 9, 1982; October 13, 1984; October 11, 1986; October 15, 1988. Coding: 1 if a toss-up election for the House of Representatives, 0 otherwise.

PARTICIPATION IN GOVERNMENTAL POLITICS: ESTIMATED EQUATIONS

Table C-1 Causes of Writing to Congress, 1973–1990 (Ordinary Least Squares Estimates)

Variable	Coefficient	Standard Error
Social Involvement		
Percentage of population that was officer of a club or organization	.300	.091
Mobilization by Political Leaders		
Percentage of population that worked for political party	.318	.138
Percentage of senators and representatives serving first two years of term	−.084	.016
Number of bills introduced in year, natural logarithm	.676	.233
Presidential speeches in last week requesting letters to Congress	1.072	.715

Table C-1 (*continued*)

Variable	Coefficient	Standard Error
Mobilization Around Issues		
Watergate period	1.435	.553
Unemployment rate, month prior	.277	.088
Presidential budget request as a percentage of last year's budget	−3.884	2.746
Presidential budget request as a percentage of last year's budget, squared	.020	.014
Mobilization Around Opportunities		
Number of days in session in last four weeks	.035	.018
Number of bills on the floor, natural logarithm	.263	.066
(Constant)	189.984	136.554

Adjusted R^2 = .44
Standard error of the regression = 1.33
Durbin-Watson statistic = 1.65
Number of cases = 172
Source: Appendix A.

Table C-2   Causes of Attending a Local Meeting on a Town or
School Affair, 1973–1990 (Ordinary Least Squares
Estimates)

Variable	Coefficient	Standard Error
Social Involvement		
Percentage of population that served on committee of local club or organization	.628	.122
Percentage of population that served as an officer of a club or organization	.327	.106
Mobilization Around Issues		
School-aged children per thousand voting-age population	.026	.003
Change in real, per capita property tax collections	.027	.012
Mobilization Around Opportunities		
Holiday in last four weeks	−.180	.166
Percentage of the voting-age population in areas with school budgets due, month prior	.021	.005
(Constant)	2.673	.983

Adjusted R^2 = .64
Standard error of the regression = 1.28
Durbin-Watson statistic = 1.80
Number of cases = 172
Source: Appendix A.

Table C-3   Causes of Signing a Petition, 1973–1990 (Ordinary
Least Squares Estimates)

Variable	Coefficient	Standard Error
Social Involvement		
Percentage of population that was officer of a club or organization	.690	.147
Mobilization by Political Leaders		
Percentage of population that worked for a political party	1.071	.198
Percentage of senators and representatives serving first two years of term	−.103	.026
Mobilization Around Issues		
Change in real, per capita property tax collections	.031	.021
Mobilization Around Opportunities		
Percentage of population in areas with school budgets due, month prior	.034	.008
Percentage of population in states with ballot access petitions due, month prior	.030	.013
(Constant)	25.451	1.311

Adjusted R² = .45
Standard error of the regression = 2.19
Durbin-Watson statistic = 1.80
Number of cases = 172
Source: Appendix A.

Table C-4   Causes of Writing to Congress, 1976
(Probit Estimates)

Variable	Coefficient	Standard Error	Effect on Probability of Writing (in Percent)
Resources			
Education	.557	.174	12.0
Age	.043	.016	4.4
Age squared (× .01)	−.046	.017	
Women	−.168	.092	−3.7
Blacks	−.382	.174	−7.3
Mexican-Americans and Puerto Ricans	−1.040	.615	−14.4
External efficacy	.267	.117	5.7
Social Involvement			
Currently unemployed	−.443	.299	−8.1
Joined with others to work on a national problem	.810	.136	22.7
Joined with others to work on a local problem	.521	.102	12.9
Mobilization by Political Leaders			
Contacted by a party	.337	.096	7.8
Represented in the Senate by a newly elected senator	−.205	.110	−4.3
(Constant)	−2.431	.381	

Likelihood Ratio Index = .18
Percentage of cases correctly predicted = 84.7 (null model = 81.7)
Chi-square = 213.0 with 12 degrees of freedom (probability < .001)
Number of cases = 1,238
Source: Appendix A.

Table C-5 Causes of Attending Local Meetings, 1976
(Probit Estimates)

Variable	Coefficient	Standard Error	Effect on Probability of Attending (in Percent)
	Resources		
Education	.575	.138	12.5
External efficacy, local referent	.152	.093	3.2
Internal efficacy, local referent	.249	.084	5.4
	Social Involvement		
Joined with others to work on a local problem	1.025	.079	28.7
	Mobilization Around Issues		
Children of school age	.551	.075	12.8
(Constant)	−1.994	.102	

Likelihood Ratio Index = .20
Percentage of cases correctly predicted = 82.9 (null model = 80.9)
Chi-square = 362.7 with 5 degrees of freedom (probability < .001)
Number of cases = 1,873
Source: Appendix A.

Table C-6   Causes of Signing a Petition, 1976
(Probit Estimates)

Variable	Coefficient	Standard Error	Effect on Probability of Signing (in Percent)
Resources			
External efficacy	.304	.085	9.2
Social Involvement			
Currently employed	.142	.073	4.2
Family income	.622	.127	18.7
Joined with others to work on a national problem	.428	.114	14.0
Joined with others to work on a local problem	.676	.081	22.9
Mobilization by Political Leaders			
Contacted by a party	.239	.075	7.4
Represented in the House by a newly elected representative	−.144	.078	−4.2
Represented in the Senate by a newly elected senator	−.240	.082	−7.0
Mobilization Around Issues			
Children of school age	.133	.073	4.0
(Constant)	−1.388	.092	

Likelihood Ratio Index = .13
Percentage of cases correctly predicted = 73.5 (null model = 70.2)
Chi-square = 259.0 with 9 degrees of freedom (probability < .001)
Number of cases = 1,663
Source: Appendix A.

PARTICIPATION IN ELECTORAL POLITICS: ESTIMATED EQUATIONS

Table D-1   Causes of Voter Turnout, 1956–1988 Presidential Election Years (Probit Estimates)

Variable	Coefficient	Standard Error	Effect on Probability of Voting (in Percent)
Resources			
Income	.550	.059	15.8
Education	.584	.053	16.6
Unemployed	−.095	.063	−2.7
Age	.054	.005	29.0
Age squared ($\times$ .01)	−.040	.005	
Internal efficacy	.102	.033	2.9
External efficacy	.360	.035	10.6
Evaluation of Parties and Candidates			
Strength of party identification	.364	.046	10.6
Affect for a party	.423	.079	11.4
Care which party wins presidential election	.219	.030	6.4
Affect for presidential candidate	.201	.065	5.6

(continued)

Table D-1   *(continued)*

Variable	Coefficient	Standard Error	Effect on Probability of Voting (in Percent)
Social Involvement			
Years in community, natural logarithm*	.096	.016	10.7
Church attendance	.518	.037	15.1
Homeowners*	.265	.029	7.5
Currently working	.075	.033	2.1
Mobilization by Parties			
Contacted by a party	.283	.033	7.8
Mobilization by Campaigns			
Close presidential election	.384	.147	3.0
Perceived closeness of election	.057	.032	1.6
Gubernatorial election	.179	.033	5.0
Presidential primary election	−.131	.030	−3.7
Mobilization by Social Movements			
Civil rights movement actions	.041	.008	7.3
Legal Organization of Elections			
Literacy tests × blacks	−.500	.188	−16.0
Poll tax × blacks	−.319	.238	−10.2
Periodic registration × blacks	−.387	.146	−11.6

Table D-1 *(continued)*

Variable	Coefficient	Standard Error	Effect on Probability of Voting (in Percent)
1965 Voting Rights Act × blacks	.582	.211	26.4
1965 Voting Rights Act × whites	.332	.110	19.5
Voter registration closing date	−.003	.001	−5.6

Other Demographic Variables

Live in Southern state	−.542	.034	−16.3
Live in border state	−.217	.051	−6.1
Blacks	−.150	.051	−4.4
Mexican-Americans and Puerto Ricans	−.194	.103	− 5.7
(Constant)	−2.417	.111	

Likelihood Ratio Index = .23
Percent of cases correctly predicted = 75.7 (null model = 68.4)
Chi-square = 3,245.5 with 31 degrees of freedom (probability < .001)
Number of cases = 11,310
*Coefficient reported for equation reestimated for 1968–1988 presidential election years only.
Source: Appendix B.

Table D-2   Causes of Trying to Persuade Others How to Vote, 1956–1988 Presidential Election Years (Probit Estimates)

Variable	Coefficient	Standard Error	Effect on Probability of Persuading (in Percent)
Resources			
Income	.177	.052	5.7
Education	.427	.048	13.9
Age	−.006	.001	−10.9
Internal efficacy	.172	.029	5.6
External efficacy	.152	.034	4.8
Evaluation of Parties and Candidates			
Strength of party identification	.244	.044	7.8
Affect for a party	.396	.070	13.3
Care which party wins presidential election	.336	.030	10.7
Affect for presidential candidate	.678	.059	22.9
Social Involvement			
Currently working	.056	.030	1.8
Mobilization by Parties			
Contacted by a party	.346	.029	11.6

Table D-2 *(continued)*

Variable	Coefficient	Standard Error	Effect on Probability of Persuading (in Percent)
Mobilization by Campaigns			
Close presidential election	.911	.138	7.8
Perceived closeness of election	.044	.030	1.4
Other Demographic Variables			
Women	−.202	.028	−6.5
(Constant)	−1.268	.025	

Likelihood Ratio Index = .14
Percent of cases correctly predicted = 70.3 (null model = 66.8)
Chi-square = 2,033.4 with 14 degrees of freedom (probability < .001)
Number of cases = 11,426
Source: Appendix B.

Table D-3 Causes of Working for a Political Party or Candidate, 1956–1988 Presidential Election Years (Probit Estimates)

Variable	Coefficient	Standard Error	Effect on Probability of Working (in Percent)
Resources			
Income	.222	.098	1.8
Education	.356	.083	2.9
Age	.019	.009	1.6
Age squared (× .01)	−.019	.010	
Internal efficacy	.194	.048	1.7
External efficacy	.184	.064	1.4
Evaluation of Parties and Candidates			
Strength of party identification	.391	.082	3.0
Affect for a party	.352	.111	3.4
Care which party wins presidential election	.214	.058	1.7
Affect for presidential candidate	.431	.097	4.0
Social Involvement			
Church attendance*	.152	.062	1.2

Table D-3 *(continued)*

Variable	Coefficient	Standard Error	Effect on Probability of Working (in Percent)
Mobilization by Parties			
Contacted by a party	.498	.046	4.8
Mobilization by Campaigns			
Close presidential election	.451	.237	1.0
Perceived closeness of election	.096	.053	.8
Mobilization by Social Movements			
Civil rights movement actions × whites	.029	.011	1.8
(Constant)	−3.667	.605	

Likelihood Ratio Index = .07
Percent of cases correctly predicted = 95.5 (null model = 95.5)
Chi-square = 291.2 with 15 degrees of freedom (probability < .001)
Number of cases = 11,333
*Coefficient reported for equation reestimated for 1968–1988 presidential election years only.
Source: Appendix B.

Table D-4   Causes of Contributing Money to a Political Party
or Candidate, 1956–1988 Presidential Election
Years (Probit Estimates)

Variable	Coefficient	Standard Error	Effect on Probability of Contributing (in Percent)
Resources			
Income	.974	.076	14.8
Education	.647	.065	9.8
Age	.009	.001	9.0
Internal efficacy	.160	.038	2.5
External efficacy	.188	.049	2.8
Evaluation of Parties and Candidates			
Strength of party identification	.354	.063	5.1
Affect for a party	.409	.089	7.0
Care which party wins presidential election	.240	.043	3.5
Affect for presidential candidate	.207	.077	3.3
Social Involvement			
Currently working	.125	.040	1.9
Mobilization by Parties			
Contacted by a party	.396	.037	6.6

Table D-4 *(continued)*

Variable	Coefficient	Standard Error	Effect on Probability of Contributing (in Percent)
Mobilization by Campaigns			
Close presidential election	.798	.188	3.2
Perceived closeness of election	.079	.042	1.2
Mobilization by Social Movements			
Civil rights movement actions	.031	.009	3.1
Other Demographic Variables			
Live in Southern state	−.217	.045	−3.2
Live in border state	−.306	.073	−4.3
(Constant)	−3.491	.259	

Likelihood Ratio Index = .14
Percent of cases correctly predicted = 89.8 (null model = 89.5)
Chi-square = 1,070.4 with 16 degrees of freedom (probability < .001)
Number of cases = 11,380
Source: Appendix B.

Table D-5 Causes of Voter Turnout, 1974–1986 Midterm
Election Years (Probit Estimates)

Variable	Coefficient	Standard Error	Effect on Probability of Voting (in Percent)
Resources			
Income	.151	.087	4.6
Education	.895	.079	27.0
Unemployed	−.283	.077	−8.5
Age	.052	.007	25.7
Age squared (× .01)	.041	.007	
External efficacy	.082	.041	2.5
Evaluation of Parties and Candidates			
Strength of party identification	.570	.063	17.5
Care which party wins congressional elections	.646	.040	20.7
Social Involvement			
Years in community, natural logarithm	.194	.020	23.3
Church attendance	.334	.052	10.2
Homeowners	.180	.049	5.5
Mobilization by Parties			
Contacted by a party	.340	.044	10.4

Table D-5 (*continued*)

Variable	Coefficient	Standard Error	Effect on Probability of Voting (in Percent)
Mobilization by Campaigns			
Unopposed House seat	−.134	.056	−4.0
Open House seat	.124	.064	3.7
Toss-up House election	.200	.106	6.0
Other Demographic Variables			
Live in Southern state	−.323	.048	−9.8
Live in border state	−.277	.071	−8.4
Blacks	−.283	.070	−8.5
Mexican-Americans and Puerto Ricans	−.312	.142	−9.3
(Constant)	−3.350	.333	

Likelihood Ratio Index = .29
Percent of cases correctly predicted = 72.9 (null model = 51.2)
Chi-square = 2,0591.1 with 19 degrees of freedom (probability < .001)
Number of cases = 5,124
Source: Appendix B.

Table D-6 Causes of Trying to Persuade Others How to Vote, 1974–1986 Midterm Election Years (Probit Estimates)

Variable	Coefficient	Standard Error	Effect on Probability of Persuading (in Percent)
Resources			
Income	.144	.075	3.5
Education	.820	.073	19.6
Age	−.006	.001	−9.2
Evaluation of Parties and Candidates			
Strength of party identification	.580	.061	13.7
Care which party wins congressional election	.579	.041	14.1
Social Involvement			
Years in community, natural logarithm	.043	.018	3.9
Mobilization by Parties			
Contacted by a party	.427	.040	11.3
Mobilization by Campaigns			
Gubernatorial election	.158	.048	3.7
Other Demographic Variables			
Women	−.237	.038	−5.8
(Constant)	−2.066	.070	

Likelihood Ratio Index = .14
Percent of cases correctly predicted = 80.2 (null model = 79.5)
Chi-square = 929.2 with 9 degrees of freedom (probability < .001)
Number of cases = 6,542
Source: Appendix B.

Table D-7   Causes of Working for a Political Party or
Candidate, 1974–1986 Midterm Election Years
(Probit Estimates)

Variable	Coefficient	Standard Error	Effect on Probability of Working (in Percent)
Resources			
Education	.501	.111	4.3
Age	.012	.011	2.2
Age squared (× .01)	−.016	.011	
External efficacy	.119	.064	1.1
Evaluation of Parties and Candidates			
Strength of party identification	.522	.102	4.3
Care which party wins congressional election	.453	.070	3.7
Social Involvement			
Years in community, natural logarithm	.080	.032	2.6
Church attendance	.114	.080	1.0
Mobilization by Parties			
Contacted by a party	.595	.061	6.1
Mobilization by Campaigns			
Open House seat	.176	.086	1.7
(Constant)	−3.369	.541	

Likelihood Ratio Index = .08
Percent of cases correctly predicted = 95.0 (null model = 95.0)
Chi-square = 185.3 with 10 degrees of freedom (probability < .001)
Number of cases = 5,835
Source: Appendix B.

Table D-8   Causes of Contributing Money to a Political Party
or Candidate, 1974–1986 Midterm Election Years
(Probit Estimates)

Variable	Coefficient	Standard Error	Effect on Probability of Contributing (in Percent)
Resources			
Income	.999	.105	15.5
Education	.745	.097	10.9
Age	.010	.002	10.4
External efficacy	.162	.053	2.5
Evaluation of Parties and Candidates			
Strength of party identification	.474	.083	6.9
Care which party wins congressional election	.246	.055	3.7
Mobilization by Parties			
Contacted by a party	.278	.052	4.5
Mobilization by Campaigns			
Toss-up Senate election	.220	.078	3.7
Toss-up House election	.151	.113	2.5
Other Demographic Variables			
Women	−.167	.051	−2.6
Live in Southern state	−.127	.059	−1.9
Live in border state	−.155	.098	−2.3
(Constant)	−3.237	.242	

Likelihood Ratio Index = .13
Percent of cases correctly predicted = 89.6 (null model = 89.4)
Chi-square = 472.1 with 12 degrees of freedom (probability < .001)
Number of cases = 5,371
Source: Appendix B.

MOBILIZATION AND PARTICIPATION IN ELECTORAL POLITICS: ESTIMATED EQUATIONS

Table E-1 Causes of Being Contacted by a Political Party, 1956 to 1988 Presidential Election Years (Probit Estimates)

Variable	Coefficient	Standard Error	Effect on Probability of Being Contacted (in Percent)
	Resources		
Income	.316	.051	9.5
Education	.615	.046	18.6
Age	.012	.001	22.1
	Attachment to Parties		
Strength of party identification	.182	.039	5.3
	Social Involvement		
Years in community, natural logarithm*	.060	.015	6.9
Church attendance	.121	.034	3.6
Homeowners*	.144	.037	4.2
Union family	.063	.030	1.9

(continued)

287

Table E-1   (*continued*)

Variable	Coefficient	Standard Error	Effect on Probability of Being Contacted (in Percent)
Mobilization by Campaigns			
Close presidential election	.160	.128	1.3
Gubernatorial election	.071	.029	2.1
Unopposed House seat	−.165	.041	−4.7
Open House seat	.125	.044	3.9
Mobilization by Social Movements			
Civil rights movement actions	.023	.006	4.3
Other Demographic Variables			
Women socialized before 1920	−.151	.025	−4.4
Live in Southern state	−.131	.032	−3.8
Southern blacks before 1964	−.681	.231	−15.4
(Constant)	−1.847	.039	

Likelihood Ratio Index = .05
Percent of cases correctly predicted = 75.3 (null model = 75.3)
Chi-square = 704.7 with 16 degrees of freedom (probability < .001)
Number of cases = 12,606
*Coefficient reported for equation reestimated for 1968–1988 presidential election years only.
Source: Appendix B.

Table E-2 Causes of Being Contacted by a Political Party, 1974
to 1986 Midterm Election Years (Probit Estimates)

Variable	Coefficient	Standard Error	Effect on Probability of Being Contacted (in Percent)
Resources			
Income	.298	.072	9.5
Education	.711	.065	22.0
Age	.006	.001	12.1
Attachment to Parties			
Strength of party identification	.231	.053	7.2
Social Involvement			
Years in community, natural logarithm	.075	.017	9.1
Church attendance	.201	.044	6.3
Homeowners	.231	.043	7.2

(*continued*)

Table E-2   (*continued*)

Variable	Coefficient	Standard Error	Effect on Probability of Being Contacted (in Percent)
Mobilization by Campaigns			
Toss-up gubernatorial election	.054	.045	1.7
Toss-up Senate election	.228	.057	7.5
Toss-up House election	.168	.091	5.5
Open House seat	.164	.055	5.3
Other Demographic Variables			
Live in Southern state	−.141	.038	−4.4
(Constant)	−2.020	.056	

Likelihood Ratio Index = .07
Percent of cases correctly predicted = 71.7 (null model = 71.4)
Chi-square = 547.5 with 12 degrees of freedom (probability < .001)
Number of cases = 6,534
Source: Appendix B.

MEASURING INEQUALITY
IN POLITICAL PARTICIPATION

To assess the nature and level of inequality in political participation requires a measure of inequality that permits comparisons across groups, across forms of political participation, and across time. In this appendix we describe our measure, show how to interpret it, and identify its properties.[1]

Underrepresentation and Overrepresentation

We begin by partitioning the population into mutually exclusive and exhaustive groups. POP_i will stand for the percentage of the *population* that falls into group i of a k-fold partition. Next, we tally the number of *participants* that come from each group and let $PART_i$ stand for group i's share of the participants.

To learn whether a group is under- or overrepresented among the participants, we compare the group's share of the participants to its share of the population as a whole:

$$RATIO_i = PART_i / POP_i.$$

---

[1] Every measure of inequality—ours included—is arbitrary, incomplete, and embedded with normative assumptions. See Amartya Sen, *On Economic Inequality* (Oxford: Clarendon Press, 1973); Douglas Rae, Douglas T. Yates, Jr., Jennifer L. Hochschild, Joseph Morone, and Carole Fessler, *Equalities* (Cambridge: Harvard University Press, 1981).

A ratio of 1.0 means that the group is *just-represented*—its share of the participants equals its share of the population.[2] A ratio larger than 1.0 means that the group is *overrepresented* in the pool of participants, and a ratio of less than 1.0 means that the group is *underrepresented*. The more the ratio exceeds 1.0, the more overrepresented the group; the more the ratio falls below 1.0, the more underrepresented.

The following table illustrates these simple calculations for educational inequalities among those who worked for a political party or candidate in a presidential election year between 1952 and 1988.

Education	Percent of Population	Percent of Participants	Representation Ratio
Grades 0–8	20.1	9.6	.48
Grades 9–11	16.3	8.1	.50
High school diploma	32.8	28.5	.87
Some college	16.8	22.4	1.33
College degree	14.0	31.5	2.25

Those with 0–8 years of formal schooling are grossly underrepresented: They make up 20.1 percent of the population, but only 9.6 percent of the participants; their share of the participant pool is only 48 percent of their share of the population. College graduates, on the other hand, are overrepresented by 2.25 times: They make up only 14 percent of the population, but 31.5 percent of the participants.

---

[2] Put differently, participants are representative of the population when they constitute fair samples of the population—when they accurately reflect or mirror the population as a whole. See Marie Collins Swabey, *The Democratic State* (Cambridge: Harvard University Press, 1937), pp. 20–29, and Hanna Fenichel Pitkin, *The Concept of Representation* (Berkeley: University of California Press, 1967), pp. 60–80. Understanding whether participants are representative of the population is a different task from assessing whether a legislator represents her constituency. In the case of a legislator, part of the task of understanding representation would surely include an examination of what the agent has done with the grant of authority from her constituents. In the case of political participation, the population does not select the participants; the participants are not agents for the rest of the population; there are no mechanisms of accountability.

Differences among groups in their rates of political participation are, of course, what produces under- and overrepresentation.[3] When every group participates at the same rate, the ratio is 1.0 for each group. The more a group's participation rate lags behind that of the other groups, the more underrepresented it will be. The more active it is compared to the other groups, the more overrepresented it will be.

Inequality Among Groups

By themselves, the ratios do not reveal the amount of inequality in political participation, only whether each group is over- or under-represented compared to an ideal of proportional representation. We learn how much inequality there is across groups by looking at the relationship between each group's standing and its level of representation. How do the ratios change as educational attainment increases, for example?

· A simple way to assess these intergroup inequalities is to compare the representation ratios for the two groups that anchor the ends of the distribution.[4] We denote the ratio of these representation ratios as EQ.

$$EQ = RATIO_b / RATIO_t$$

where

$RATIO_b$ = the representation ratio for the group at the bottom of the distribution;

$RATIO_t$ = the representation ratio for the group at the top of the distribution.

[3]In fact, the ratio for each group is mathematically equivalent to the group's participation rate divided by the participation rate for the entire population.

[4]One could get more sophisticated and estimate an equation describing the relationship between the partitioning variable and the representation ratios: $RATIO_i = \exp(a + b \times Education_i + u_i)$, where $RATIO_i$ is the observed representation ratio for group i, $Education_i$ is the level of education for group i, and u_i is a stochastic error term. The estimated coefficients could then be used to calculate the change in the ratio that occurs as one moves from the bottom to the top of the partitioning variable. Nonlinearities in the relationship could be accommodated as well. This

EQ is easy to interpret. When the groups at the bottom and the top are represented among the participants in proportion to their share of the population, EQ is 1.0. When EQ falls below 1.0, the coefficient shows the amount by which the group at the bottom of the continuum is underrepresented compared to the group at the top. A coefficient of .5, for example, would mean that the group at the bottom is underrepresented by half, compared to the group at the top. A coefficient of 1.5 would mean that the group at the bottom is overrepresented by 50 percent compared to the group at the top.[5]

Returning to our earlier example of educational equalities in campaign work, EQ = .48/2.25 = .23, meaning that the least educated are represented among the participants at 23 percent of the rate of college graduates.

Some Properties of EQ

Our measure of inequality differs importantly from most of the more familiar measures of inequality.[6] The Gini Coefficient, for example, counts every pair of differences among the groups. Schutz's Relative Mean Deviation and the Coefficient of Variation look at all the

---

(continued)

approach would take into account information about the representation ratios for the categories that lie between the low and high ends of the continuum. In practice, however, when the partitioning variable is divided into only three to five categories, and the relationship between the partitioning variable and the representation ratios is relatively linear, this alternative technique does not offer much improvement over our simpler method.

[5] EQ is mathematically equivalent to the ratio of the participation rates of the bottom category to the top category and thus can also be interpreted as how much the participation rate of the bottom lags behind that of the top.

[6] For a sampling see Hugh Dalton, "The Measurement of the Inequality of Incomes," *Economic Journal* 30 (September 1920), pp. 348–61; Partha Dasgupta, Amartya Sen, and David Starrett, "Notes on the Measurement of Inequality," *Journal of Economic Theory* 6 (April 1973), pp. 180–87; Mark Fossett and Scott J. South, "The Measurement of Intergroup Income Inequality: A Conceptual Review," *Social Forces* 61 (March 1983), pp. 855–71; Serge-Christophe Kolm, "Unequal Inequalities, II," *Journal of Economic Theory* 13 (August 1976), pp. 82–111; Sen, *On Economic Inequality*; and Loren K. Waldman, "Types and Measures of Inequality," *Social Science Quarterly* 58 (September 1977), pp. 229–41.

differences between each group and the average group. The problem, though, is that when calculating the intergroup differences, these measures are blind to each group's value on the partitioning variable. Big differences among the ratios produce a large Gini Coefficient whether or not they are associated with values of the partitioning variable. Consider these two cases:

	Ratios of Over- or Underrepresentation	
Education	Case A	Case B
0–8	.35	1.60
9–11	.60	.35
High school diploma	1.00	2.60
Some college	1.60	.60
College degree	2.60	1.00
Measures of Inequality		
Gini Coefficient	.45	.45
Coefficient of variation	.33	.33
Relative mean deviation	.36	.36
EQ	.13	1.60

In Case A, representation is strongly related to the level of formal education: The least educated are grossly underrepresented; the most educated are heavily overrepresented. In Case B there is very little systematic relationship between educational attainment and representation. Most inequality measures do not distinguish between these two cases; ours does.

Beyond its face validity, EQ has several attractive properties. First, EQ is scale invariant, meaning that it is insensitive to aggregate shifts in the level of participation. Thus, every group's participation can drop by the same proportion (say 10 percent) and the value of EQ will remain unchanged.

Scale invariance is an important property from two vantage points. When making comparisons over time, scale invariance ensures that a change in EQ comes from a change in the relative inequality across groups, not in the level of participation. Similarly, when comparing rare political actions to more common ones, scale invariance ensures that the different values of EQ stem from different amounts of inequality, not differences in how likely people are to engage in the activities.[7]

Second, EQ does not vary with the size of the groups into which the population has been divided. EQ does not get bigger when an overrepresented group shrinks; it does not get smaller when an underrepresented group grows. When an underrepresented group contracts, there are fewer under-represented people in the polity, so one might be tempted to say that inequality has been reduced, but we think it would be perverse to conclude that by decreasing the number of blacks in the population one had reduced racial inequality in participation. EQ does not make this mistake. It changes only when inequalities among the groups change, not when their size changes. The property of invariance with respect to group size also allows us to compare inequalities across different partitionings of the population (for example, to compare class inequality to racial inequality).[8]

Finally, our measure meets the Pigou-Dalton condition.[9] When the group at the bottom of the distribution participates more at the expense of the group at the top, EQ will move closer to 1.0, indicating greater equality.[10]

[7]Measures that are based on the *difference* between a group's share of the participants and its share of the population, rather than on the *ratio*, are not scale invariant.

[8]Unlike EQ, the representation ratios by themselves are sensitive to changes in each group's share of the population, meaning that the ratios cannot be used to make comparisons over time or across divisions of the population.

[9]Dalton, "The Measurement of the Inequality of Incomes," p. 351.

[10]As Dalton himself noted, there is an obvious limiting condition. The assumption is that the transfer from the better off to the worse off is not sufficient to reverse the relative positions of the two and hence to introduce inequality, but in the opposite direction. If we were to calculate EQ by the method described in note 4, the Pigou-Dalton condition would hold more generally than described here.

REFERENCES

Abramson, Paul R. *Political Attitudes in America.* San Francisco: W. H. Freeman, 1983.

Abramson, Paul R. and John H. Aldrich. "The Decline of Electoral Participation in America." *American Political Science Review* 76 (September 1982), pp. 502–21.

Abramson, Paul R. and William Claggett. "Racial Differences in Self-Reported and Validated Turnout in the 1988 Presidential Election." *Journal of Politics* 53 (February 1991), pp. 186–97.

Adams, John W. and Alice Bee Kasakoff. "Estimates of Census Underenumeration Based on Genealogies." *Social Science History* 15 (Winter 1991), pp. 527–43.

Aldrich, John. "Some Problems in Testing Two Rational Models of Participation." *American Journal of Political Science* 20 (November 1976), pp. 713–33.

Alinsky, Saul D. *Reveille for Radicals.* Chicago: University of Chicago Press, 1946.

Almond, Gabriel A. and Sidney Verba. *The Civic Culture.* Princeton: Princeton University Press, 1963.

Alt, James E. "Race and Voter Registration in the South Before and After the Voting Rights Act." In Chandler Davidson and Bernard Grofman, eds., *The Impact of the Voting Rights Act in the South.* Princeton: Princeton University Press, forthcoming.

Applebome, Peter. "Fearing Duke, Voters in Louisiana Hand Democrat Fourth Term." *New York Times*, November 18, 1991, p. A1.

_____. "On Eve of Louisiana, Nothing is Certain." *New York Times*, November 15, 1991, p. A21.

Ashenfelter, Orley and Stanley Kelley, Jr. "Determinants of Participation in Presidential Elections." *Journal of Law and Economics* 18 (December 1976), pp. 695–731.

Axelrod, Robert. *The Evolution of Cooperation.* New York: Basic Books, 1984.

Balch, George I. "Multiple Indicators in Survey Research: The Concept of 'Sense of Political Efficacy.' " *Political Methodology* 1 (Spring 1974), pp. 1–43.

Ball, Howard, Dale Krane, and Thomas P. Lauth. *Compromised Compliance: Implementation of the 1965 Voting Rights Act.* Westport, Conn.: Greenwood Press, 1982.

Baltz, Dan. "Candidates, Public Depend Less on News Media for the Message." *Washington Post*, May 19, 1992, p. A2.

Barnes, Samuel H., Max Kaase et al., *Political Action: Mass Participation in Five Western Democracies.* Beverly Hills: Sage, 1979.

Barrow, Clyde W. "Unions and Community Mobilization: The 1988 Massachusetts Prevailing Wage Campaign." *Labor Studies Journal* 14 (Winter 1989), pp. 18–39.

Barry, Brian. *Sociologists, Economists and Democracy.* London: Collier-Macmillan, 1970.

Batson, C. D. and J. S. Coke. "Empathic Motivation for Helping Behavior." In J. T. Cacioppo and R. E. Petty, eds., *Social Psychophysiology: A Sourcebook.* New York: Guilford Press, 1983, pp. 417–33.

_____. "Empathy: A Source of Altruistic Motivation for Helping?" In J. P. Rushton and R. M. Sorrentins, eds., *Altruism and Helping Behavior.* Hillsdale, N.J.: Lawrence Erlbaum, 1981, pp. 167–87.

Bauer, Raymond A., Ithiel de Sola Pool, and Lewis Anthony Dexter. *American Business and Public Policy: The Politics of Foreign Trade.* 2nd ed. Chicago: Aldine-Atherton, 1972.

Beck, Paul Allen. "A Socialization Theory of Partisan Realignment." In Richard G. Niemi and associates, eds., *The Politics of Future Citizens.* San Francisco: Jossey-Bass, 1974, pp. 199–219.

Bem, Daryl J. "Self-Perception: An Alternative Interpretation of Cognitive Dissonance Phenomena." *Psychological Review* 74 (May 1967), pp. 183–200.

Bennett, Stephen E. *Apathy in America, 1960–1984: Causes and Consequences of Citizen Political Indifference.* Dobbs Ferry, N.Y.: Transnational Publishers, 1986.

Bennett, W. Lance. *The Governing Crisis: Media, Money, and Marketing in American Elections.* New York: St. Martin's Press, 1992.

Bensel, Richard and Elizabeth Sanders. "The Impact of the Voting Rights Act on Southern Welfare Systems." In Benjamin Ginsberg and Allan Stone, eds., *Do Elections Matter?* New York: M. E. Sharpe, 1986, pp. 52–78.

Berelson, Bernard R., Paul F. Lazarsfeld, and William N. McPhee. *Voting.* Chicago: University of Chicago Press, 1954.

Bernard, Bertram M. *Election Laws of the Forty-eight States.* New York: Oceana Publications, 1950.

Berry, Jeffrey M. *The Interest Group Society.* New York: Scott, Foresman, 1989.

Birnbaum, Jeffrey H. and Alan S. Murray. *Showdown at Gucci Gulch: Lawmakers, Lobbyists and the Unlikely Triumph of Tax Reform.* New York: Random House, 1987.

Black, Earl. *Southern Governors and Civil Rights: Racial Segregation as a Campaign Issue in the Second Reconstruction.* Cambridge: Harvard University Press, 1976.

Blumenthal, Sidney. *The Permanent Campaign: Inside the World of Elite Political Consultants.* New York: Basic Books, 1981.

Blydenburgh, John C. "A Controlled Experiment to Measure the Effects of Personal Contact Campaigning." *Midwest Journal of Political Science* 15 (May 1971), pp. 365–81.

Bonner, Ethan. *Battle for Justice: How the Bork Nomination Shook America.* New York: W. W. Norton and Co., 1989.

Boyd, Richard W. "Decline of U.S. Voter Turnout: Structural Explanations." *American Politics Quarterly* 9 (April 1981), pp. 133–59.

———. "Election Calendars and Voter Turnout." *American Politics Quarterly* 14 (January 1986), pp. 89–104.

Bradburn, Norman M., Lance J. Rips, and Steven K. Shevell. "Answering Autobiographical Questions: The Impact of Memory and Inference in Surveys." *Science* 236 (April 10, 1987), pp. 157–61.

Brehm, John. "Opinion Surveys and Political Representation." Ph.D. dissertation, University of Michigan, 1990.

Brody, Richard A. "The Puzzle of Political Participation in America." In Anthony King, ed., *The New American Political System*. Washington, D.C.: American Enterprise Institute, 1978, pp. 287–324.

Brody, Richard A. and Benjamin I. Page. "Indifference, Alienation, and Rational Decisions." *Public Choice* 13 (Summer 1973), pp. 1–17.

Brody, Richard A. and Paul M. Sniderman. "From Life Space to the Polling Place: The Relevance of Personal Concerns for Voting Behavior." *British Journal of Political Science* 7 (July 1977), pp. 337–60.

Brown, Ronald E. and Monica Wolford. "Religious Resources and African American Political Action." Paper presented at the annual meeting of the American Political Science Association, 1991.

Burnham, Walter Dean. "The Appearance and Disappearance of the American Voter." In Richard Rose, ed., *Electoral Participation: A Comparative Analysis*. Beverly Hills: Sage, 1980, pp. 35–73.

_____. "The Changing Shape of the American Political Universe." *American Political Science Review* 59 (March 1965), pp. 7–28.

_____. "The Class Gap." *New Republic*, May 9, 1988, pp. 30–33.

_____. *The Current Crisis in American Politics*. New York: Oxford University Press, 1982.

_____. "Shifting Patterns of Congressional Voting Participation in the United States." Paper presented at the annual meeting of the American Political Science Association, 1981.

_____. "Theory and Voting Research: Some Reflections on Converse's 'Change in the American Electorate.'" *American Political Science Review* 68 (September 1974), pp. 1002–23.

_____. "The Turnout Problem." In A. James Reichley, ed., *Elections American Style*. Washington, D.C.: Brookings Institution, 1987, pp. 97–133.

Burns v. Forston. 410 U.S. 686 (1973).

Button, James W. *Black Violence: Political Impact of the 1960s Riots.* Princeton: Princeton University Press, 1978.

Byrne, D. *The Attraction Paradigm.* New York: Academic Press, 1971.

Cain, Bruce E. and Ken McCue. "The Efficacy of Registration Drives." *Journal of Politics* 47 (November 1985), pp. 1221–30.

Caldeira, Gregory A. and Samuel C. Patterson. "Contextual Influences on Participation in U.S. State Legislative Elections." *Legislative Studies Quarterly* 7 (August 1982), pp. 359–82.

Caldeira, Gregory A., Samuel C. Patterson, and Gregory A. Markko. "The Mobilization of Voters in Congressional Elections." *Journal of Politics* 47 (May 1985), pp. 490–509.

Calvo, Maria Antonia and Steven J. Rosenstone. *Hispanic Political Participation.* San Antonio: Southwest Voter Research Institute, 1989.

Campbell, Angus. "Surge and Decline: A Study of Electoral Change." *Public Opinion Quarterly* 24 (Fall 1960), pp. 397–418.

Campbell, Angus, Philip E. Converse, Warren E. Miller, and Donald E. Stokes, *The American Voter.* New York: John Wiley and Sons, 1960.

Cannell, Charles F., Kent H. Marquis, and Andre Laurent. "A Summary of Studies of Interviewing Methodology." n.d.

Carton, Paul. *Mobilizing the Black Community: The Effects of Personal Contact Campaigning on Black Voters.* Washington, D.C.: Joint Center for Political Studies, 1984.

Cassel, Carol A., and David B. Hill. "Explanations of Turnout Decline: A Multivariate Test." *American Politics Quarterly* 9 (April 1981), pp. 181–95.

Cassel, Carol A. and Robert C. Luskin. "Simple Explanations of Turnout Decline." *American Political Science Review* 82 (December 1988), pp. 1321–30.

Cavanagh, Thomas E. "Changes in American Voter Turnout, 1964–1976." *Political Science Quarterly* 96 (Spring 1981), pp. 33–65.

_____. "Research on American Voter Turnout: The State of the Evidence." Paper presented at the Conference on Voter Participation, Carnegie Endowment for International Peace, 1981.

Cavanagh, Thomas E. and Lorn S. Foster. *Jesse Jackson's Campaign: The Primaries and the Caucuses.* Washington, D.C.: Joint Center for Political Studies, 1984.

Chester, Edward W. *Radio, Television, and American Politics.* New York: Sheed and Ward, 1969.

Citrin, Jack. "Comment: The Political Relevance of Trust in Government." *American Political Science Review* 68 (September 1974), pp. 973–88.

Clark, Peter B. and James Q. Wilson. "Incentive Systems: A Theory of Organizations." *Administrative Science Quarterly* 6 (September 1961), pp. 129–66.

Clubb, Jerome M., William H. Flanigan, and Nancy H. Zingale. *Partisan Realignment.* Beverly Hills: Sage, 1980.

Cody, Caroline. "The Politics of Textbook Publishing, Adoption, and Use." In David L. Elliot and Arthur Woodward, eds., *Textbooks and Schooling in the United States.* Chicago: National Society for the Study of Education, 1990, pp. 127–45.

Cohen, Jeffrey E. "Change in Election Calendars and Turnout Decline: A Test of Boyd's Hypothesis." *American Politics Quarterly* 10 (April 1982), pp. 246–54.

Colby, David C. "A Test of the Relative Efficacy of Political Tactics." *American Journal of Political Science* 26 (November 1982), pp. 741–53.

Collins, Sheila D. *The Rainbow Challenge.* New York: Monthly Review Press, 1986.

Congressional Quarterly. *Guide to U.S. Elections.* 2nd ed. Washington, D.C.: Congressional Quarterly Press, 1985.

Converse, Philip E. "Change in the American Electorate." In Angus Campbell and Philip E. Converse, eds., *The Human Meaning of Social Change.* New York: Russell Sage, 1972, pp. 263–337.

_____. *The Dynamics of Party Support: Cohort-Analysing Party Identification.* Beverly Hills: Sage, 1976.

Converse, Philip E. and Richard Niemi. "Non-Voting Among Young Adults in the United States." In William J. Crotty et al., eds., *Political Parties and Political Behavior.* 2nd ed. Boston: Allyn and Bacon, 1971, pp. 443–66.

Converse, Philip E. and Roy Pierce. *Political Representation in France.* Cambridge: Harvard University Press, 1986.

Conway, M. Margaret. *Political Participation in the United States.* 2nd ed. Washington, D.C.: Congressional Quarterly Press, 1991.

Conway, M. Margaret and Judith Garber. "Stability and Change in Political Participation: A Panel Analysis." Paper presented at the annual meeting of the Southern Political Science Association, 1983.

Cook, Rhodes. "In the Wake of Louisiana Defeat Duke Eyes National Bid." *Congressional Quarterly Weekly Report,* November 23, 1991, pp. 3475–79.

Cover, Albert D. "Contacting Congressional Constituents: Some Patterns of Perquisite Use." *American Journal of Political Science* 24 (February 1980), pp. 125–35.

Cover, Albert D. and Bruce S. Brumberg. "Baby Books and Ballots: The Impact of Congressional Mail on Constituent Opinion." *American Political Science Review* 76 (June 1982), pp. 347–59.

Cox, Gary W. "Closeness and Turnout: A Methodological Note." *Journal of Politics* 50 (August 1988), pp. 768–75.

Craig, Stephen C. "Efficacy, Trust, and Political Behavior: An Attempt to Resolve a Lingering Conceptual Dilemma." *American Politics Quarterly* 7 (April 1979), pp. 225–39.

Craig, Stephen C. and Michael A. Maggiotto. "Measuring Political Efficacy." *Political Methodology* 8 (1982), pp. 85–109.

Creighton, James L. *The Public Involvement Manual.* Cambridge: Abt Books, 1981.

Crepaz, Markus M. L. "The Impact of Party Polarization and Postmaterialism on Voter Turnout." *European Journal of Political Research* 18 (March 1990), pp. 183–205.

Crewe, Ivor. "Electoral Participation." In David Butler, Howard R. Penniman, and Austin Ranney, eds., *Democracy at the Polls.*

Washington, D.C.: American Enterprise Institute, 1981, pp. 216–63.

Crotty, William J. *Political Reform and the American Experiment*. New York: Thomas Y. Crowell, 1977.

Cumming, Elaine and William E. Henry. *Growing Old: The Process of Disengagement*. New York: Basic Books, 1961.

Dahl, Robert A. *A Preface to Democratic Theory*. Chicago: University of Chicago Press, 1956.

———. *Who Governs? Democracy and Power in an American City*. New Haven: Yale University Press, 1961.

Dalton, Hugh. "The Measurement of the Inequality of Incomes." *Economic Journal* 30 (September 1920), pp. 348–61.

Dasgupta, Partha, Amartya Sen, and David Starrett. "Notes on the Measurement of Inequality." *Journal of Economic Theory* 6 (April 1973), pp. 180–87.

Dawson, P. A. and J. E. Zinser. "Political Finance and Participation in Congressional Elections." *Annals of the American Academy of Political and Social Science* 425 (May 1976), pp. 59–73.

DeBats, Donald A. "Hide and Seek: The Historian and Nineteenth-Century Social Accounting." *Social Science History* 15 (Winter 1991), pp. 545–63.

DeGregorio, Christine and Jack E. Rossotti. "The Nomination of Judge Robert H. Bork to the United States Supreme Court: A Case Study in Contemporary Interest Group Politics." Paper presented at the annual meeting of the American Political Science Association, 1990.

Denver, D. T. and H. T. G. Hands. "Marginality and Turnout in British General Elections." *British Journal of Political Science* 4 (January 1974), pp. 17–35.

Derfner, Armand. "Racial Discrimination and the Right to Vote." *Vanderbilt Law Review* 26 (April 1973), pp. 523–84.

Dexter, Lewis Anthony. "What Do Congressmen Hear: The Mail." *Public Opinion Quarterly* 20 (Spring 1956), pp. 16–27.

Dionne, E. J. *Why Americans Hate Politics*. New York: Simon & Schuster, 1991.

Downs, Anthony. *An Economic Theory of Democracy.* New York: Harper & Row, 1957.

Dunn v. Blumstein. 405 U.S. 330 (1972).

Eisinger, Peter. "Black Employment in Municipal Jobs: The Impact of Black Political Power." *American Political Science Review* 76 (June 1982), pp. 380–92.

Eldersveld, Samuel J. "Experimental Propaganda Techniques and Voting Behavior." *American Political Science Review* 50 (March 1956), pp. 154–65.

Eldersveld, Samuel J. and Richard W. Dodge. "Personal Contact or Mail Propaganda? An Experiment in Voting and Attitude Change." In Daniel Katz, Dorwin Cartwright, Samuel Eldersveld, and Alfred M. Lee, eds., *Public Opinion and Propaganda.* New York: Dryden Press, 1954, pp. 532–42.

Erickson, Bonnie H., and T. A. Nosanchuk. "How an Apolitical Association Politicizes." *Canadian Review of Sociology and Anthropology* 27 (May 1990), pp. 206–19.

Fainstein, Norman I. and Susan S. Fainstein. *Urban Political Movements: The Search for Power by Minority Groups in American Cities.* Englewood Cliffs, N.J.: Prentice-Hall, 1974.

Fenno, Richard F., Jr. *Home Style: House Members in Their Districts.* Boston: Little, Brown and Co., 1978.

———. *The United States Senate: A Bicameral Perspective.* Washington: American Enterprise Institute, 1982.

Ferejohn, John and Morris Fiorina. "Closeness Counts Only in Horseshoes and Dancing." *American Political Science Review* 69 (September 1975), pp. 920–25.

Fessler, Pamela. "Compromise Explored on Social Security." *Congressional Quarterly Weekly Report*, May 30, 1981, pp. 936–37.

———. "Tactics of New Elderly Lobby Ruffle Congressional Feathers." *Congressional Quarterly Weekly Report*, June 2, 1984, pp. 1310–13.

Finkel, Steven E. "Reciprocal Effects of Participation and Political Efficacy: A Panel Analysis." *American Journal of Political Science* 29 (November 1985), pp. 891–913.

Finkel, Steven E. and Karl-Dieter Opp. "Party Identification and Participation in Collective Action." *Journal of Politics* 53 (May 1991), pp. 339–71.

Fiorina, Morris P. *Congress: Keystone of the Washington Establishment.* New Haven: Yale University Press, 1977.

Foley, John, Dennis A. Britton, and Eugene B. Everett, Jr. *Nominating a President: The Process and the Press.* New York: Praeger, 1980.

Fossett, Mark, and Scott J. South. "The Measurement of Intergroup Income Inequality: A Conceptual Review." *Social Forces* 61 (March 1983), pp. 855–71.

Fowler, Linda L. and Ronald G. Shaiko. "Contact with Congress: A New Attentive Constituency." Paper presented at the Conference on Citizen Participation, Tallinn, Estonia, U.S.S.R., 1987.

Franklin, Charles H. "Incumbent Visibility over the Election Cycle." Paper presented at the Stanford/Hoover Conference on Senate Elections, 1991.

Frantzich, Stephen E. *Write Your Congressman: Constituent Communications and Representation.* New York: Praeger, 1986.

Freedman, Paul. "Mobilization and Participation." Unpublished manuscript, University of Michigan, 1992.

Gamson, William A. *The Strategy of Social Protest.* Homewood, Ill.: Dorsey Press, 1975.

Gans, Curtis B. "The Empty Ballot Box: Reflections on Nonvoters in America." *Public Opinion* (September/October 1978), pp. 54–57.

———. "MacNeil/Lehrer Report." Public Broadcasting Service, November 7, 1978.

Garrow, David J. *Protest at Selma: Martin Luther King, Jr. and the Voting Rights Act of 1965.* New Haven: Yale University Press, 1978.

Gerlach, Luther P. and Virginia H. Hine. *People, Power, Change: Movements of Social Transformation.* Indianapolis: Bobbs-Merrill, 1970.

Giles, Michael W. and Marilyn K. Dantico. "Political Participation and Neighborhood Social Context Revisited." *American Journal of Political Science* 26 (February 1982), pp. 144–50.

Gilliam, Franklin D. "Influences on Voter Turnout for U.S. House Elections in Non-Presidential Years." *Legislative Studies Quarterly* 10 (August 1985), pp. 339–51.

Gimpel, Jim. "Year-End Wrap-up on the Drug Mail from Indiana." Report, Office of Senator Daniel Coats, January 1990.

Ginsberg, Benjamin. "A Post Election Era?" *PS: Political Science & Politics* (March 1989), pp. 18–20.

Ginsberg, Benjamin and Martin Shefter. *Politics by Other Means: The Declining Importance of Elections.* New York: Basic Books, 1990.

Glass, David, Peverill Squire, and Raymond E. Wolfinger. "Voter Turnout: An International Comparison." *Public Opinion* (December/January 1984), pp. 49–55.

Godwin, R. Kenneth. "Money, Technology, and Political Interests: The Direct Marketing of Politics." In Mark P. Petracca, *The Politics of Interests: Interest Group Politics Transformed.* Boulder: Westview Press, 1992, pp. 308–25.

Goergen, Christian. "Explaining Turnout in 1988: About the Importance of Perceiving Differences between Parties and Candidates." Paper presented at the annual meeting of the Midwest Political Science Association, 1991.

Gosnell, Harold F. *Getting Out the Vote: An Experiment in the Stimulation of Voting.* Chicago: University of Chicago Press, 1927.

Graber, Doris A. *Mass Media and American Politics.* 3rd. ed. Washington, D.C.: Congressional Quarterly Press, 1989.

Greenstone, J. David. *Labor in American Politics.* Chicago: University of Chicago Press, 1977.

Grofman, Bernard and Chandler Davidson, eds. *Controversies in Minority Voting: The Voting Rights Act in Perspective.* Washington, D.C.: Brookings Institution, 1992.

Guinn v. United States. 238 U.S. 347 (1915).

Hamilton, Charles V. *The Bench and the Ballot: Southern Federal Judges and Black Voters.* New York: Oxford University Press, 1973.

Hansen, John Mark. *Gaining Access: Congress and the Farm Lobby, 1919–1981.* Chicago: University of Chicago Press, 1991.

———. "The Political Economy of Group Membership." *American Political Science Review* 79 (March 1985), pp. 79–96.

Hansen, John Mark and Steven J. Rosenstone. "Participation Outside Elections." Report submitted to the Board of Overseers, National Election Study, October 1983.

Hansen, Lawrence. *Our Turn: Politicians Talk about Themselves, Politics, the Public, the Press, and Reform.* Washington, D.C.: Centel Corporation, 1992.

Hardin, Russell. *Collective Action.* Baltimore: Resources for the Future, 1982.

Harper v. *Virginia State Board of Elections.* 383 U.S. 663 (1966).

Harris, Joseph P. *Registration of Voters in the United States.* Washington, D.C.: Brookings Institution, 1929.

Havard, William C. "The South: A Shifting Perspective." In William C. Havard, ed., *The Changing Politics of the South.* Baton Rouge: Louisiana State University Press, 1972, pp. 3–36.

Hayghe, Howard V. "Volunteers in the U.S.: Who Donates the Time?" *Monthly Labor Review* (February 1991), pp. 17–23.

Herity, Thomas and John D. Brady. "Saving Money with a PC." *Campaigns and Elections* (March/April 1988), p. 53.

Hertzke, Allen D. "The Role of Churches in Political Mobilization: The Presidential Campaigns of Jesse Jackson and Pat Robertson." In Allan J. Cigler and Burdett A. Loomis, eds., *Interest Group Politics,* 3rd ed. Washington, D.C.: Congressional Quarterly Press, 1991.

Hofstadter, Richard. *The Age of Reform.* New York: Random House, 1955.

Holmes, Stephen A. "Perot Encounters a Maze of Ballot Rules." *New York Times,* May 14, 1992, p. A10.

Huckfeldt, Robert. "Political Participation and the Neighborhood Context." *American Journal of Political Science* 23 (June 1979), pp. 579–92.

Huckfeldt, Robert and John Sprague. "Networks in Context: The Social Flow of Political Information." *American Political Science Review* 81 (December 1987), pp. 1198–1216.

———. "Political Parties and Electoral Mobilization: Political Structure, Social Structure, and the Party Canvass." *American Political Science Review* 86 (March 1992), pp. 70–86.

Huenefeld, John. *The Community Activist's Handbook: A Guide to Organizing, Financing, and Publicizing Community Campaigns.* Boston: Beacon Press, 1970.

Hughes, Sallie. "On Election Day, Memories, Fears Weigh on Voters." *Miami Herald*, November 17, 1991, p. A31.

Huntington, Samuel P. and Joan M. Nelson. *Political Participation in Developing Countries: No Easy Choice.* Cambridge: Harvard University Press, 1976.

"The Impeachment Lobby: Emphasis on Grass Roots Pressure." *Congressional Quarterly Weekly Report*, May 25, 1974, pp. 1368–74.

Jackman, Robert W. "Political Institutions and Voter Turnout in the Industrial Democracies." *American Political Science Review* 81 (June 1987), pp. 405–23.

Jacobson, Gary. *The Politics of Congressional Elections.* 3rd ed. New York: HarperCollins, 1992.

Jennings, M. Kent and Gregory B. Markus. "Political Involvement in the Later Years: A Longitudinal Survey." *American Journal of Political Science* 32 (May 1988), pp. 302–16.

Kaase, Max. "Mass Participation." In M. Kent Jennings and Jan W. van Deth, eds., *Continuities in Political Action.* New York: Walter de Gruyter, 1990, pp. 23–64.

Kahn, Si. *Organizing.* New York: McGraw-Hill, 1982.

Karnig, Albert K. and Susan Welch. *Black Representation and Urban Policy.* Chicago: University of Chicago Press, 1980.

Katosh, John P. and Michael W. Traugott. "The Consequences of Validated and Self-Reported Voting Measures." *Public Opinion Quarterly* 45 (Winter 1981), pp. 519–35.

Katz, Elihu. "The Two-Step Flow of Communication: An Up-to-Date Report on an Hypothesis." *Public Opinion Quarterly* 21 (Spring 1957), pp. 61–78.

Katz, Elihu and Paul F. Lazarsfeld. *Personal Influence: The Part Played by People in the Flow of Mass Communications.* Glencoe, Ill.: Free Press, 1955.

Keech, William R. *The Impact of Negro Voting: The Role of the Vote in the Quest for Equality.* Chicago: Rand McNally, 1968.

Kelley, Stanley, Jr., Richard E. Ayres, and William G. Bowen. "Registration and Voting: Putting First Things First." *American Political Science Review* 61 (June 1967), pp. 359–79.

Kenny, Christopher B. "Political Participation and Effects from the Social Environment." *American Journal of Political Science* 36 (February 1992), pp. 259–67.

Kernell, Samuel. *Going Public: New Strategies of Presidential Leadership.* Washington: Congressional Quarterly Press, 1986.

Key, V. O., Jr. *Politics, Parties, and Pressure Groups.* 5th ed. New York: Thomas Y. Crowell Co., 1964.

_____. *Southern Politics in State and Nation.* New York: Vintage, 1949.

_____. "A Theory of Critical Elections." *Journal of Politics* 17 (February 1955), pp. 3–18.

Kinder, Donald R. and D. Roderick Kiewiet. "Economic Discontent and Political Behavior: The Role of Personal Grievances and Collective Economic Judgments in Congressional Voting." *American Journal of Political Science* 33 (May 1979), pp. 495–527.

_____. "Sociotropic Politics: The American Case." *British Journal of Political Science* 11 (February 1981), pp. 129–61.

Kingdon, John W. *Congressmen's Voting Decisions.* 3rd ed. Ann Arbor: University of Michigan Press, 1989.

Kleppner, Paul. *Chicago Divided: The Making of a Black Mayor.* Dekalb, Ill.: Northern Illinois University Press, 1985.

_____. *Who Voted? The Dynamics of Electoral Turnout, 1870–1980.* New York: Praeger, 1982.

Knack, Stephen. "Civic Norms, Social Sanctions, and Voter Turnout." *Rationality and Society* 4 (April 1992), pp. 133–56.

———. "Social Connectedness and Voter Participation: Evidence from the 1991 NES Pilot Study." Unpublished manuscript, Center for the Study of Public Choice, George Mason University, January 1992.

Knights, Peter R. "Potholes in the Road of Improvement? Estimating Census Underenumeration by Longitudinal Tracing: U.S. Census, 1850–1880." *Social Science History* 15 (Winter 1991), pp. 517–26.

Kolbert, Elizabeth. "Campaign Ads Replace Campaigning in California." *New York Times*, May 22, 1992, p. A2.

Kolm, Serge-Christophe. "Unequal Inequalities, II." *Journal of Economic Theory* 13 (August 1976), pp. 82–111.

Korte, Charles and Stanley Milgram. "Acquaintanceship Networks between Racial Groups: Application of the Small World Method." *Journal of Personality and Social Psychology* 15 (June 1970), pp. 101–8.

Kousser, J. Morgan. *The Shaping of Southern Politics: Suffrage Restriction and the Establishment of the One-Party South, 1880–1910.* New Haven: Yale University Press, 1974.

Kramer, Gerald H. "The Ecological Fallacy Revisited: Aggregate-versus Individual-Level Findings on Economics and Elections and Sociotropic Voting." *American Political Science Review* 77 (March 1983), pp. 92–111.

———. "The Effects of Precinct-Level Canvassing on Voting Behavior." *Public Opinion Quarterly* 34 (Winter 1970), pp. 560–72.

Lamiel, Patty "The People's Lobby." In Lee Staples, ed., *Roots to Power: A Manual for Grassroots Lobbying.* New York: Praeger, 1984, pp. 188–97.

Lane, Robert E. *Political Life: Why and How People Get Involved in Politics.* New York: Free Press, 1959.

LaPalombara, Joseph. "Political Participation as an Analytical Concept in Comparative Politics." In Sidney Verba and Lucian W. Pye, eds. *The Citizen and Politics: A Comparative Perspective.* Stamford, Conn.: Greylock Publishers, 1978, pp. 167–94.

Latane, B., and J. M. Darley. *The Unresponsive Bystander: Why Doesn't He Help?* New York: Appleton-Crofts, 1970.

Lavrakas, Paul J. and Elicia J. Herz. "Citizen Participation in Neighborhood Crime Prevention." *Criminology* 20 (November 1982), pp. 479–98.

Lawson, Steven F. *Black Ballots: Voting Rights in the South, 1944–1969.* New York: Columbia University Press, 1976.

_____. *In Pursuit of Power: Southern Blacks and Electoral Politics, 1965–1982.* New York: Columbia University Press, 1985.

_____. *Running for Freedom: Civil Rights and Black Politics in America Since 1941.* Philadelphia: Temple University Press, 1991.

Lazarsfeld, Paul F., Bernard Berelson, and Hazel Gaudet. *The People's Choice.* New York: Columbia University Press, 1948.

League of Women Voters Education Fund. "Easy Does It: Registration and Absentee Voting Procedures by State." Washington, D.C.: The League of Women Voters Education Fund, 1976, 1980, 1984, 1988.

Leighley, Jan "Participation as a Stimulus of Political Conceptualization." *Journal of Politics* 53 (February 1991), pp. 198–211.

_____. "Social Interaction and Contextual Influences on Political Participation." *American Politics Quarterly* 18 (October 1990), pp. 459–75.

Lipset, Seymour Martin and William Schneider. *The Confidence Gap.* New York: Free Press, 1983.

Loomis, Burdett A. "A New Era: Groups and the Grass Roots." In Allan J. Cigler and Burdett A. Loomis, eds., *Interest Group Politics.* Washington, D.C.: Congressional Quarterly Press, 1983, pp. 169–90.

Lupfer, Michael and David E. Price. "On the Merits of Face-To-Face Campaigning." *Social Science Quarterly* 53 (December 1972), pp. 534–43.

Malchow, Hal and Fran May. "Television Watch Parties: 1984's Fund Raising Innovation." *Campaigns and Elections* (Fall 1985), pp. 18–22.

Marston v. Lewis. 410 U.S. 679 (1973).

Martinez, Valerie J. "Old-Age Interest Groups and Grassroots Mobilization." Paper presented at the annual meeting of the American Political Science Association, 1991.

Mathiowetz, Nancy A. "The Problem of Omission and Telescoping Error: New Evidence from a Study of Unemployment." *Proceedings of the Section on Survey Research Methods, American Statistical Association* (1985), pp. 482–84.

Matthews, Donald R. and James W. Prothro. *Negroes and the New Southern Politics.* New York: Harcourt, Brace and World, 1966.

Mayhew, David R. *Congress: The Electoral Connection.* New Haven: Yale University Press, 1974.

———. *Placing Parties in American Politics: Organization, Electoral Settings, and Government Activity in the Twentieth Century.* Princeton: Princeton University Press, 1986.

McAdam, Doug. *Political Process and the Development of Black Insurgency, 1930–1970.* Chicago: University of Chicago Press, 1982.

McGerr, Michael E. *The Decline of Popular Politics: The American North, 1865–1928,* New York: Oxford University Press, 1986.

McGuigan, Patrick B. and Dawn H. Weyrich. *Ninth Justice: The Fight for Bork.* Washington: Free Congress Foundation, 1990.

Milbrath, Lester W. and M. L. Goel. *Political Participation.* 2nd ed. Chicago: Rand McNally, 1977.

Milgram, Stanley. "Interdisciplinary Thinking and the Small World Problem." In Muzafer Sherif and Carolyn W. Sherif, *Interdisciplinary Relationships in the Social Sciences.* Chicago: Aldine Publishing Co., 1969, pp. 103–20.

Miller, Arthur H., Patricia Gurin, Gerald Gurin, and Oksana Malanchuk. "Group Consciousness and Political Participation." *American Journal of Political Science* 25 (August 1981), pp. 494–511.

Miller, Tim. "Why Congress Wants Computers." *Washington Post Magazine,* May 15, 1983, p. 21.

Miller, Warren E. "Disinterest, Disaffection, and Participation in Presidential Elections." *Political Behavior* 2 (November 1980), pp. 7–32.

———. "The Puzzle Transformed: Explaining Declining Turnout." Unpublished manuscript, Arizona State University, April 1991.

Moe, Terry M. *The Organization of Interests.* Chicago: University of Chicago Press, 1980.

Moffett, James. *Storm in the Mountains.* Carbondale: Southern Illinois University Press, 1988.

Morris, Aldon D. *The Origins of the Civil Rights Movement: Black Communities Organizing for Change.* New York: Free Press, 1984.

Moynihan, Elizabeth B. "Mail Call on Capitol Hill." *New York Times Magazine,* November 15, 1981, pp. 135–65.

Murphy, Michelle M. "Elderly Lobby Group Continues to Thrive but Image on Capitol Hill Still Tarnished." *Congressional Quarterly Weekly Report,* March 26, 1988, pp. 778–79.

Nagel, Jack. *Participation.* Englewood Cliffs, N.J.: Prentice-Hall, 1987.

National School Boards Association. "School-Community Communication: School Board Members and Their Constituents." Research Report 1980-1, National School Boards Association, 1980.

Neter, John and Joseph Waksberg. "A Study of Response Errors in Expenditure Data from Household Interviews." *Journal of the American Statistical Association* 59 (March 1964), pp. 18–55.

Nisbett, Richard and Lee Ross. *Human Inference: Strategies and Shortcomings of Social Judgment.* Englewood Cliffs, N.J.: Prentice-Hall, 1980.

Nisbett, Richard E. and Timothy D. Wilson. "Telling More Than We Can Know: Verbal Reports of Mental Processes." *Psychological Review* 84 (May 1977), pp. 231–59.

Norrander, Barbara. "Turnout in the 1988 Presidential Primaries: Testing Alternative Models." Paper presented at the annual meeting of the Midwest Political Science Association, 1989.

Novak, Robert. "MacNeil/Lehrer Report." Public Broadcasting Service, November 7, 1978.

Obershall, Anthony. *Social Conflict and Social Movements.* Englewood Cliffs, N.J.: Prentice-Hall, 1973.

Olson, Mancur, Jr. *The Logic of Collective Action.* Cambridge: Harvard University Press, 1965.

Ornstein, Norman J. and Shirley Elder. *Interest Groups, Lobbying and Policymaking.* Washington: Congressional Quarterly Press, 1978.

Ornstein, Norman J., Thomas E. Mann, and Michael Malbin. *Vital Statistics on Congress, 1989–1990*. Washington: American Enterprise Institute, 1990.

Ornstein, Norman J. and Michael Robinson. "The Case of Our Disappearing Congress." *TV Guide*, January 11, 1986, pp. 4–10.

Parker, Frank. *Black Votes Count: Political Empowerment in Mississippi After 1965*. Chapel Hill: University of North Carolina Press, 1990.

Pateman, Carole. *Participation and Democratic Theory*. Cambridge: Cambridge University Press, 1970.

Patterson, Samuel C. and Gregory A. Caldeira. "Getting Out the Vote: Participation in Gubernatorial Elections." *American Political Science Review* 77 (September 1983), pp. 675–89.

Peirce, Neil R. and Peter C. Choharis. "The Elderly as a Political Force—26 Million Strong and Well Organized." *National Journal*, September 11, 1982, pp. 1559–62.

Penick, Betye K. Eidson. *Surveying Crime*. Washington, D.C.: National Academy of Sciences, 1976.

Perry, James M. "Call It New Media, Teledemocracy or Whatever; It's Changing the Way the Political System Works." *Wall Street Journal*, June 24, 1992, p. A20.

Pertschuk, Michael and Wendy Schaetzel. *The People Rising: The Campaign Against the Bork Nomination*. New York: Thunder's Mouth Press, 1989.

Peterson, Mark A. *Legislating Together: The White House and Capitol Hill from Eisenhower to Reagan*. Cambridge: Harvard University Press, 1990.

Phillips, Kevin P. and Paul H. Blackman. *Electoral Reform and Voter Participation*. Washington, D.C.: American Enterprise Institute, 1975.

Pierce, John C. and Nicholas P. Lovrich. "Survey Measurment of Political Participation: Selective Effects of Recall in Petition Signing." *Social Science Quarterly* 63 (March 1982), pp. 164–71.

Pitkin, Hanna Fenichel. *The Concept of Representation*. Berkeley: University of California Press, 1967.

Piven, Frances Fox and Richard A. Cloward. *Why Americans Don't Vote*. New York: Pantheon Books, 1988.

Pollock, Philip H., III. "Organizations as Agents of Mobilization: How Does Group Activity Affect Political Participation?" *American Journal of Political Science* 26 (August 1982), pp. 485–503.

Polsby, Nelson W. *Consequences of Party Reform*. New York: Oxford University Press, 1983.

Polsby, Nelson W. and Aaron Wildavsky. *Presidential Elections: Contemporary Strategies of American Electoral Politics*. 8th ed. New York: Free Press, 1991.

Pomper, Gerald M. *Elections in America: Control and Influence in Democratic Politics*. New York; Dodd, Mead and Company, 1970.

Pomper, Gerald M. and Loretta Sernekos. "The 'Bake Sale' Theory of Voting Participation." Paper presented at the annual meeting of the American Political Science Association, 1989.

Powell, G. Bingham, Jr. "American Voter Turnout in Comparative Perspective." *American Political Science Review* 80 (March 1986), pp. 17–43.

———. *Contemporary Democracies*. Cambridge: Harvard University Press, 1982.

Presser, Stanley, Michael Traugott, and Santa Traugott. "Vote 'Over' Reporting in Surveys: The Records or the Respondents." Paper presented at the International Conference on Measurement Errors, Tucson, 1990.

Price, David E. and Michael Lupfer. "Volunteers for Gore: The Impact of a Precinct-Level Canvass in Three Tennessee Cities." *Journal of Politics* 35 (May 1973), pp. 410–38.

Public Broadcasting Service. "Summer of Judgment: The Watergate Hearings." July 27, 1983.

Radcliff, Benjamin. "The Welfare State, Turnout, and the Economy: A Comparative Analysis." Paper presented at the annual meeting of the Midwest Political Science Association, 1991.

Rae, Douglas W., Douglas T. Yates, Jr., Jennifer Hochschild, Joseph Morone, and Carole Fessler. *Equalities*. Cambridge: Harvard University Press, 1981.

Rauch, Jonathan. "Interest Groups Preparing for Worst as They Lobby Against Budget Cuts." *National Journal,* December 15, 1984, pp. 2380–85.

Reid, T. R. *Congressional Odyssey: The Saga of a Senate Bill.* New York: W. H. Freeman, 1980.

Reiter, Howard L. "Why is Turnout Down?" *Public Opinion Quarterly* 43 (Fall 1979), pp. 297–311.

Rich, Wilbur C. and Abraham Wandersman. "Participation in Block Organizations." *Social Policy* 14 (Summer 1983), pp. 45–47.

Riker, William H. *Democracy in the United States.* New York: Macmillan, 1953.

Riker, William H. and Peter C. Ordeshook. *An Introduction to Positive Political Theory.* Englewood Cliffs, N.J.: Prentice-Hall, 1973.

———. "A Theory of the Calculus of Voting." *American Political Science Review* 62 (March 1968), pp. 25–42.

Robinson, John P. "Interpersonal Influence in Election Campaigns: Two-Step Flow Hypotheses." *Public Opinion Quarterly* 40 (Fall 1976), pp. 304–19.

Robinson, John P. and Philip E. Converse. "Social Change Reflected in the Use of Time." In Angus Campbell and Philip E. Converse, eds., *The Human Meaning of Social Change.* New York: Russell Sage Foundation, 1972, pp. 17–86.

Robinson, John P., Philip E. Converse, and Alexander Szalai. "Everyday Life in Twelve Countries." In A. Szalai, ed., *The Use of Time: Daily Activities of Urban and Suburban Populations in Twelve Countries.* The Hague, Netherlands: Mouton, 1972, pp. 113–44.

Robinson, Michael J. "Three Faces of Congressional Media." In Thomas E. Mann and Norman J. Ornstein, eds., *The New Congress.* Washington: American Enterprise Institute, 1981, pp. 55–96.

Robinson, Michael J. and Margaret A. Sheehan. *Over the Wire and on TV.* New York: Russell Sage Foundation, 1983.

Rosenau, James N. *Citizenship Between Elections: An Inquiry into the Mobilizable American.* New York: Free Press, 1974.

Rosenstone, Steven J. "Economic Adversity and Voter Turnout." *American Journal of Political Science* 26 (February 1982), pp. 25–46.

———. "Separate and Unequal: Report of the 1989 Detroit Area Study." Unpublished manuscript, University of Michigan, 1989.

Rosenstone, Steven J., Roy L. Behr, and Edward H. Lazarus. *Third Parties in America: Citizen Response to Major Party Failure*. Princeton: Princeton University Press, 1984.

Rosenstone, Steven J., John Mark Hansen, and Donald R. Kinder. "Measuring Change in Personal Economic Well-Being." *Public Opinion Quarterly* 50 (Summer 1986), pp. 176–92.

Rosenstone, Steven J. and Raymond E. Wolfinger. "The Effect of Registration Laws on Voter Turnout." *American Political Science Review* 72 (March 1978), pp. 22–45.

Rusk, Jerrold G. "Comment: The American Electoral Universe: Speculation and Evidence." *American Political Science Review* 68 (September 1974), pp. 1028–49.

Rusk, Jerrold G. and John J. Stucker. "The Effect of the Southern System of Election Laws on Voting Participation." In Joel H. Silbey, Allan G. Bogue, and William H. Flanigan, eds., *The History of American Electoral Behavior*. Princeton: Princeton University Press, 1978, pp. 198–250.

Sabato, Larry J. *Campaigns and Elections*. Glenview, Ill.: Scott, Foresman/Little, Brown, 1989.

———. *The Rise of Political Consultants*. New York: Basic Books, 1981.

Salamon, Lester. "Mississippi Postmortem: The 1971 Elections." *New South* 27 (Winter 1972), p. 45.

Salamon, Lester M. and Stephen Van Evera. "Fear, Apathy, and Discrimination: A Test of Three Explanations of Political Participation." *American Political Science Review* 67 (December 1973), pp. 1288–1306.

Salisbury, Robert H. *Citizen Participation in the Public Schools*. Lexington, Mass.: Lexington Books, 1980.

———. "An Exchange Theory of Interest Groups." *Midwest Journal of Political Science* 13 (February 1969), pp. 1–32.

Sampson, E. E. and C. A. Insko. "Cognitive Consistency and Conformity in the Autokinetic Situation." *Journal of Abnormal and Social Psychology* 68 (February 1964), pp. 184–92.

Scammon, Richard. *America Votes.* Washington, D.C.: Government Affairs Institute, 1986, 1990.

Schattschneider, E. E. *The Semi-Sovereign People: A Realist's View of Democracy in America.* New York: Holt, Rinehart and Winston, 1960.

Schlozman, Kay. "What Accent the Heavenly Chorus? Political Equality and the American Pressure System." *Journal of Politics* 46 (November 1984), pp. 1006–32.

Schlozman, Kay Lehman and John T. Tierney. "More of the Same: Washington Pressure Group Activity in a Decade of Change." *Journal of Politics* 45 (May 1983), pp. 351–77.

_____. *Organized Interests and American Democracy.* New York: Harper & Row, 1986.

Schlozman, Kay Lehman and Sidney Verba. *Injury to Insult: Unemployment, Class and Political Response.* Cambridge: Harvard University Press, 1979.

Schumpeter, Joseph A. *Capitalism, Socialism, and Democracy.* New York: Harper & Row, 1950.

Sears, David O. and Jack Citrin. *Tax Revolt: Something for Nothing in California.* Cambridge: Harvard University Press, 1982.

Sen, Amartya. *On Economic Inequality.* Oxford: Clarendon Press, 1973.

Shaffer, Stephen D. "A Multivariate Explanation of Decreasing Turnout in Presidential Elections, 1960–1976." *American Journal of Political Science* 25 (February 1981), pp. 68–95.

The Shameful Blight: The Survival of Racial Discrimination in Voting in the South. Washington, D.C.: The Washington Research Project, 1972.

Sharpless, John B. and Ray M. Shortridge. "Biased Underenumeration in Census Manuscripts." *Journal of Urban History* 1 (August 1975), pp. 409–39.

Silver, Brian D., Barbara A. Anderson, and Paul R. Abramson. "Who Reports Voting." *American Political Science Review* 80 (June 1986), pp. 613–24.

Simmons, H. W., N. N. Berkowitz, and R. J. Moyer. "Similarity, Credibility and Attitude Change: A Review and a Theory." *Psychological Bulletin* 73 (January 1970), pp. 1–16.

Smith, Constance E. *Voting and Election Laws.* New York: Oceana Publications, 1960.

Smith v. *Allwright.* 321 U.S. 649 (1944).

Snow, David A. "Social Networks and Social Movements." *American Sociological Review* 45 (October 1980), pp. 787–801.

Squire, Peverill, Raymond E. Wolfinger, and David P. Glass. "Residential Mobility and Voter Turnout." *American Political Science Review* 81 (March 1987), pp. 45–65.

Stanley, Harold W. *Voter Mobilization and the Politics of Race: The South and Universal Suffrage, 1952–1984.* New York: Praeger, 1987.

———. Personal communication, 1984.

Steckel, Richard H. "The Quality of Census Data for Historical Inquiry: A Research Agenda." *Social Science History* 15 (Winter 1991), pp. 579–99.

Stiles, Skip. "A Field Guide to Capitol Hill: Recognize Strange Inhabitants, Learn the Jargon." *Roll Call,* May 18, 1987, p. 20.

Stone, Walter J. *Republic at Risk: Self-Interest in American Politics.* Pacific Grove, Calif.: Brooks/Cole Publishing Co., 1990.

Strate, John M., Charles J. Parrish, Charles D. Elder, and Coit Ford, III. "Life Span Civic Development and Voting Participation." *American Political Science Review* 83 (June 1989), pp. 444–64.

Strate, John M., Charles J. Parrish, Charles D. Elder, and Thomas Jankowski. "Life Span Civic Development and Campaign Participation." Paper presented at the annual meeting of the American Political Science Association, 1990.

Sundquist, James L. *Dynamics of the Party System.* Washington, D.C.: Brookings Institution, 1973.

Swabey, Marie Collins. *The Democratic State.* Cambridge: Harvard University Press, 1937.

Tate, Katherine. "Black Political Participation in the 1984 and 1988 Presidential Elections." *American Political Science Review* 85 (December 1991), pp. 1159–76.

Tate, Katherine and Ronald E. Brown. "The Black Church and Political Participation Revisited." Paper presented at the annual meeting of the Midwest Political Science Association, 1991.

Taylor, Paul "The Death of Withholding, or How Bankers Won Big." *Washington Post*, July 31, 1983, p. A12.

Teixeira, Ruy. *Why Americans Don't Vote: Turnout Decline in the United States, 1960–1984.* New York: Greenwood Press, 1987.

Thompson, Kenneth H. *The Voting Rights Act and Black Electoral Participation.* Washington, D.C.: Joint Center for Political Studies, 1982.

Tilly, Charles. *From Mobilization to Revolution.* Reading, Mass.: Addison-Wesley, 1978.

Travers, Jeffrey and Stanley Milgram. "An Experimental Study of the Small World Problem." *Sociometry* 32 (December 1969), pp. 425–43.

U.S. Attorney General. *Report of the Attorney General of the United States, 1966.* Washington, D.C.: U.S. Government Printing Office, 1966.

U.S. Bureau of the Census. "Studies in the Measurement of Voter Turnout." *Current Population Reports, Special Studies.* Series P-23, No. 168, November 1990.

U.S. Commission on Civil Rights. *Political Participation.* Washington, D.C.: U.S. Government Printing Office, May 1968.

———. *The Voting Rights Act: The First Months.* Washington, D.C.: U.S. Government Printing Office, 1965.

———. *The Voting Rights Act: Ten Years After.* Washington, D.C.: U.S. Government Printing Office, January 1975.

———. *The Voting Rights Act: Unfulfilled Goals.* Washington, D.C.: U.S. Government Printing Office, September 1981.

U.S. Commission on Civil Service. *Annual Report of the U.S. Civil Service Commission, 1966.* Washington, D.C.: U.S. Government Printing Office, 1966.

U.S. Congress, House of Representatives. *Hearings before a Subcommittee of the Committee on Appropriations of the House of Representatives.* "Legislative Branch Appropriations for 1976." 94th Congress, 1st session, 1975.

_____. "Legislative Branch Appropriations for 1979." 95th Congress, 2d session, 1978.

_____. "Legislative Branch Appropriations for 1981." 96th Congress, 2d session, 1980, part 2.

_____. "Legislative Branch Appropriations for 1982." 97th Congress, 1st session, 1981.

_____. "Legislative Branch Appropriations for 1983." 97th Congress, 2d session, 1982, part 2.

_____. "Legislative Branch Appropriations for 1984." 98th Congress, 1st session, 1983, part 2.

_____. "Legislative Branch Appropriations for 1987." 99th Congress, 2d session, 1986, part 2.

_____. "Legislative Branch Appropriations for 1991." 101st Congress, 2d session, 1990, part 2.

U.S. Congress, House of Representatives. Committee on House Administration. "Report of the Committee on House Administration Task Force to Investigate the Operation and Management of the Office of the Postmaster." 102d Congress, 2d session, July 21, 1992.

_____. "U.S. House of Representatives Election Law Guidebook 1988." House Document 100–208, 100th Congress, 2d session, 1988.

U.S. Department of Commerce. "Studies in Measurement of Voter Turnout." *Current Population Reports, Special Studies,* P-23, No. 168. Washington, D.C.: U.S. Government Printing Office, November 1990.

U.S. President's Commission on Registration and Voting Participation. *Report of the President's Commission on Registration and Voting Participation,* November 1963.

Uhlaner, Carole Jean. "Political Participation and Discrimination: A Comparative Analysis of Asians, Blacks and Latinos." In William

Crotty, ed., *Political Participation and American Democracy.* New York: Greenwood Press, 1991, pp. 139–70.

―――. "Rational Turnout: The Neglected Role of Groups." *American Journal of Political Science* 33 (May 1987), pp. 390–422.

―――. "'Relational Goods' and Participation: Incorporating Sociability into a Theory of Rational Action." *Public Choice* 62 (September 1989), pp. 253–85.

Uhlaner, Carole J., Bruce E. Cain, and D. Roderick Kiewiet. "Political Participation of Ethnic Minorities in the 1980s." *Political Behavior* 11 (September 1989), pp. 195–321.

Unger, Donald G. and Abraham Wandersman. "Neighboring and Its Role in Block Organizations: An Exploratory Report." *American Journal of Community Psychology* 11 (June 1983), pp. 291–300.

V.E.P. News, 2 (January 1968), p. 1.

Verba, Sidney and Norman H. Nie. *Participation in America: Political Democracy and Social Equality.* New York: Harper & Row, 1972.

Verba, Sidney, Norman H. Nie, and Jae-on Kim. *Participation and Political Equality: A Seven-Nation Comparison.* New York: Cambridge University Press, 1978.

Verba, Sidney and Gary Orren. *Equality in America: The View from the Top.* Cambridge: Harvard University Press, 1985.

Vogel, David. *Fluctuating Fortunes: The Political Power of Business in America.* New York: Basic Books, 1989.

Voter Education Project. "What Happened in the South, 1966." Atlanta: Voter Education Project, December 14, 1966.

Waldman, Loren K. "Types and Measures of Inequality." *Social Science Quarterly* 58 (September 1977), pp. 229–41.

Walker, Jack L., Jr. *Mobilizing Interest Groups in America: Patrons, Professions, and Social Movements.* Ann Arbor: University of Michigan Press, 1991.

―――. "Three Modes of Political Mobilization." Paper presented at the annual meeting of the American Political Science Association, 1984.

Wandersman, Abraham and Gary A. Giamartino. "Community and Individual Difference Characteristics as Influences on Initial Participation." *American Journal of Community Psychology* 8 (April 1980), pp. 217–28.

Wandersman, Abraham, John F. Jakubs, and Gary A. Giamartino. "Participation in Block Organizations." *Journal of Community Action* 1 (September/October 1981), pp. 40–47.

Waste, Richard J. *The Ecology of City Policymaking.* New York: Oxford University Press, 1989.

Watters, Pat and Reese Cleghorn. *Climbing Jacob's Ladder: The Arrival of Negroes in Southern Politics.* New York: Harcourt, Brace and World, 1967.

Weisberg, Herbert F. and Bernard Grofman. "Candidate Evaluations and Turnout." *American Politics Quarterly* 9 (April 1981), pp. 197–219.

Wilcox, Clyde. *God's Warriors: The Christian Right in Twentieth Century America.* Baltimore: Johns Hopkins University Press, 1992.

Williams, Mike. "Louisiana Blacks See Danger in Duke Victory." *Atlanta Journal and Constitution*, November 12, 1991, p. A3.

Wilson, James Q. *Political Organizations.* New York: Basic Books, 1973.

Winkle, Kenneth. "The U.S. Census as a Source in Political History." *Social Science Quarterly* 15 (Winter 1991), pp. 565–77.

Wolfinger, Raymond E. *The Politics of Progress.* Englewood Cliffs, N. J.: Prentice-Hall, 1974.

Wolfinger, Raymond E., David P. Glass, and Peverill Squire. "Predictors of Electoral Turnout: An International Comparison." *Policy Studies Review* 9 (Spring 1990), pp. 551–74.

Wolfinger, Raymond E. and Steven J. Rosenstone. *Who Votes?* New Haven: Yale University Press, 1980.

Woodward, C. Vann. *The Strange Career of Jim Crow.* 2nd ed. New York: Oxford University Press, 1966.

Yadlosky, Elizabeth. "Voting Laws of the Fifty States and the District of Columbia." U.S. Library of Congress, Legislative Reference Service, May 18, 1964.

Zeigler, Harmon, Harvey J. Tucker, and L. A. Wilson II. "Communication and Decision Making in American Public Education: A Longitudinal and Comparative Study." In Jay N. Scribner, ed., *The Politics of Education*. Chicago: National Society for the Study of Education, 1977, pp. 218–54.

Zipp, John F. "Perceived Representativeness and Voting: An Assessment of the Impact of 'Choices' vs. 'Echoes.'" *American Political Science Review* 79 (March 1985), pp. 50–61.

Zuckerman, Alan S. and Darrell M. West. "The Political Bases of Citizen Contacting: A Cross-National Analysis." *American Political Science Review* 79 (March 1985), pp. 117–31.

INDEX

African-Americans
  and civil rights movement, 189–96
  and mobilization, 78, 168, 173,
    220–21, 223–24, 244
  and participation in elections, 43,
    44, 58–60, 173n, 204, 219–24,
    244–46
  and participation in government, 43,
    44, 77–78
  and voter registration, 197–205, 208
Age
  generational hypothesis, 139, 140
  life-cycle hypothesis, 137–39, 140–41
  life-experience hypothesis, 137, 140.
  See also experience with politics
Age cohorts, 139–40, 140n–41n
Alienation. *See* confidence in government
American Association of Retired
    Persons (AARP), 115
American Bankers Association, 110
American Medical Association (AMA),
    107
Americans for Democratic Action
    (ADA), 85
Anderson, John, 124
Attending local meetings
  activism in, 42–54
  causes of, 72–77, 80–83, 86–88,
    101–6, 118, 122–23, 125–27
  inequalities in, 236, 238–40
  trends in, 4, 63, 65, 67–69, 125–27

Ballot access petitions, 123–25
Barry, Brian, 11
Benefits of participation. *See* rewards
    of participation
Blacks. *See* African-Americans

Bork, Robert, 109–10
Boyd, Richard, 187
Brody, Richard A., 3, 212
Budgets
  federal, 113–14
  local, 122–23
Building Trades Council, 84
Bush, George, 98, 99, 168, 216, 218

Calendars
  congressional, 118–22
  effect on mobilization, 34–35
  election, 124, 178–79, 183–84,
    185–88
  local budgeting, 122–23
Carter, Jimmy, 19, 98, 99, 100, 180,
    216, 218, 223
Chiles, Lawton, 115
Church attendance, 158–59, 167, 222
Churches, and mobilization, 110,
    167n, 194
Citizen duty, 19–20, 30n, 146–47
Citrin, Jack, 150
Civic responsibility. *See* citizen duty
Civil Rights Act of 1964, 189, 191,
    221, 246
Civil rights movement, 188–96, 203,
    220–21, 244
Class. *See* resources; income; education
Closeness of elections. *See* competitive
    elections
Closing date, 207–208, 219–20
Collective benefits. *See* rewards of
    participation
Competitive elections
  and mobilization, 35, 169–70, 174,
    179–82, 183–85, 218

327